Mr. Sulu Grabbed My Ass,
and Other Highlights
from a Life in Comics, Novels,
Television, Films and Video Games

Mr. Sulu Grabbed My Ass,
and Other Highlights
from a Life in Comics, Novels,
Television, Films and Video Games

PETER DAVID

McFarland & Company, Inc., Publishers
Jefferson, North Carolina

All photographs are from the author's collection.

LIBRARY OF CONGRESS CATALOGUING-IN-PUBLICATION DATA

Names: David, Peter (Peter Allen) author.
Title: Mr. Sulu grabbed my ass, and other highlights from a life in comics, novels, television, films and video games / Peter David.
Description: Jefferson : McFarland & Company, Inc., Publishers, 2021. | Includes index.
Identifiers: LCCN 2020048442 | ISBN 9781476683546 (paperback : acid free paper) ∞ ISBN 9781476641546 (ebook)
Subjects: LCSH: David, Peter (Peter Allen)—Anecdotes. | Novelists, American—20th century—Biography. | Cartoonists—United States—Biography.
Classification: LCC PS3554.A92144 Z46 2021 | DDC 813/.54 [B]—dc23
LC record available at https://lccn.loc.gov/2020048442

BRITISH LIBRARY CATALOGUING DATA ARE AVAILABLE

ISBN (print) 978-1-4766-8354-6
ISBN (ebook) 978-1-4766-4154-6

© 2021 Second Age, Inc. All rights reserved

No part of this book may be reproduced or transmitted in any form or by any means, electronic or mechanical, including photocopying or recording, or by any information storage and retrieval system, without permission in writing from the publisher.

Front cover image: Peter David at a Comic Con

Printed in the United States of America

McFarland & Company, Inc., Publishers
Box 611, Jefferson, North Carolina 28640
www.mcfarlandpub.com

Contents

When I First Thought About Writing This…	1
Thanks, Hitler, I Guess	8
I Was Will Smith's Bodyguard	17
Make Mine Marvel	27
Becoming a Part-Time Writer	40
Becoming a Full-Time Writer	52
The Kids	64
Kathleen Gets Her Own Chapter	82
Worst Trip to Disney Ever	95
Star Trek I: The Fandom Menace	105
Harlan	114
Star Trek II: First Contact	128
The Name of the Place Is Babylon 5	139
Once Upon a Time, in a School in Outer Space	156
Comics Stuff	167
Fans	182
"But I Digress"	187
Various Things	194
Looking Back	205
Index	215

When I First Thought About Writing This...

I was at the New York Friar's Club.

Let me say that again: I was at the New York Friar's Club.

Part of me still could not believe it. When I had grown up in the 1960s and 1970s, the Friar's Club roasts were first broadcast as part of the Kraft Music Hall. They included such luminaries as Johnny Carson, Don Rickles and Jerry Lewis. These were eventually replaced by the Dean Martin roasts, and over the decades the Friar's Club returned to the televised roasting scene on Comedy Central. And there I was, invited to participate in that tradition.

The invitation had come from none other than the target of that evening's roast, George Takei—Mr. Sulu himself.

I had known George for many years. Hell, his was the first autograph I managed to snag when I went to my very first *Star Trek* convention. I'd gotten him to sign a poster that I'd gotten who-knows-where.

My first more professional encounter had come many years later, when I was writing the *Star Trek* comic book for DC Comics. George had signed on to write an annual, but he had no experience with writing comics, and so I was assigned to aid him in putting it together. I happened to be in California for God-knows-what reason, and so I swung by his domicile at the appointed hour.

This may sound like a cliché, but within five minutes I had figured out that he was gay.

I was introduced to Brad Altman, his assistant. I glanced around the apartment and saw no pictures of any females except his mother. The place was extremely tidy. George was immaculately dressed. As we discussed the story, he made it clear that he wanted it to be a metaphor about AIDS, an epidemic then still in its infancy, and had only turned serious in the public imagination because Rock Hudson had died of it several years earlier. All this went through my head and I thought,

"Hunh. George is gay." It was no big deal; I certainly didn't give a damn. It was just a new piece of information that I filed away.

Over the years our friendship grew. I once again happened to be in Los Angeles when George was filming *Star Trek VI: The Undiscovered Country*. He invited me to the set and I eagerly showed up. He greeted me wearing a make-up bib on his uniform and when he brought me over to the bridge set, he smiled and gestured proudly, "My ship." It was as if, to him, it wasn't a set; it was genuine. Grace Lee Whitney was there as Janice Rand, which surprised the hell out of me.

Some minutes later, George asked me to go over his scene with him. It's not as if it was a testament to my performance ability; actors will ask anyone who can read to go over lines with them. It was the scene where Sulu contacts Kirk, and in the sequence he identified himself as "Captain Sulu."

Now some years earlier author Vonda McIntyre, in her Star Trek novel *The Entropy Effect*, published by Pocket Books, had introduced the name "Hikaru" as Sulu's first name. George had always liked it, but since it had never been spoken on screen, the name was not official. I said to George, "You know, Kirk never introduces himself as Captain Kirk. He always says, Captain James Kirk. This would be the ideal time to establish Hikaru as his first name by having him say, 'Captain Hikaru Sulu.'" George said, "That's a great idea. Let's ask Nick."

Nick, of course, was Nicholas Meyer, the famed author of *The Seven Percent Solution*, who had saved the Trek film franchise with *Star Trek II: The Wrath of Khan* and had co-written the script for, and was directing, *Trek VI*. George walked me over to Meyer, who was sitting in a director's chair watching playbacks on a TV screen. George was standing right next to me as he said, "Nick, this is my friend, Peter David." He then took a step back and stood me in front of him as he said, "He has a suggestion." So basically, I was suddenly a human roadblock between him and Meyer. Thanks, George.

So I pitched the idea to him. He rolled the name around. "Hikaru Sulu. Hikaru Sulu. Captain Hikaru Sulu." Then he nodded and said, "Okay. Go with it."

The thing was, that moment in the scene where George used Sulu's full name wound up on the editing room floor. But now that he had the license to do so, George started dropping it in everywhere he could.

Flash forward some months and I was at the screening of the film for *Star Trek* licensees. I had been pitching my editor, Kevin Ryan of Pocket Books, on the idea of doing a novel focusing on Sulu, but Kevin—who was there along with a number of other Pocket employees—wasn't interested. In the very first scene, we open with Captain Sulu lifting a cup of tea while we hear the following in voiceover:

"Star Date 9521.6. Captain's log, U.S.S. *Excelsior*. Hikaru Sulu, commanding."

Well, the Pocket Books contingent exploded. Finally, *finally*, something from the books was now official, by Paramount's own rules. The movie itself was tremendously entertaining and after the showing, Kevin came up to me and said, "Peter! Captain Sulu novel! Let's talk!"

Some time later, that novel, *The Captain's Daughter*, was published. Flash forward many years. I walked into my local bowling alley for my Wednesday night league and almost immediately a couple of guys came running up to me. Understand that no one there knew what I did for a living. I didn't show up Wednesdays to be fabulous. I showed up to bowl. The bowling alley was the one place I could socialize without being a *New York Times* bestselling author and comic book maven. But the guys, all excited, were firing questions at me, overlapping with each other. I answered them as fast as I could.

"Are you the Peter David who writes *Star Trek* novels?"

"Uh ... yeah."

"Do you know George Takei?" They pronounced it Tuh-Ky.

"Yes, and it's Tuh-Kay."

"You wrote a book called *The Captain's Daughter*?"

"Yessss." I had no idea what the hell was going on and asked.

Well, it turned out that George had been on the Howard Stern show that day, and talk had turned to *Trek* novels. They asked if there were any that George liked, and he said, "Well, I really like one called *The Captain's Daughter* that was written by my friend, Peter David."

That was that. George had effectively "outed" me to everyone at my bowling alley. The rest of the evening, people kept coming by and asking me the same questions that the first guys had. Apparently, everyone listened to Howard Stern. Some of them even asked me in bewilderment, "What are you doing here?" Maybe they thought I should be just hanging around with movie stars or something, I dunno.

Of course, it was on the Stern show that George most prominently came to terms with publicly becoming a gay icon. So when he and Brad were going to get married, they invited my wife Kathleen and me to the wedding. Why not? They had attended ours. Some months before we'd gotten married, we had been at breakfast with George and Brad, who were in Long Island, where I live, for a concert tour where George was narrating *Lord of the Rings*. We said, "What are you doing Memorial Day?" George said, "We're at a convention in Atlanta." I couldn't believe the luck and said, "As it so happens, we're getting married in Atlanta!"

4   Mr. Sulu Grabbed My Ass, and Other Highlights

Some years later I was seated in the fifth row at George's wedding. To my left was Kathleen. To my right was Harlan Ellison and his wife, Susan. We were in a lecture hall in a Japanese Cultural Center. Standing at the front of the room were Nichelle Nichols and Walter Koenig. All of a sudden, at the top of the long flights of stairs that led downward, George and Brad appeared. They were wearing matching tuxedos— white jackets and black trousers—and they strolled down the stairs to the tune "One Singular Sensation" from *A Chorus Line*. I desperately wanted to laugh but Kathleen was elbowing me in the ribs. I could see that Harlan was biting the inside of his cheek to keep himself together. The wedding ceremony itself was wonderful and amazing. Despite the claims of many anti-gay marriage advocates, the ground did not open up and swallow anyone.

It was also around that time that George was going to be roasted by the Friar's Club. The fact that they were no longer being broadcast had apparently not deterred the Friars from doing in-house roasts, and George asked if I would be willing to be part of the presentation. He wanted a friendly face on the panel, I guess.

I don't remember the names of any of the other comics who were on the panel save one: Gilbert Gottfried. Like everyone else, I knew Gilbert only from his loud-mouthed public persona. When he was not on, however, I was astounded to learn that he was quite soft-spoken and intelligent. The Gilbert Gottfried the public knows is a comedic persona he has invented. Upon learning that Gilbert was going to be one of the presenters, I asked the organizer nervously if I was going to be following him. The organizer laughed and said, "No one follows Gilbert. He's always last." That was fine with me.

Kathleen and newlywed Brad were seated in the audience and I sat several seats down from George as the various comedians got up and made hilarious comments about George. George has a distinctive laugh and it was definitely on display that evening. Eventually it was my turn. The audience's reception was polite but not overwhelming. None of them knew me. I wasn't a comic.

But I was ready.

I got up and began speaking:

> Unlike the rest of the gentlemen and ladies here, I am not a comedian and I am prepared to prove that.
>
> I know what I'm expected to do here. Make a variety of jokes, preferably off-color, about our guest of honor. About his career, about his personal life. Cut him down to size, telling ourselves we do it out of affection when, really, we just kind of like being mean.
>
> I can't bring myself to do it, not because I think I'm morally superior or sticking

to the high road. It's simply because, bottom line, our guest's body of work has meant too much to me for too much of my life. And life is too short, y'know? Too short to waste an opportunity to speak well of someone when they're still here to enjoy it.

The truth is that this man's work has meant a great deal to me. I admit it: a first-generation *Star Trek* fan. I watched our honored guest's heroics as he guided the Starship *Enterprise* through its five-year mission.

Sure, the series could be cornball at times ... like, when it was on. But that did not detract one iota from what our honoree contributed to the series and to the role. A role he played with sincerity, with style, with flair. He and his heroics helped fire the imagination of young viewers to explore space, to envision what it would like to adventure into the unknown. Many of them went on to become NASA engineers, technicians, even astronauts. I'm supposed to make fun of him, but instead I can only congratulate him for everything that his work has done for me ... for all of us.

And you might have thought that his career would have ended with *Star Trek*, but no. Since then he has continued with a vital and exciting career on stage, in movies, and of course, television. Whether he's busting bad guys as TJ Hooker or defending them as Denny Cra...

I stopped dead. Puzzlement crossed my face as I started riffling through the pages. There were some confused chuckles from the audience, but no one was sure what was going on. Then, with a look of utter annoyance, I said, "Aw shit, this is my rejected speech from the William Shatner roast."

Well, the place went nuts. The Friar's Club exploded with laughter. George was braying with hysterics. I maintained my look of irritation but inside my head was overwhelmed with joy. I had brought down a room of professional comedians. They had thought I was giving a genuine speech of love for George; they had even applauded once or twice in the course of it. But the fact was that it had all been a set up, and if anyone was going to appreciate being so totally hosed, it was going to be the members of the Friar's Club. I looked directly at them and said:

> Great. Just ... great. Everyone else is roasting the final frontier fegaleh, and I pulled the wrong speech. I am so sorry. This is just so embarrassing. I thought I had the right speech. My brain just ... *pbtthhh.*

Quickly I started thumbing through the pages.

> Let me see if there's anything salvageable here. Hold on: "Multiple Emmy award winning...." No. "Beloved by millions...." No. "The classic definition of a man's man."

I now had to embark on the trickiest part of the speech. If I had just said that I had the wrong speech, I couldn't keep reading off it. That would make no sense. One has to stick to the story one is presenting. So I crumbled up the rest of the pages and tossed them aside, saying,

6   Mr. Sulu Grabbed My Ass, and Other Highlights

"Y'know, I think I'm just gonna wing it here." From that point on, I had to proceed entirely from memory. Which I did:

> This is what happens when you get older. Brain farts. I've turned fifty, which, if you're a guy, you know what comes next. My last check-up, my doctor said, "So, Peter, time to schedule a colonoscopy." Ah, fifty, that magical age when doctors suddenly become obsessed with shoving things up your ass. Of course, Doctor Takei here was a bit precocious in that regard. When other seven-year-old boys were playing doctor by saying, "Okay, Emily, take your shirt off so I can listen to your heart," seven-year-old George's line was, "Okay, Bobby, bend over, spread your legs and grab your ankles. First we'll check your prostate, and then I'm going to get my dad's colonoscopy kit."
>
> George's parents, God rest 'em, had no clue. When George got older, and he told them he had decided he was going to be an actor, his father said, "Actor? I don't understand. Based on what Bobby's parents said, we thought you were going to be a proctologist. And by the way, stop using my plumbing snake to give colonoscopies because Bobby's parents are complaining. Actor? What a queer decision."
>
> I've actually known George personally for well over twenty years. We met in an interesting way. I pulled over to help him because he'd been in a fender bender. See, there was this strip mall along the road and it had a big sign up on the roadside advertising the various stores. And among the stores was a supermarket called Giant. Maybe you've heard of it. And they also had an athletic supply store called Dick's. Consequently the sign on the roadside read "Giant Dicks,"* and George, who was driving a Suzuki Samurai, had slammed on the brakes because he wanted to go check it out. As a result, the Samurai was rear ended by a Mercury Mountaineer. Of course, being George's car, the Samurai kinda liked it, as did the Mountaineer. So they collided again and the bumper meshed with the tail and it took ten minutes to separate the rear-ending Samurai and Mountaineer, although it did provide inspiration for George's next movie, "Blokeback Mountain." And everything was fine, except half a mile down the road there was a BJ's and the car got totaled.
>
> George was in the closet for most of that time although I'm not sure who he thought he was fooling. When you write a 300-page autobiography and the only woman you talk about is your mother, you're either gay or you're Oedipus. I mean, come on. George, even *Star Trek* fans figured it out, and a lot of them are so clueless about women, their idea of foreplay is saying, "Permission to come aboard."
>
> I guess George's credulity has always been the most charming thing about him. The most famous of course is Howard Stern's repeatedly hosing him about Schwarzenegger. Me, I visited him on the set of *Star Trek VI* and he brought me over to the bridge set of the Excelsior and he pointed with such genuine pride and said, "There it is: My ship." And there's guys hammering shit into place and hanging lights and I'm going, "George. It's not a ship; it's a movie set." "No. It's my ship." How can you not love that measure of self-delusion?
>
> And I know what I said earlier about roasts being mean-spirited, but here's the

---

*In point of fact, this was based on something from real life. I had driven past a mall some time before that which indeed had a big sign advertising a store called "Giant," and also "Dick's," and so it read "Giant Dick's." Where do writers get ideas? From the world around them.

truth. And George, I know this is confusing and even disorienting for you because you're not accustomed to having men expressing affection while facing you so...

At which point, I turned my back to him and thrust my buttocks toward him. Now what I was supposed to say was:

> I just want to say on behalf of everyone here, we love you, and respect you for the phenomenal talent you are. You just go right on believing that.

But I have no idea if I ever actually said that. Because presented with a target, George reached out with both hands and started squeezing my ass.

Kathleen and Brad didn't see it because of the angle of the podium. A month or so later, though, they got it on DVD, and the camera picked it up just fine because Brad howled in shock and said, "*You grabbed his ass*?!?"

Yes, he did.

And as I stood there, what went through my mind was: *What in the hell kind of life have I led that brought me to this moment? Maybe I should write it down.*

And that's exactly what I'm doing.

Enjoy the ride.

Thanks, Hitler, I Guess

Because honestly, it feels kind of weird to be thanking Adolf Hitler for anything. He was easily the most evil individual of the 20th century, so it seems odd to be giving him a shout-out of any sort. On the other hand, if it weren't for him, I wouldn't be here. Seriously? Is that history's lesson? Six million people had to die for me to show up? That doesn't seem remotely just.

The reason Hitler is relevant and important to my being here is because if it were not for him, my father, Gunter David, would likely have grown to manhood in Berlin where he was born and the odds of him meeting my mother would have reduced somewhat.

My father was born in 1929 to Martin and Hela David, two German citizens. Martin ran a women's shoe store in downtown Berlin. Decades later, I would be in Berlin for a convention and I went to the exact address where the store had been; there's now a movie theater there that plays foreign films. I don't mean American; I mean really foreign films whose titles I can't even understand.

One day in the early 1930s, my grandfather was minding his own business in the store when a brick was thrown through his window. People outside yelled, "Dirty Jews!" Martin turned to Hela and said, "Get the boy ready. We're leaving."

You need to understand how brave it was for him to realize that his country was spinning right down the tubes and that it was not going to be safe for them to remain there. All his neighbors insisted he was overreacting. "Nothing's going to happen. It will blow over. They're just Nazis." That's why these days I never hesitate to describe someone as a Nazi; to bring Godwin's Law into a discussion when it seems appropriate and invoke Nazis. Because once upon a time, being a Nazi just meant you were loud and obnoxious and could easily be ignored or dismissed out of hand. There was no reason to become alarmed at their activities because you figured their actions were simply some manner of social aberration.

So all the neighbors dismissed the actions of the Nazis out of hand. And all the neighbors died in concentration camps.

Meanwhile my father's family fled to London and then Paris before finally settling in what was then called Palestine (and still called Occupied Palestine by some) but would eventually become Israel.

There my father became fascinated by American movies. Once he became old enough, he went to America with the determination to become a movie star. Indeed, he did embark upon an acting career, but quickly discovered that he was too insecure to deal with the endless rejections of auditions. He attended San Mateo Junior College in California and wound up training to become a journalist.

He also met a young woman named Dalia Rojansky.

Dalia, born in Haifa in 1933, was the daughter of Aaron and Claire Rojansky. Aaron was a partner in a CPA firm in Israel and also the first tenor in the Israeli opera, so that was pretty cool. Dalia was an absolutely brilliant woman, especially when it came to mathematics. She graduated from Barnard College in New York. She had a classmate named Joan Molinsky who went on to some fame when she became a comedienne and changed her name to Joan Rivers. Mathematics was her thing, and she actually worked with Watson and Crick on their DNA research.

She wound up being introduced to Gunter by a mutual friend.

And boy, Aaron Rojansky didn't like him. At all. He just felt this kid wasn't good enough for his daughter. They wound up eloping in secret and then Dalia snuck back home that evening, which is where she spent her wedding night. Eventually I guess they managed to screw their nerve to the sticking post and admitted that they had gotten married, which probably didn't go over all that well.

My father claimed that it was my birth that changed everything. That Aaron, or as I called him, Sabra Aaron ("Sabra" is a term that refers to anyone who is born on Israeli soil) absolutely adored me and was very impressed that my father had produced such a remarkable offspring. I don't think I was anything special but go argue with your grandfather.

Unfortunately, my mother never got on with my grandmother Hela. My grandfather passed away in the 1960s and my grandmother wound up moving to a nearby apartment, and she and my mother would argue incessantly. I never understood what they were talking about because they would speak in German, specifically to avoid my knowing what they were saying. To this day, if I resent my parents for anything, it's that they made a point of avoiding teaching me any of the languages they spoke. I could know English, German and Hebrew, because they were fluent in all, and if they'd taught me when my brain was young and absorbent, I'd be familiar with all of them. But no. Every time I'd pick up some words, they'd quickly switch to another language to keep me in the dark. Thanks, guys.

Indeed, many years later at that same Germany science fiction convention I mentioned earlier, I was speaking to a room full of fans and telling them that I knew no German. As I was speaking, two guys started arguing about something. I kept talking and their German-spoken argument became louder and louder and finally in frustration I shouted, "*Was ist los?*" ("What's the matter?") Everything stopped dead and I said in surprise, "Where did *that* come from?" I thought about it a moment and then said, "Oh, of course. When I was growing up, my father would always be saying, 'Was ist los, Mutter?'" ("What's the matter, mother?") Well, the place roared with laughter. The guys who had been arguing were immediately fine with each other again, sharing in the amusement. Apparently, that's a very common question for Germans.

We lived in a small town in New Jersey called Bloomfield, on a street called Albert Terrace. I still remember when they planted saplings along the street, and my father told me they'd be big trees in twenty, thirty years. That seemed like an infinity of time. Yet a few years ago, I happened to drive down Albert Terrace, just to see it, and was astounded to see massive trees lining the entire street.

My first exposure to comic books was Harvey comics that my barber kept at his shop. I knew nothing about comics. In reading *Casper*, when he would turn invisible, that was rendered as a series of broken lines. I thought it was some sort of play-along feature and I would take a pencil and connect the dots. After I got a haircut, my mother would typically take me next door to a restaurant to get ice cream. The restaurant's name is Holsten's. It's still there and has gained notoriety as the place where Tony Soprano went for what might have well been his last meal in the final episode of *The Sopranos*. If you go with a party of four, you can still sit at his table, which is marked with a plaque.

Some years back I was in a comic book store and a mother was there with her kids. One of the kids came back excited and said to his mother, "Mom! There are Teenage Mutant Ninja Turtle Comic books *too*!" I found this immensely amusing. There hadn't been any movies yet up to that point, but the Turtles were in an incredibly successful TV series, and the poor ignorant boy had no idea that the Turtles had originated in comic books.

But then I thought about it and realized that I had likewise learned about superhero comics through television: specifically through the George Reeves' "Adventures of Superman" series. At the end of every episode, the announcer would proclaim, "Superman is based on the character appearing in Superman magazines!" Not comic books, but magazines. This I found fascinating. There were magazines about him? This was the age before DVRs or DVDs or VHS tapes. The only time I could enjoy a Superman adventure was when he was on TV, 4:30 in the afternoon, period. But magazines? I could pick them up and read them whenever I wanted to. I eventually found out that there was a magazine store a few streets over, and they had plenty of comic books. It's where I discovered the world of DC heroes, including Supergirl, Batman, and one hero whose name I pronounced "A-KEW-uh-Man." I eventually asked my Dad what "A-KEW-uh" meant and he corrected my pronunciation to "AH-kwuh-man." (Did I ever dream I would eventually cut off Aquaman's hand and replace it with a harpoon? Hardly.)

My first exposure to Marvel Comics came from when I was visiting my cousin Danny, the son of my mother's brother (about whom the less said, the better.) Danny showed me his stack of comics and one of them was *Fantastic Four Annual #3*, the marriage of Reed Richards and Sue Storm. Any long-time fans will remember that virtually every major Marvel hero and villain showed up. What was interesting was that I was able to read and understand every single thing that happened in that issue, despite my complete lack of familiarity with the characters. When one considers that nowadays fans have trouble making their way through a single, twenty-page comic book and comprehending the story, that's quite an accomplishment. The one thing I didn't understand was the bit at the end, when Stan Lee and Jack Kirby showed up at the wedding and were refused entry. I had paid no attention to the credits and so had no idea who the top-hatted, formally dressed men were. Of course, I had no idea that years later I would meet Jack and become friends with Stan. I often imagine what it would be like to go back in time and tell my younger self what my life would be like. I wouldn't have believed it.

With my interest in the Marvel Universe stirred, I picked up *Marvel Tales* and *Marvel Collectors Items Classics*, which featured reprints of the older stories. Each of them cost a princely twenty-five cents. Nowadays if new fans want to read up on old titles, they have to buy trade paperback collections for twenty bucks and up. So, if anyone wants to know why we have so much trouble pulling in new, young readers, keep in mind that the tools that enabled me to get current with old issues no longer exist. That has to be discouraging for the up-and-comers.

I did not remain an only child forever. Eventually I got a younger brother, Walter Charles, and a younger sister, Ronni Beth, who eventually shortened her name to Beth. In my parents' later years, Beth wound up having them move to within a five-minute drive of her and she pretty much took care of them as their health declined. My father passed away three years ago, and my mother two years later. My father, who was so afraid of death for so much of his life, welcomed it by the end, and my mother's dementia riddled brain was so far gone that she had no idea what was going on.

But I'm getting ahead.

Was my father the perfect father? No. I don't know anyone who is the perfect father. Of course, having read Joe Straczynski's autobiography, I can tell you he was certainly not the worst father. That would be Joe's. Go read *Becoming Superman* by Joe and you'll understand.

My dad was all for sharing his interests with me, but wasn't the slightest bit inclined to get involved in anything that interested me. Although he did wind up watching one episode of *Star Trek*. It was "Patterns of Force," the one in which they're on a world populated by Nazis. He wandered past, saw it, said, "Nazis?!" I said, "Yeah. It's a whole planet of them." He sat right down and watched the rest of the episode with me.

He also took me to my first comic book convention. We were watching the evening news one Friday and they reported about this comic con that was going on in New York City. It was organized by Phil Seuling and it was incredibly popular. Jack Kirby, who at that time was occupied with the "New Gods" comics for DC, was a guest. I stared longingly at the screen but said nothing.

"Would you like to go?" my dad asked.

My head snapped around. "Really?!"

"I'll take you tomorrow," he said. Considering we were living in Pennsylvania at the time, that was not a short trip, but I was up for it. The next day, good as his word, he drove us up to New York and I actually got to meet the King himself. I remember asking him how to pronounce the name of his formidable villain, Darkseid: As DarkSEED or DarkSIDE. The latter, as it turns out. I'm big on knowing how to pronounce things.

(Funny aside: Many, many years later I was attending a convention in Portland, Oregon. My convention escort and I were approaching the venue and this kid came running up to me and asked, "Is it pronounced Sub-muhREEENer or Sub-MAREinner." I told him it was the second one. He also asked me how to pronounce Bill Sienkiewicz [Sin-KEV-itch] and Fabian Nicieza [Nee-see-AY-suh] and a few others. Finally, satisfied, he turned away, and I said, "Oh, and you didn't ask, but it's pronounced Moon Ka-NIG-it." He stared in confusion. "I thought it was Moon Knight." I said, "Ah, but you have to remember to use the Egyptian pronunciation." He ran off toward a group of friends who were waiting for him to come back with the information. My companion said, "You're evil." I said, "Just wait." We watched him convey the info to his friends, and they all nodded, taking it in, and I knew exactly when he got to Moon Knight because their faces fell and they looked confused and were shaking their heads. Another young life ruined; my work there was done.)

Was my dad supportive of my career choice? Well, when I was in my late teens, I will always remember him saying, "Your hobbies are nice, but you can't make a living out of science fiction and comic books." Which is of course exactly what I did. On the other hand, in later years he adored my success. Every time I'd have a new book come out, he'd go to his local bookstore and have my mother take pictures of him standing next to the display.

The major problem I had with my father was that he hit me. I assume that's how he was raised and once that behavior is ingrained, it's hard to get rid of. He wouldn't punch me or beat me, but he would slap me. Sometimes to really frighten me he would yank out his belt. He told me in later years that he never actually hit me with it; he would make loud noise with it by hitting furniture, but to my young mind there was no difference. I lived in constant fear of doing something that would provoke him to violence.

I'll never forget the day that ended.

I was in my very late teens. My younger brother Wally had done something that pissed my father off, and Dad was chasing him down the hallway. I couldn't just stand there and watch my kid brother get slapped around. I stepped in between them, shouting for my father to back off. Infuriated that I was getting in his way, he brought his right hand around to hit me.

I caught it by the wrist.

We stood there in the hallway, strength against strength. It wasn't a fair contest. I was a mature young man and my dad was in his late middle age, never worked out, and had the upper body strength of a trout. I immobilized him. A shocking realization swept over both of us: I was stronger than he was. He could no longer slap me around with impunity. I would fight back and I would win.

Just like that, all the rage dissipated. His jaw went slack in astonishment that, in an instant, a lifetime of physical domination over his children had ended. They had a protector who could stand up to him and defeat him. As he stared at me as if seeing me for the first time, I released my grip on his wrist. He took a few steps back, still staring at me, then turned and walked into his bedroom and shut the door.

He never hit any of us again.

In his later years, my father gave great thought to his conduct in raising me, and apparently decided that he was lacking. Every time we'd get together, he'd apologize to me about some offense that he was

My sister Beth and me with my parents, Gunter and Dalia, celebrating my dad's 80th birthday.

certain I still held against him even though invariably I had no recollection of it. He did the best he could and that's all you can ask of a person.

My mother was great.

She never lost her temper with me (she left matters of discipline to my dad) and she was the one from whom I got my sense of humor. Every Passover the same thing would happen at our sedars: I would crack jokes and my mother would laugh and crack jokes back and my dad would get so fed up that he'd storm away from the table and swear we'd never do another sedar. And the following year my mom and I would swear that we'd behave ourselves, and we'd try to, but never did.

Her only problem was that she'd grown up in Israel, and food refrigeration was not always the best. So her mother drilled into her the notion that you should overcook everything because that way germs couldn't survive. So most foods she made, she cooked them for so long that the taste was burned right out of them. I remember one Thanksgiving where she was cooking the turkey and it was, by any measure, ready. The breast was at 165 degrees, the little "done" pin had popped out. It was ready to take out. My mother insisted it needed more cooking time. My siblings and I staged a rescue in which Wally distracted her in the hallway while Beth and I launched a SWAT-esque raid on the turkey. As we rescued it from the oven, my mother caught on to what we were doing and tried to stop us. "No, no, we have to leave it in for another hour!" she cried. We managed to convince her otherwise. That was the year I discovered that you actually have to carve a drumstick off a turkey rather than just snap it off, which was how it had always been when my mother was able to cook at her preferred length.

As I grew up, I was certain that I was going to be a reporter like my dad. I began my studies at Temple University. I still remember one journalism class where the teacher was going to pretend that he was a police sergeant who was briefing the class on a crime that we were then to write up as a story. We were instructed to interrupt with questions at any time. He began dictating, "The victim, John Smith, was found at—"

My hand immediately shot up. "Spell the victim's name, please," I said.

Students sitting around me moaned. *What a stupid question*, they must have figured.

Without blinking an eye, but with a very slight smile, the teacher said, "First name J-O-N, second name S-M-Y-T-H-E."

I was rewarded with surprised mutters and the sounds of pencils scratching out the incorrectly spelled name. I grinned. You couldn't fool me that easily.

When I was nineteen, I wound up getting a job at a weekly newspaper called *The Germantown Courier*. One of the assignments that was my regular beat was that I was supposed to go down to the local police station and flip through the police calendar. I was then to write up stories based upon what interesting crimes had happened in Germantown that week. It was a job that could occasionally inspire amusement. One week some guy stole some washing machines out of the back of a Sears truck. I wrote that the thief had made a clean getaway. The editor cut that line. I thought it was funny.

One particular week, I was flipping through the police pad and there was nothing. I mean nothing. Minor crap. A stolen bicycle. There wasn't a thing for me to turn into a story.

Then I got to the last page and my eyes opened wide.

A fourteen-year-old girl had been raped and sodomized.

And my very first reaction was, *Good! Something to write about!*

And as that thought went through my head, my brain suddenly split right down the middle. It was as if one half was studying the other half. The one that was doing the studying said, *How could you think* Good!? *This poor girl is going to be scarred for life, and your first reaction is* Good *because you have a story? What the hell is wrong with you?*

And that was the first point at which I realized I wasn't going to be able to do reporting for a living.

Real life isn't like movies. You typically don't have a realization and then change overnight. I continued studying journalism, eventually moving from Temple University to NYU for reasons I'll go into later. But when I graduated with my B.A. in journalism, I couldn't find any jobs locally. I would have to move far out of the New York area, and I was not enamored of that idea.

So, I stayed put and decided to explore getting jobs in other venues.

Which is how I wound up being Will Smith's bodyguard.

Okay, that didn't actually happen immediately. It happened many, many years later.

But when one thinks about one's life, one rarely considers it in strict chronological context. One tends to jump around, thinking about how one thing leads to another.

So: I was Will Smith's bodyguard. Except not really. Let me explain...

I Was Will Smith's Bodyguard

My book agent, Andy Zack, called me one day and said he had a proposal for a novelization for me to write.

Let me talk about novelizations for a moment, since the subject has been broached. I always like Alan Dean Foster's take on turning the scripts of movies or television programs into books. He said that if you took a screenplay and turned it into a really good book, you were considered—at best—a talented hack. If you took a book and turned it into a really good screenplay, you could get an Oscar.

I've done lots of novelizations, including some that came out better than the movie. Producer Michael Uslan, for instance, said he wished he'd filmed my novelization of *The Return of Swamp Thing* rather than the script they used. The process of writing one always goes the same way: a publisher who has optioned the novelization rights contacts me and I agree to do it. It's pretty straightforward.

What Andy was proposing, however, was very different. He said an actor wanted to hire me to produce a novelization of a screenplay for a movie he had written for his brother in law that he was going to make. He wanted to talk to me on the phone about doing the job.

I said, "Andy, that's ridiculous. Why would I take this meeting? Some guy wants to hire me instead of a publisher? That's absurd."

Andy said, "I think you should take the meeting."

"For a screenplay that some actor has written for his brother in law?"

"Yeah."

"What's the actor's name?"

"Caleeb Pinkett." That's not a typo. Pronounced "Caleb" but two "ee's."

"I never heard of Caleeb Pinkett," I said impatiently. "I've heard of Jada Pinkett, but not Caleeb."

"Jada's his sister."

That stopped me. "Jada Pinkett is his sister."

"Right."
"Jada Pinkett Smith is his sister."
"Uh-huh."
"So his brother in law is Will Smith."
"Right."
"I'll take the meeting," I said.

We had the phone call, and Caleeb gave me a break down of the project. Titled "The Mark of Cain," it posited that the original Cain was also the first vampire ever created, and Will was going to play him. We batted ideas around, and there were some places where I thought he had good notions, and others where I thought they could be changed or improved. He seemed more interested in the things I didn't like than in the things I did.

I wound up hearing back from Andy after the conversation. Caleeb liked me. He wanted me to write the novelization. More, he wanted me to come out and meet with him and Will ... in China, which was where Will was at the time, involved in the filming of *The Karate Kid* remake starring his son.

So I had to go and get my passport updated as they prepared the visa for me to go to China.

Which never happened, because Will came back from China. Out of nowhere, to make up for the fact that I had to go and do stuff with my passport and then miss out on a trip to China, Will's people sent me a bottle of wine. I was impressed. Then, out of curiosity, I priced out the bottle and was astounded to learn it sold for around $500. Holy crap!

So instead they flew me out business class to Los Angeles, where Caleeb was supposed to meet up with me at my hotel. Instead, while standing on line at National to pick up my car, I got a phone call telling me there had been a change in plans and I was supposed to go to Will's house. Whoa!

I drove to the address they gave me. Now: remember the original *King Kong?* Remember those giant gates that were supposed to keep Kong out? That's what was waiting for me at the end of the driveway. I tapped on the intercom and announced myself. The doors slowly swung open and about ten feet in, there was a guard station like you'd find at Disney World. I rolled up and the guard, pointing to the vast vista before us, said, "Okay, you head down the driveway, past the guest house, bear left at the tennis courts, turn right at the lake, and come around to the parking area."

I sat there, unable to move, trying to wrap myself around the sheer immensity of the place. The guard looked at me curiously. "I'm sorry," I said, "I just need a moment to process this."

A grin split his face. "I understand. The exact same thing happened to me the first day I got here."

I followed the directions and pulled into the back of the house. Caleeb answered the door, a cheery looking young man, quite handsome (you can find his picture on IMDB). He led me to an area with a table that could be used to either eat at or work at. There were people working in the kitchen that I realized were cooks, and they immediately asked me solicitously if I was hungry. They assured me they could prepare whatever I wanted. I politely declined.

Then a few moments later, Will walked in.

Now I had very carefully considered what I would say to him because I figured that would set the tone of the relationship. If I geeked out, told him what a big fan I was, then I figured I would diminish my standing. If I just said, "Nice to meet you," that was hardly original and since my stock in trade was ideas, unoriginality didn't seem the best way to proceed.

So when Will—whose head was shaved as it would later be for *Suicide Squad*—walked in, I looked up, blinked, and said, "Oh, you're *that* Will Smith."

Will immediately roared with laughter. "I didn't assume; it's a very common name," I added, to which he replied, "It certainly is."

We got to work.

It was certainly the most unique novelizing assignment I had ever taken on, because typically the scripts I adapted were finished. In this case, both Will and Caleeb clearly considered the script to be in flux, and they were very interested in my views on how to improve it.

At no time did I ever give voice to what I thought would be the best way to improve it: Get someone else to star in it.

That's no knock on Will's acting ability. I'm sure he could have acted the hell out of it. What concerned me was whether audiences would accept Will in the role of King of All Evil. Viewers were accustomed to Will as the wise-ass hero. Either that or a flawed but likable man who wound up learning stuff through the film that improved him. I was dubious as to whether audiences would accept Will Smith as the originator of (A) vampires and (B) murder. But I felt that was outside the purview of my job, and so I kept that opinion to myself.

I was amazed by how open Will and Caleeb were to my suggestions. I mean, it was Caleeb's script and Will was a multi-millionaire movie star. I was just some writer from New York. Yet they took seriously everything I had to offer. At one point I made a suggestion that had Will and Caleeb saying, "We'd have to rewrite the entire third act. Let's get the board!" And they went and wheeled out this large board covered with file cards and notes that they had used to plot out the script.

At one point we took a break and I brought my computer outside to get some air. I remembered that my third daughter, Ariel, had just begun her education at Sacred Heart University in Connecticut. I used my computer to do a FaceTime chat with her. She was in her dorm room with a friend, Emma, and she didn't know where I was. We chatted and then Will emerged from the house and looked at me oddly because I was sitting there talking to my computer. "I'm doing a FaceTime chat with my daughter, Ariel, who just started college," I called, and then I grinned. "Wanna say hi?"

"Sure," said Will and he trotted over.

He stuck his face into camera and I said, "Ariel, this is my friend, Will."

Ariel's eyes widened and her jaw dropped in shock. As for Emma ... remember the poster for the movie *Scanners?* With the guy whose head is about to explode? That was Emma.

"Hey, Ariel," said Will. "So how's college?"

"Ariel!" she said, apparently because her brain had locked up and hadn't managed to assimilate what Will was saying to her. I just sat there, grinning.

Later on, they showed me a cut-together scene from *Karate Kid*, the part in which Jackie Chan confronts a group of toughs in an alleyway. "Notice how he never hits them," Caleb pointed out. "He sets them against each other." Which he did; it was a very well choreographed sequence.

Then at one point they said to me, "We're going to be flying up to Seattle this evening. Trey's [Will's eldest son, in high school at that point] football team is heading up there for a playoff. You want to come? We'd totally understand if you didn't."

Now the truth was that I had been awake since 4 a.m. Eastern time, and I was completely exhausted. But there was no way I was going to pass up on that. "Sure," I said.

"Okay. We'll be heading up at 5 p.m."

As time passed and we continued to work, I was noticing that time was ticking along. From where we were it was going to take forty-five minutes to an hour to reach LAX, so when it hit 4 p.m. I said nervously, "Shouldn't we get going? If the plane is taking off at 5 p.m...."

"It'll wait for us," Will said confidently.

That was, of course, when I realized. We were going on a private airplane. I'd never flown on one in my life. I had to admit, I was interested in what it would be like.

It was freaking cool, is what it was. The passengers were Will,

Caleeb, Will's body man, whose name I've forgotten: let's call him Sam. And me, of course. It was a marvelous plane, complete with our own stewardess and fully stocked with food for meals. The seats were unbelievably comfortable. We continued to discuss *Cain*, so it was a working trip, and easily the best flight I'd ever taken.

We arrived at a private airport in Seattle and a car was waiting for us. It drove us over to the football field where the game was just under way. The four of us clambered out of the car and entered at the far end of the field, making our way around it to go to the benches at sidelines.

The crowd spotted Will and erupted in cheers. Both sides of the stadium, the home team and the visitors, went nuts when they saw that Will was there.

As the volume of the crowd went through the roof in hysterics, I said to Caleeb, "Sorry. This always happens when I go places."

A few minutes later, my wife Kathleen called me on my cell phone and said, "You've been spotted at the game."

"I know," I said. Then I frowned. "How did you know?"

"Someone is Tweeting about it. They just wrote, 'Will Smith just arrived with his three bodyguards.'"

"Really?" It was certainly an apt description for Sam, but me? I turned to Caleeb and said, "According to the Twitterverse, you and I are Will's bodyguards." Caleeb grinned at that.

We didn't go and sit up in the seats. They were crammed with fans that would have been all over Will. Instead we stood down on the field near the team, and we moved up and down the field as Trey's team battled their opponents. Meanwhile, TV news crews kept coming over and tried to get to Will, but Sam kept them at bay. "Will is here just to watch his son's game," Sam said in a patient but firm tone. "He doesn't want this evening, or the coverage, to be about him." I thought that was remarkably sensitive of Will, to be concerned about taking the spotlight away from his son.

Trey's team won, thank God. I was not looking forward to the prospect of a plane ride back with a cranky Will Smith. When we returned to the private airport for our plane, there was a mob of Will fans waiting at the gate, perhaps hoping he'd come out and hobnob with them. He didn't. I couldn't blame him. In this day and age, you have no idea if one of the fans has a gun in his pocket and a dream of achieving immortality by being the guy who gunned down Will Smith.

I wrote the novelization, and did a second draft of it, and was well paid for it.

Time passed. And then one day Caleeb approached me about a new project that they were working on.

It was called *After Earth*. It was going to star Will and Jaden together, which would seem to any reasonable person to be box office gold. Will and Jaden were going to play a space ranger and his son who wind up trapped on an Earth of the future, one where the whole of humanity had left during a nuclear war and the world was overrun by monstrous animals who wanted to destroy them. I thought, "It can't miss."

Caleeb needed two things. First, he needed a team of writers to craft a bible for the film. This was intended to be a launching point for a full franchise, one that would be a vehicle for Jaden much as *Men in Black* was for Will. They had a television spin-off in the works that Ron Moore was involved with. But they needed a back story for the world, one that could be distributed to everyone—Moore, licensees, whoever—so that we could all be on the same page. That seemed reasonable to me.

Second, they had a book deal with Del Rey to publish a novelization and collection of novellas designed to be a prequel. They needed someone to write those, too.

"I've got it covered," I told Caleeb with confidence. "I have a couple of guys I can work with. We'll handle everything. Oh: who's directing it?"

"M. Night Shyamalan," he said.

My heart crashed into my feet. I knew we were dead before we were even in lift off.

Understand, this is not a comment on Night's talent. God knows he had turned out a string of awful movies. On the other hand, he had turned out some great ones, too. So the quality of the movie itself was a coin flip. That wasn't what concerned me. What worried me was that the movie had suddenly become a hundred times harder to sell. It didn't matter that Will and Jaden were starring in it. The moment the trailers said M. Night Shyamalan, audiences were going to groan and say, "No way." Whatever the box office gold Will's name had was going to be X'd out by Night's. The audiences were going to say, "Yeah, it's a Will Smith movie, but I hate Shyamalan." Reviewers were going to be sitting in wait to lob grenades at it and Will and Jaden were going to be caught in the crossfire.

But that was tomorrow's problem. I had a bible to write.

I immediately contacted Mike Friedman and Bob Greenberger. I had cowritten several *Star Trek* novels with them, and we also annually collaborated on *Mystery Trekkie Theater 3000* for the Shore Leave convention, where we would throw insults and snarks at a *Trek* episode. They seemed the ideal partners for the venture, and they immediately signed on. We were sent the script and after we had time to read it, we got together, we collaborated, and we started pounding out the back story.

We gave Overbrook Entertainment (Will's company) more than they bargained for. The bible was something like three hundred pages long, starting with the creation of Earth and going into the far-flung future of *After Earth*. It was an astoundingly impressive science fiction package. It provided the entire basis we needed for the prequel anthology, which was titled "A Perfect Beast."

I also managed to score a hell of a deal for myself. Caleeb wanted me to come up with a story for the *After Earth* sequel, and I managed to convince him (and Will) to let me write the entire script. I was thrilled for the opportunity. This could finally be my big break into Hollywood.

Some time later, Will was filming *Men in Black 3* and we were invited to come watch. That night they were filming under a section of the FDR Drive nearby some piers, and wife Kathleen, daughter Caroline (aged nine) and I went to watch.

When Will arrived on set, there was a flood of fans following him and being kept back by a string of security guards. He came over and greeted us. Caroline was sitting on a seat, seeming rather indifferent to Will's presence.

Left to right: Me, Bob Greenberger, Will Smith and Mike Friedman.

"Caroline's a little disappointed," I admitted to him in a low voice. "She was hoping Jaden or Willow would be here."

Will immediately let out a loud sort of ululating cry, as if he were making bird noises or something. And from a tent a short distance away, Willow and Jaden emerged.

Caroline's face became incandescent. She descended from her chair and her little body was trembling as the younger Smiths approached. "You want to give Jaden a hug?" Will asked.

Immediately Caroline sped toward him and slammed into him with such velocity that she nearly knocked the Karate Kid on his ass. Willow, not to be outdone, opened her arms and said, "How about me?" She hugged Willow as well, but her attention was entirely focused on Jaden.

After *MIB3*, Will and Jaden proceeded to start shooting *After Earth*. At one point, Will and company were shooting at a lot near Philadelphia and we were invited to come down and meet the crew. Bob, Mike and I rolled down with Kathleen and Caroline in tow. We arrived on the set and I was ushered into Will's trailer. I walked in, didn't see him...

And Will leaped out from hiding and shouted "Boo!" at me.

I jumped two feet in the air and when I regained enough of my wits to speak, I shouted, "Really? *Really?* You get paid millions of dollars to be in movies and *that's* how you entertain yourself?!?" Ha-Freaking-Ha.

After shooting concluded for the day, we hung out at the offices for a while and watched Night play ping-pong with various cast members. Caroline was ten by that point and it was abundantly clear that she was now totally enamored of Jaden. At one point, Jaden was playing Night, and every time the ball would fall on the floor, Caroline would scamper over, pick it up and bring it to Jaden. Never to Night. Didn't matter whose ball it was; she gave it to Jaden. It was adorable.

I was busy writing my novelization of the film and was about a third of the way through it when I was felled with a stroke (more about that later). My typing speed dropped from one hundred twenty words a minute to eight. There was just no way I was going to be able to finish the novelization. Del Rey was ready to cancel it, but Bob and Mike stepped in. They took over the work and between the two of them, banged out the rest of the book. Despite my offer to have their names on it, they took no cover credit and they also took none of the advance money. How's that for friends?

So eventually *After Earth* debuted. My script for the sequel was ready to go.

And the film tanked.

First of all, as I feared, it was targeted because of Night. His name was almost non-existent in the promotion exactly to avoid people being scared off, but word got out. Either people didn't go because it was Night, or they trashed the film. People who had no issues with Jaden's performances in *The Karate Kid* or *The Pursuit of Happyness* suddenly decided he didn't know how to act.

Even better were the people who loudly declared that they would have no truck with a film where nepotism was on full display. Right, right. Just like they shunned *Paper Moon* with Ryan O'Neal and his daughter Tatum. And Billy Ray and Miley Cyrus in *Hannah Montana: The Movie.* Martin and Charlie Sheen in *Wall Street.* Henry Fonda and his daughter Jane in *On Golden Pond.* It seemed to me that Night's presence caused most people to put on their hate hats and look for anything and everything they could bitch about.

With Jaden Smith during the afterparty at the launch of *After Earth*.

I also couldn't help but note that Will's character was essentially unlikable. His relationship with his son was icy and he seemed disinterested in human emotion. It was, of course, so that he could have a character arc, but as I originally feared when I first learned of *Mark of Cain*, audiences were put off by Will playing basically an asshole.

Ultimately the film took in $243 million overall over a budget of $130 million. By any stretch of accounting, that meant the film was successful, even when you factor in that a film has to make 150 percent of its budget to turn a profit. But apparently that wasn't satisfactory, and the film was dismissed as a bomb even though it indisputably made money.

Several days after the film opened, Caleeb called me and said they were cancelling all the other *After Earth* projects. There would be no more books or comic books planned, the Ron Moore pilot was D.O.A., and naturally my screenplay would never be filmed. I also found out that

Mark of Cain was dead. Apparently, the studios had come to the same conclusion that I had: Audiences didn't want to see a Will Smith that they had trouble rooting for.

That was pretty much the last conversation I ever had with Caleeb.

But hey, at least I was his brother-in-law's bodyguard for a while.

Make Mine Marvel

When I was working for *The Germantown Courier*, I had given up reading comics. I had basically outgrown them some years earlier, as was not atypical for comic book readers when they hit puberty. But one day as I was walking by a local newsstand, I saw a large tabloid publication that featured, to my shock, Superman squaring off against Spider-Man. Now if you could have told nineteen-year-old me that decades later I would be involved in writing an entire crossover series with Marvel heroes squaring off against DC, I would have ... well, actually, I'd have gone Marty McFly on you and gotten as much information about upcoming sporting events as I could. In any event, that didn't come up, but I did buy the tabloid because I was genuinely interested.

And some time after that, at that same newsstand, I discovered that there was a brand-new *X-Men* book. It was issue #95, and I recognized almost none of the characters. But I bought it and read it and all my old love for comic books came roaring back to me. Those two issues pulled me back in. Later I went to a comic book convention where I picked up #94 for pretty much cover price, and the *Giant Sized X-Men #1* for a dollar. I just checked on eBay and someone is selling both those issues together for $1500. Six months later I picked up a copy of *Incredible Hulk #181*, the first appearance of Wolverine, also for a buck. That one is now on eBay for $1000 at the low end and as high as $3200. Jesus.

I continued reading both Marvel and DC comics well into my twenties. Meanwhile I had decided not to become a reporter, but I was determined to try and stay connected to publishing in some way, shape or form.

Fortunately, I had a talent that benefited me: I could type. Fast. Very fast. Like 120 words a minute fast. That skill landed me at E.P. Dutton, where I worked for a woman named Gloria Mosesson as her secretary. She had her own book imprint, Elsevier Nelson. I managed to have a comic book encounter even in those circumstances, because one day we received a letter and book in the mail that told us one of our books—*Star*

Chase—was a line-for-line plagiarism of another book called *Escape Across the Cosmos* by Gardner Fox. I of course knew Fox as being one of the main architects of the DC Universe. I compared the two novels and found that the letter writer was absolutely correct. I informed Gloria of the theft and she assigned me to get in touch with Fox. I contacted DC and they put me in touch with him. I managed to remain professional and tell Fox that we were going to be sending him a check for the book, the same amount that we had paid the "author," and that any future editions of the book (there were none) would have his name on it. Fox took it quite well; to him it was found money on a book that had come out nearly twenty years ago.

My other fun moment at Dutton was when I discovered the original Winnie-the-Pooh animals were wrapped in a bag in a closet. The same toys that Christopher Robin Milne had loved. I got permission at one point to take them out of the bags and my then-wife and I played with them. Those same toys now sit in a special display at the New York Public Library, staring out at the world through glass.

Eventually I left Gloria Mosesson right after she fired me. Basically, Elsevier Nelson acquired a new Canadian owner and I was sure that the then-office manager was working to get dirt on Gloria (she criticized them relentlessly) so Gloria would be fired. Gloria sided with the office manager and fired me.

It was the lowest moment in my life. I will never forget meeting up for the commute home with my then wife, whose was seven months pregnant with our first daughter, Shana. She could tell, even from a distance, that something was wrong and I had to tell her that I was out of work with no medical coverage and no means of covering the expenses for the baby.

Some months later, the Canadians fired Gloria and put the office manager in charge. I thought that was hilarious because I was already employed again, working for the sales department of Playboy Paperbacks.

Despite what the title might suggest, Playboy Paperbacks was a high quality publisher. We handled books by authors such as Anne Tyler (*The Accidental Tourist*), Morgan Llewelyn (*Lion of Ireland*) and a novelization of a very popular comic book series called *Elfquest: Journey to Sorrow's End* by Wendy and Richard Pini. I worked in the direct sales department for a great guy named Paul Hurowitz. I also became friends with the science fiction editor, Sharon Jarvis (who would later go on to become my first literary agent).

Eventually, though, Playboy wound up having to sell off the book division. We had a month to find other employment because all the division's assets were being purchased by Ace. They were acquiring the books and contracts, but all the people were going to be out of work.

And Paul wasn't going to be able to help me find another job because Paul had died some months earlier. He picked up pneumonia during a road trip. I was devastated when he passed away, and now with Playboy going out of business, that entire portion of my life was ending.

Now: I had acquired in my *Star Trek* convention going (more about *Star Trek* later) a friend named Howie Weinstein, author of the *Star Trek: The Animated Series* script "The Pirates of Orion" and some novels as well. Knowing that I needed money from any source, he put me together with a guy named Bob Greenberger who was, at the time, editor of a magazine called *Comics Scene*. *Comics Scene* was a comic-related magazine published by *Starlog*. Both are now long gone, but at the time they were quite a powerful force in the industry, and I was more than happy to talk to anyone who could kick work my way.

Bob was pleased to chat with me, and he had the exact article in mind for me to write. The direct sales market was a relatively new concept, having first risen its head in the 1970s through the business acumen of distributor Phil Seuling. Up until then, comics were low-priority items distributed through Independent Distributors. They placed them into news stores, 7-Elevens and such. They were low discount and fully returnable, which is why it took months for publishers to know how books were selling. Titles could actually be cancelled and then publishers would find out months later that sales were doing quite well.

Seuling had come up with a different approach. He wanted to buy comics directly from the publishers non-returnable, but at a significantly higher discount. Also, as opposed to newsstands that adhered to the concept of "on-sale" dates, the direct sales stores would put their books out on the stands the moment they got them.

It's fair to say that the direct market saved the comics industry. Wholesale books slowly devolved into a mere accessory as direct sales grew to the point where it was that market driving the industry. In addition to Phil's Sea Gate Distributors, other distributors began popping up all over the country. Diamond Comics, Capital City, Pacific, Glenwood, Comics Unlimited and up to a dozen more over time.

Bob wanted to do a story about it and how its rise had changed the comics publishing industry. Since I was already working in publishing sales, he figured that I would be a natural to write the story.

I immediately began researching, speaking to such folks as Paul Levitz at DC Comics, Phil Seuling and anyone else I could find. The last interview I was slated to do was with Carol Kalish, who was the assistant direct sales manager at Marvel under Mike Friedrich. I arranged for an interview and came in.

Carol was an attractive blonde-ish brunette in her mid–20s, with an easy manner and a relentless intellect. I came into her office at 3 p.m. and we spoke until 6—both our throats were raw. We really enjoyed each other's company. At the end of the interview, as I was packing up my stuff, Carol asked where I worked. I told her. "How did you get time off to come and do this interview?"

"Playboy Paperbacks is being shut down," I said. "So I told my boss I was going out for an interview. He assumed I meant job interview and just said, 'Good luck.'"

Carol's eyes lit up. "So ... you're going to be out of a job?"

"By the end of the month, yeah."

She leaned forward and said, "I'm being promoted to sales manager at the end of the month, and I'm going to need an assistant. Would you be interested in interviewing?"

I blinked like a deer in the headlights. "Well ... okay ... sure. But let me call my editor on this story to make sure that's not going to present a conflict."

When I got home, I phoned Bob and told him the situation. Would being hired by Marvel present any conflict of interest?

"Can you write the story before the job interview?"

"Absolutely," I said.

"Okay but be sure not to make Marvel a disproportionate part of the story."

So I wrote the story and some days later I returned to Marvel, this time to be the subject of the interview. It may well be the first time in history where a potential employee interviewed his potential boss first. I came in wearing a suit to look as professional as possible.

I walked into Carol's office and she was sitting behind her desk, putting together a model kit. "Is that a pterodactyl?" I asked as I sat.

"No, it's Rodan!" she said cheerfully. And she proceeded to tell me Rodan's entire origin as a part of the Godzilla monster universe. As she spoke, she reached across her desk for a piece of the model and her rolling chair skidded out from under her. She hit the floor with a loud thud. I sat there, stunned, thinking, *What the hell...?*

She scrambled back into the chair, righted herself, folded her hands and said to me briskly, "So ... why do you want to work at Marvel Comics?" as if she had not been on the floor seconds earlier.

I thought about it for a moment and said, "Do you see this suit? It's a winter suit. This is pretty much the last month I can wear it and I don't have a summer suit. So if I have to keep job searching, I'll need to buy a summer suit because this one is too warm. I really can't afford that right now, so I'd like to get this job to avoid spending that money."

She considered that, nodded and said, "Good answer." She bounded to her feet and said, "Come on. I want to introduce you to Ed," meaning Ed Shukin, her boss and the head of independent sales.

Two days later, Carol phoned me up. I had the job.

After that, things got interesting.

* * *

I spent five years as Marvel's assistant direct sales manager and eventually sales manager, when Carol was promoted to vice president of direct sales. Our jobs didn't really change, just our titles. Eventually I wound up with two assistants as well, my secretary Sandy Schechter, a personable red-headed woman, and Fred Baumann, a young general assistant who was at the disposal of everyone in direct sales. I'll never forget the time that Carol had lent him twenty bucks for something (I think it was a card game) and on pay day he walked into the office with the money to repay her. She had a distributor in with her and Fred placed the twenty on her desk and said, "Thank you for letting me work here another week, Ms. Kalish," and walked out, leaving Carol stunned and the distributor roaring with laughter.

Did Carol and I always get on? Good lord, no. She was strong-willed with many firm opinions and a mind that was very hard to change. Sometimes I got the feeling that she disagreed with me just to be arbitrary. One day we were coming back from lunch and she kept disagreeing with me about so many points that suddenly I said, out of the blue, "Black!" Without hesitation she shot back, "White!" "I *knew* it!" I shouted.

My first major undertaking as the assistant direct sales manager was to attend the Chicago Comic Con. It was one of the most mentally exhausting endeavors I had ever undertaken. I had breakfast, lunch and dinner meetings with retailers and distributors, and I can say with no exaggeration that every single one of those guys hated Marvel. Or if not hated, at least had major complaints. No one had anything positive to say. They complained about discounts, co-op advertising, reorders, every possible subject under the sun. I wanted to blow my brains out, it was just so fatiguing. Maybe it was just because I was the new guy and they had all collectively decided to beat me into submission, but by the time I left the convention, you could have poured me into my airplane seat with a spoon.

However, although getting to know the retailers and distributors was an exhausting undertaking, I was also getting to know the creators whom I had grown up reading. I'll never forget the first time I met Chris Claremont, the man whose writing had pulled me back into comics in the first place.

"Mr. Claremont, I'm Peter David, the assistant direct sales manager, it's a pleasure to meet you."

"Yeah, nice to meet you too. Now can you step out of the way of the copier, I need to Xerox some stuff."

Over time I met all the editors, who seemed polite and interested in my talents whenever they wanted to promote their various titles and stories. Denny O'Neill came to me describing a storyline he wanted to do that would hit Tony Stark hard with his alcoholism. I came up with the promo line, "His armor can protect him from anything ... except himself." Denny loved that line and we went with it.

Then there was the time that Walt Simonson came in with his first drawing of Beta Ray Bill. The tag line was, "What have they done to the Mighty Thor?!" Some months later he brought in a drawing of Thor as a frog and naturally we went with, "What have they done to the Mighty Thor now!?"

Meanwhile Carol was determined to improve the quality of the direct sales market. She kept opening up new distributors, which drove the older ones nuts because, y'know, more competition. Carol didn't care. Her greatest fear was that one distributor would wind up driving the others out and we would wind up with only one. Which is, of course, exactly what happened. To this day I worry that Diamond will run into major financial problems and fold up shop. Then what? My guess is that Disney will buy them.

She noticed that many retailers didn't even have cash registers; they just operated out of a cigar box. She introduced a cash register program that I helped oversee, introducing retailers to the notion of using cash registers. It might seem self-evident to an outsider, but to many comic retailers, it was an entirely new concept. I'll never forget one retailer at a convention who I was introducing to the idea. I worked with him for twenty minutes, doing a series of transactions on it, and at the end I totaled out what would have been his day of sales. He stared at it and said, "What's this amount here? $123?"

I glanced at it and said, "That's the amount of money you gave away in discounts."

His jaw dropped. "Really?"

"Yup."

He immediately ordered a cash register and also said he was going to cut back on, or do away with, discounts completely.

Soon I met Stan Lee. Stan was no longer working in the office at the time, having relocated to the west coast, but every so often he would come back to do business. And every time I ran into him in the hallway, I would introduce myself again because his lousy memory was absolutely legendary. The fifth time I met him, I said, "Hey, Stan." And he said, "Hi..." and then paused and said, "Peter!"

I thought, *My God, Stan Lee remembers my name. I've arrived.*

Then there was 1986, the year that the Mets were battling it out to get into the World Series that they would eventually win. They had made it to the division finals and were squaring off against the Houston Astros for the sixth game of a seven-game series. This was considered a must-win for the Mets because, if they lost, the series would be tied and they would have to face Astros Ace Mike Scott, who had dominated them in the two previous games.

In those days, on occasion, those games were played during the daytime. As the game approached the ninth inning, a number of us—including me—assembled in Jim Shooter's office. None of us wanted to go home and not see the Mets win the game. The Mets had been down three to one for the entirety of the game, but in the top of the ninth inning they scored three to tie it, and when the Astros failed to score, it sent the game into extra innings.

Chris Claremont walked in and asked what the score was.

"Tied at three," we said.

"Well, they better wrap it up because the American league championship game starts at eight."

We collectively scoffed. The game was already going into extra innings. The ALCS was at 8 p.m. Three hours later? It wasn't even going to be close.

Inning after inning passed. The Mets scored a run in the top of the 14th and we thought, "Thank God," but then the Astros came back in the bottom with a response run and the game continued. Finally, in the 16th inning, the Mets scored three and we were convulsed with joy. And then the damned Astros came back with two runs and they had runners on the corners with two outs.

And all we could think was, *Jesus, don't let Claremont be right* as the clock inched toward eight straight up.

Then Jesse Orosco struck out the batter and a cheer erupted. Not just from us, but outside. There was a P.C. Richards on the corner and every television in the window was tuned to the game, and mobs of people were standing there watching it. One of the best ballgames I ever saw. That anyone ever saw.

I also pitched for the Marvel softball team. My best moment was one game where the other team had, through a series of errors on my

(From left) Gwen, Caroline, Ariel, me and Kathleen standing outside Citi Field to see a Mets game. The photograph was taken by Gwen's husband, Heath.

team's part, managed to load the bases with one out. Our lead was in jeopardy. I made the next pitch and the result was a line drive right back at me. Reacting instantly, I grabbed the ball on the fly. Then I immediately pivoted and shoveled the ball to first base, doubling off the runner. End of the inning.

One time I brought my daughter, Shana, to the Marvel offices, for take your daughter to work day. She was maybe five years old. I brought her around to meet the editors, and while I was in Louise Simonson's office, Jim Shooter stepped in behind her. Sensing there was someone there, she turned and all she could see were his legs. Rather than backing up, she tilted backwards to try and see the face of the well-over-six-feet Shooter. Instead of managing to spy his face, she instead tumbled backwards and hit the floor, which we all thought was funny as hell.

Later on, I was in my office and I turned to see what Shana was up to.

She was gone. At some point I'd been looking down, buried in work, and she had chosen that moment to wander out of my office.

Immediately I sprinted out of my office and as I did, I ran past Alice, the secretary to Mike Hobson, executive vice-president of Marvel. I said, "Did you see a little girl wander past here?"

"Yes," Alice said immediately. "She's in with Mike."

I stopped dead. "She's what?"

"She walked into Mike's office."

"Was there anyone in there with him?"

She nodded. "Jim Galton."

Oh, holy crap. My daughter had strolled into a meeting being held between the president and vice-president of Marvel Comics. That was it. I was dead. I was fired.

And suddenly Shana strolled out, her arms filled with books and Marvel toys. "Bye, Mike!" she said cheerfully. Shana had a way with people.

Most of my average days were spent dealing with whatever issues or problems the distributors had. On the other hand, sometimes the switchboard would toss questions over to me that they didn't want to bother editorial with. One time my phone rang and it was a kid who asked, "If Superman raced the Silver Surfer, who would win?"

"The Silver Surfer," I replied immediately.

"Okay, thanks," he said and hung up. Of course, I said the Silver Surfer. If I'd worked for DC, I would have said Superman. Obviously.

Another one of my jobs was to inspect covers. Every cover was circulated throughout the company and checked over, and my job was to make sure that the price was correct and that it lined up with the price on the UPC code or, as we called them back then, zebra labels. Mostly it was routine, although the most interesting catch I made was when I was given the cover for *Indiana Jones #1* by John Byrne. I checked the cover and code and it was fine, but for some reason I also stared at the coloring. As opposed to nowadays, where all of this stuff is done on computers, in those days the coloring was done on 8×10 Xeroxes. These were called "color guides" and were sent to the printer, where a separator did the actual coloring. Typically, when I would get the cover with the color guide attached I barely glanced at it because that wasn't my department.

In this case, though, I stared and stared because something didn't seem right. Then I spotted it. There was a menacing and rather dusky villain in the background and he had three arms. His right arm had a hand clapped over the mouth of a damsel, the left hand was holding a dagger, and the other left hand was outstretched. I flipped the black and white cover around and examined it and then looked back at the coloring. I realized at that point that the outstretched hand was likely the hand of the woman reaching toward Indy and it had simply been colored wrong by the colorist who apparently wasn't paying attention. On the other hand, maybe he *did* have three arms. It was *Indiana Jones*, so anything was possible.

I signed off on it because the price was correct, but I jotted a note on the sheet that said, "Is that bad guy supposed to have three arms in the coloring?" I handed it back to the intern and said, "Be sure Weezie [editor Louise Simonson] sees that note." He nodded and headed out.

About two minutes later, Weezie came sprinting into my office saying, "Thank you! Thank you! Thank you for spotting that! Oh my God, thank you!" I was right. The colorist had screwed up, and if I hadn't caught it, the cover would likely have gone out that way and Weezie implied that she would have gotten into big trouble with George Lucas's people.

Which isn't to say that we never had problems with Lucas. For instance, Marvel published the comic book adaptation of *Return of the Jedi*. Like any other comic, it was shipped out three weeks ahead of time—in this instance, the time being when the movie hit the theaters. Remember how I said direct sales dealers never paid attention to the on-sale dates? Well, they didn't this time either.

So when Mark Hamill, who was living in New York at the time, wandered into his local comic book store and discovered that they were selling it three weeks in advance, he immediately called George Lucas. And Lucasfilms called us and came down on us like a ton of bricks.

Carol called me into her office and said, "I want you to go to every comic book store in Manhattan and tell them to take the comic off the shelves."

I stared at her incredulously. "They won't do it!"

"I need you to see them remove it from the shelves," she insisted.

Then I understood and nodded. This wasn't really about getting the comic books off the shelves. This was an exercise in ass covering.

So I went to every Manhattan comic store. Some of the retailers knew me, some didn't. I walked in and identified myself and said, "You've put the *Return of the Jedi* special on the shelves three weeks ahead of on-sale date. You have to take it down."

"You're saying I can't sell it?" they would say in shock.

"I'm saying I need to see you take it off the shelves as I'm instructing you to do."

They would blink in puzzlement, but then they would get it. "And when you walk out the door?"

"My job is to see you take them off the shelves."

"Got it," they'd say, and they'd pull it down and put the stack behind their check out area.

"Good. Thanks," I'd say, and then I'd walk out knowing full well that as soon as I was out the door, they'd put them back out for sale. But at least the direct sales department could say that we went to every store that Mark Hamill was likely to walk into and saw them removed.

Naturally, the movie's plot details hit national news. At least it took a full news cycle for that to happen. If the Internet had existed back then, Lucas wouldn't have found out from Mark; he'd had found out from *Star Wars* fans who would have been tearing the film apart online. The one funny thing to come out of it was rumors that Marvel had fired ten people over the screw up. Ten people? If they'd fired the whole sales department, that would have been Carol, Fred, Sandy, Ed, and me. That's five. They'd have had to start firing people from subscriptions as well. In point of fact, no one was fired. We had to hunker down for a while as the storm swirled around us, but eventually the movie opened and did fine and Lucasfilm stopped caring.

I also named a character, which was exciting. I happened to be in Weezie's office when Chris Claremont was there, and they were batting around potential names for a character that would be debuting in *New Mutants*. Her name was Rahne Sinclair, and she was capable of transforming into a wolf, but she hated her power. Just hated it.

And I piped up, "If being a wolf is the bane of her existence, how about Wolfsbane?"

Chris blinked and considered that and said, "Y'know, I like that. Let's go with Wolfsbane." Which is why I've always had a fondness for that character and had great fun writing her in the pages of *X-Factor*.

The longer I worked as direct sales manager, the more comfortable I got in my job. At one convention, I had a cocktail party in my room for retailers and professionals. Being a responsible host, I wanted to make sure no one got seriously hammered, so I warned the bartender that he should monitor the drinking and give me a heads up if anyone seemed to be overdoing it. A while later, he signaled me over and said, "That guy has had three rum and Cokes in the last half hour." Who was he indicating? Dave Sim, the creator of *Cerebus the Aardvark*. I thought a moment and then said, "Okay, the next one he drinks, cut the amount of rum in half. After that, remove it entirely." The bartender nodded.

An hour and a half later, Dave was completely smashed. He was lurching around, slurring his words, hanging on people. I sidled over to the bartender and said in a low voice, "I thought you were cutting him back!"

"I did," said the bartender. "I've been giving him nothing but Coke for over an hour!"

I blinked in surprise. "Are you sure?"

"Absolutely. He should be stone cold sober."

I made my way over to Dave and asked him how he was doing. He draped an arm around me and said, "Great! I'm doing great!" His breath washed over me and it was devoid of any aroma of liquor. So Dave had apparently convinced himself that he was drunk and consequently made himself the center of the party, which I thought was hilarious.

Unfortunately, not all such retailer and pro gatherings were that entertaining.

I was supposed to be hosting a retailer gathering in, I believe it was, Atlanta, Georgia. I needed to put together a preview packet, which would consist of black and white Xeroxes of excerpts for upcoming Marvel titles. I went around to all of the editors' offices and asked for some samples for the distribution.

Denny O'Neill was, at the time, editing *Alpha Flight*. We had let rumors out that John Byrne was going to be killing off someone in the comic, and the identity was a big secret. I can tell you now, since it's thirty years later, that it was Guardian, but at the time no one knew. So Denny rifled through the art pages, which were kept in large flat file drawers, and he pulled out a sequence from the issue after Guardian dies, in which a shocked Heather, his wife, is dreaming about a rotting Guardian crashing out of his grave. "You sure about this?" I said.

"It's obviously a dream sequence, so it's not giving anything away," he said.

I said okay and took the page and added it to the Xeroxes.

Flash forward some weeks later and I'm hosting a retailer cocktail party. We have hors d'oeuvres and snacks and we also have the packages of retailer giveaways on a table along with other Marvel promotional material.

In strolls John. Everything is fine, he's making nice to all the retailers, and then he walks over and starts paging through the giveaways.

And he spots the page.

Now: Does he come over to me quietly, say, "What's this page doing in here? Get it out immediately." At which point without question I would have done as he asked?

Of course not. Instead he starts waving around the page and bellowing, "What's this page doing in here!? It gives away that Guardian dies!"

Which immediately took a quiet, lazy little gathering and turned it on its head, because none of the retailers had even really glanced through it, and those that had had assumed it was (correctly) a dream sequence and figured the events were not binding on reality. But John had just blurted out the big reveal in a manner that could not remotely be ignored. Again, thank God the Internet didn't exist because it would have been an article on "Bleeding Cool" inside of fifteen minutes.

John stormed out of the room, pausing just long enough to kick over an ashtray, leaving me stunned for a moment. The first thing I did, naturally, was gather up all the photocopied stacks and also took them out of the hands of the retailers who had already picked them up. I went into another room and ripped out the offending page from every single one. Then Tom DeFalco accompanied me to Byrne's hotel room where I apologized profusely for the mix-up and assured John that Denny had given me the pages, knowing what they were to be used for.

As soon as John got back home, he contacted Denny to verify my story.

And Denny denied it. Naturally. John must have sounded furious, and Denny threw me under the bus by stating that, hell no, he hadn't given me the pages. I must have snuck into the office, psychically known they were in the file drawer, removed them without anyone in the office seeing me, and then returned them unseen once more after photocopying them. This of course made no sense at all. But it is the version of the events that John believes to this day. His assertion was that my motivation was that I wanted to make myself seem important to the retailers because I had access to secret Marvel stuff. Which was absurd. Retailers only cared about me in terms of how I did my job in making sure their distributors got them their comics—end of story. There was no purpose in trying to elevate myself in their eyes, and certainly sticking a page of *Alpha Flight* into the middle of a retailer pack wasn't going to do it in any event. The bottom line was that Denny figured it was better that my ass get in trouble than his.

All in all, I spent five years working for Marvel in the direct sales department.

And then I became a writer.

Becoming a Part-Time Writer

Oftentimes I have encountered people who, upon learning that I am a writer, will say one of two things.

First: "I've always thought about becoming a writer, but I've never had the time."

Of course they don't have the time. They're much more involved doing important things, like earning a living or raising their children or attending meetings or doing whatever is vital to existence. So they've never had enough spare time on their hands to get involved with the whole writing thing. Someone who is actually a writer clearly has far too much time on their hands. They couldn't be like me who, at the beginning of his writing career, lived in the following manner:

Get up in the morning, grab breakfast, head into the city.

Work the entire day.

Come home around 6:30. Have dinner, spend time with the kids. Kids go to bed, spend time with the wife. Around 11 p.m., start writing until around 2 in the morning. Then go to bed and start the day all over again.

Yeah. Plenty of spare time.

Second: "I really want to become a writer. Tell me, where do you get your ideas."

When Harlan Ellison was asked that question, here was his reply:

"People ask me where I get my ideas. I always tell them, 'Schenectady.' They look at me with confusion and I say, 'Yeah, there's this idea service' in Schenectady and every week like clockwork they send me a fresh six-pack of ideas for 25 bucks. Every time I say that at a college lecture there's always some schmuck who comes up to me and wants the address of the service."

But I always give a more honest reply. I will say, "You don't become a writer and then try to figure out where to get the ideas. The fact is that your brain is wired in such a way that *not* becoming a writer isn't an option. You have to become a writer because the ideas come at you with such ferocity that not writing them down isn't an option. Instead you feel the impulse to put them down on paper (or nowadays computer screens) and get them published as far and wide as possible, ideally with my name attached in as big letters as possible."

I will give you an example.

I was watching the first *Superman* movie. As I watched the events of Superman's first night on Earth, I found myself wondering what the *Daily Planet*'s front page would have looked like the next day. Because not only did Superman save Lois Lane from certain death, he broke up two robberies and, oh yes, saved the President when he prevented Airforce One from crashing. Just imagine if he hadn't been there. What a night of catastrophe that would have been.

Then I started to think about it. Even in the comics, one had to wonder how Lois Lane, a woman catastrophically accident prone with no sense of her own mortality, had survived being a teenager. She would have been the kid you read about who died jumping from one moving train car to another, or took a bet that she wouldn't dare to try and run across the New Jersey Turnpike.

That was when the "truth" occurred to me. Nothing bad ever happened before Superman showed up, but as soon as he did, his friends' lives were thrown into chaos. What if Superman was the *cause* of it all? What if he had a power that he didn't even dream he had? What if his very presence somehow affected probabilities so that everything turned to crap whenever he was around? It made sense. He was fired away from his home as it was being destroyed. What if he has a colossal condition of survivor's guilt? What if he has a deep-seated need to make himself necessary so that no one will ever decide to get rid of him again?

This seemed to me a terrific idea for a Superman story. And then, almost as soon as I came up with it, I realized I could never write it because it would be the last Superman story ever. As soon as he realized he was causing disaster wherever he went, he would fly off into space and find a deserted world to live out his days.

But I still liked the idea. So I created substitute characters for the story, titled it "The Archetype," and sent it off to the *Magazine of Fantasy and Science Fiction*. Three weeks later, I got a contract and a check in the mail.

See? I watched a movie you've probably seen a dozen times, but I made money off it.

As I said, that's how my brain is wired. I'm always seeing things and making conjectures and asking the two most important words in a writer's language: What if? The stories just arise from there as I come up with the ways to tell the story.

So even though I was working at Marvel Comics, I still couldn't give up the notion of writing.

One would think the obvious move would be to write for Marvel. And don't think I didn't try. I would occasionally pitch ideas for *Moon Knight*, *Indiana Jones*, stuff like that. Never got anywhere. The reason was that there was a major schism between editorial and business. Editorial's thinking was very simple, you see. If you were creative, you worked for editorial. If you weren't, you worked for the business side. If you worked for the business side, you couldn't be creative because if you were, you'd be working for editorial. Q.E.D. It was a very efficient wrap-around that kept editorial secluded from the rest of Marvel.

Writing comics, therefore, was not an option.

So I wrote books.

I had acquired an agent, Sharon Jarvis, while working at Playboy. She was, at the time, the editor of science fiction, and when Playboy folded she became an agent. I had written a novel at the time called *Knight Life*. It was always said that King Arthur would return when he was needed the most. Well, it certainly seemed as if he could have been used back in the early 1980s (a time which, I must admit, seems rather halcyon compared to our current situation). So I came up with the idea that Arthur had indeed returned, that he had shown up in modern day New York City, and he would wind up running for mayor. At that point we had no publisher for it, but she was certain that she could sell it.

But she came to me with another project.

A publisher called Pinnacle Books wanted a soft-core erotic series of four books. Did I have any ideas for one?

"Soft core erotic novels?" I said incredulously. "I can't write those! I work for Marvel Comics! They'd probably fire me!"

"You'll write them under a pen name," she said. "They'll never know."

"Let me think about it," I said.

I thought about it and by the next day had come up with a series.

Her name would be Sapphire Star. What was her story? No recollection. It was over thirty years ago. I will present you with the cover copy of book one, if that will help:

> WILL THE REAL SAPPHIRE STAR PLEASE STAND UP?
> She might, if Sapphire could get off her back and up from under her latest conquest. The striking flame-haired siren is making up for lost experiences. After all, what's a poor amnesiac to do when she can't remember her latest pleasures and preferences?

But the problem is that Sapphire Star is not poor—her father could be the richest man in the world, willing to pay a fortune for his missing daughter—or the voluptuous redhead could be a brilliant imposter.

From a legendary casino in Las Vegas, across the whitewater rapids of Colorado, to the Wild Wild West, enthusiastic companions satisfy the bewitching beauty's every craving ... but Sapphire continues to search for her true identity. Is she really Sapphire Star, or is she part of the greatest scam of the century?

Sapphire Star has more lovers than Lady Chatterly, more blaze than Modesty, and more perils than Pauline. There's no one in the world like her. Now if she could only remember who she is.

Pinnacle bought it. Now I had to write four of them. Which I did.

I remember exactly one bit of business from them: that Sapphire was disappointed in the Grand Prix when she found out that it wasn't pronounced the way she thought it was.

Per my agent's advice and my own concerns, I came up with a pen name: P.J. Royce. P for Peter, J for my then-wife's middle name of Jeanne, and Royce as in Rolls Royce because I wanted something that sounded fancy.

The only person in the industry who knew I wrote them was Jerry Bingham, the cover artist who did some wonderful illustrations for them. I've never spoken about this in my life, but I figure it was over three decades ago, they've been out of print for thirty years, and I recall them as being really pretty mild; by today's standards, they'd likely be rated PG-13. If you want to go to Amazon and buy used copies somewhere, knock yourself out. They're probably terribly written but let me know what you think.

So as I cheerfully wrote soft-core porn and waited for my agent to sell *Knight Life,* my attempts to write for Marvel were politely but thoroughly rebuffed.

Let me tell you about Jim Owsley.

Owsley was a young assistant editor for Larry Hama. (He now goes by the name Christopher Priest, a name change I don't pretend to understand, especially because that's the name of an already-existing British writer, but whatever. To this day I still call him Jim or Owz.) Now Jim—and I didn't know this at the time—tended to see the world very much in a black and white manner—maybe because he was black. If someone came into Larry's office with a question, and Larry wasn't there, Jim would always say, "Can I help you?" Apparently, people would always say, "No, I'll come back," and leave.

This pissed off Jim, and he assumed it was because he was black. I'm not saying it was; it probably wasn't. Then again, at the time I didn't believe blacks who claimed that white cops were shooting them, and I was sure proven wrong on that, so what do I know? In any event, that's how he felt. This isn't speculation on my part; I know because he told me this. When? You'll see.

Now there were many times when I, as sales manager, would come into their office and need something. If Larry wasn't there, Jim would say, "Can I help you?"

"Sure," I said. Because I didn't give a damn about his skin color; I just needed help with stuff, and if he could provide it, great. Likewise, if Jim ever came to me because he needed something, I was always happy to accommodate him. I had no idea that extending simple common courtesy or treating someone like a professional lodged me so highly in Jim's estimation.

So after a few years, Jim was promoted and got an introductory assignment. He was put in charge of Spider-Man. The big guy. The one who was on all our stationery.

Suddenly everyone who had not hesitated to blow Jim off in previous years wanted his time. Why not? Everyone wanted to write Spider-Man.

And Jim took great delight in not having time for them or ignoring them or not really considering what their ideas were.

Then I walked into his office and said, "Jim, I have an idea for a Spider-Man story."

Immediately Jim said, "Close the door." I did so, he had me pull up a chair (a weird ergonomic style one) and invited me to pitch it.

"I want to have Spider-Man meet a modern version of Leopold and Loeb," I said.

"Who are they?" asked Jim.

So I described to him the case of Leopold and Loeb, two college students in 1920s Chicago who kidnapped a teen and killed him for no other reason than they felt they could. I wanted to do a story inspired by them.

Jim told me to go for it.

I did. The story was titled "Compulsion" and it ran in *Spectacular Spider-Man #103*.

Jim wanted to know what else I had.

You want to know where I get ideas? Here's another example.

In those days we had models who posed as our characters. One of the best was a guy named Scott Leva who loved playing Spider-Man. He was always so into the character, crouching and leaping everywhere. Then one day we needed a Spider-Man to attend something and Scott wasn't available. So it was decided to substitute a guy who played Captain America. (To this day I wonder if it was Jonathan Frakes, since I know that was a job he used to have.) I saw him walking around the office, and he was doing none of Scott's stunts. He was just walking around like, well, Cap. And I thought, *My God, Spider-Man's costume looks really stupid when he's just standing around or walking normally.* That triggered an entire chain of reasoning: What if Spidey was somewhere where there were no tall buildings. Basically, what if he were out in the suburbs, just walking around? Wouldn't he feel incredibly stupid?

The story practically wrote itself and saw print as "The Commuter Cometh." I have to say, I loved it when I watched *Spider-Man: Homecoming* and they had that sequence where Spidey has to sprint across somewhere in Queens with no buildings to swing from.

Jim was so happy with my work that he fired the popular Al Milgrom off *Spectacular Spider-Man* and assigned it to me.

And the bullpen erupted.

The main contention was that you didn't assign a newcomer to the flagship character. That it was something you had to work toward. But likewise, there was still a fundamental belief that a guy from direct sales had no business writing comic books. Editors darkly whispered that I would use my position in sales to promote my title. The obvious response to that would be: So? My job was to promote *all* the titles. Nevertheless, I took the accusation seriously and consequently did nothing to push my book.

Meanwhile, Jim wanted to kill off Jean DeWolff. I have no idea why. But he wanted her dead, and he wanted me to be the one who killed her. I said, "Okay," and I came up with "The Death of Jean DeWolff." I didn't call it "Who Killed Jean DeWolff?" because it wasn't a murder mystery. There was only one real suspect in the book, police detective Stan Carter. It was obviously him. To try and distract the readers from this, I used a technique that Isaac Asimov preached. If you want to make readers think a character is harmless, make him Jewish. Use Yiddish syntax in dialoguing him. Reverse the standard subject-verb-object of sentences. ("For dinner you're coming over?")

In all of fiction, the most obvious use of this technique was Yoda. When Luke Skywalker went searching for Yoda, he found this little green guy who spoke in the inverted Yiddish syntax. As a result, both Luke and the viewers figured he was just a comedy relief character and not a Jedi master.

So I did that with Stan, and it worked like a charm. Readers wrote in saying how much they liked this obvious new police contact for Spidey, having no idea that he was a shotgun-wielding maniac.

Fans also wrote in and said how upset they were that we had killed off Jean, who was declared to be their favorite character. The thing was, Jean hadn't been seen in a year. I checked every single Spider-Man fan letter during that time and *no one* asked where she was. If Mary Jane had just dropped out for no reason, fans would have been demanding to know where she was.

Yet even that widely acclaimed four-parter was criticized by editorial. When I had Spidey learn that Jean had died, I have him say, stunned, "But … my God…. I just saw her the other week." Which is what people say. I instead learned that one editor claimed that that was completely wrong. That Spidey should have ripped a lamp post out of the ground and smashed it down repeatedly shouting, "No! No! She can't be dead!" Because when a superhero finds out someone died, their natural reaction is to inflict thousands of dollars of property damage.

Interestingly, at one point we had a Spider-writer conference, and I will always remember David Michelinie coming over to me and telling me he had an idea for a character named Eddie Brock. That Eddie would be a photographer who lost his job, specifically because of my villain, the Sin-Eater, and would eventually wind up bonding with the alien costume to become a new villain called Venom. So please don't tell me that Todd McFarlane co-created Venom because he drew him with a big tongue. It was Dave.

Another thing to come out of that Spider-meeting was determining the identity of the Hobgoblin. With Roger Stern, the character's creator having departed, it was decided as a group that the Hobgoblin would be Ned Leeds, Betty's husband. Tom was assigned to lay the track work for the eventual reveal.

Flash forward some months later and Owsley comes into my office and says, "We're doing lunch today. You're going to do the story that reveals who the Hobgoblin is and I'm going to tell you who he is."

"He's Ned Leeds," I said in confusion.

"Lunch," Jim said ominously.

So we went out to lunch and Jim told me, to my shock, that Ned Leeds was being killed off in a Spider-Man/Wolverine special written by none other than Owsley.

"What?" I said incredulously. "Why are you killing off Ned?"

"To piss off DeFalco."

I started to try and talk him out of it, but he told me the book was already written and drawn. I sat there, stunned, and said, "Well then who's the Hobgoblin?"

"The Foreigner."

The Foreigner was an assassin character I had created for *Spectacular Spider-Man*. Based on Patrick McGoohan, he ran an organization of assassins and preferred to remain in the background whenever possible. DeFalco later established that he was the ex-husband of Silver Sable.

"He wouldn't be the Hobgoblin!" I declared. "First, becoming a costumed villain is totally contrary to his character. Second, we've been saying the whole time that he will be revealed to be someone who's been around for years! The Foreigner has only been around for a few months! He can't be the Hobgoblin!"

"All right," said Owsley. "Then who can he be?"

My mind raced. The problem was that Tom had been too thorough. There was a reason that Ned was the number one suspect; Tom had made it impossible for him to be anyone else. He *had* to be Ned. That was probably why just about every fan letter we got claimed it was Ned.

That's when it occurred to me.

"Do we see Ned die?" I asked.

"No," said Owsley. "Peter just finds him tied up and dead in a chair in an apartment."

"Okay," I said. "We need another villain who is afraid of the Hobgoblin. Someone who would hire the Foreigner to kill him. And the Foreigner knows that Ned is the Hobgoblin because he's the Foreigner, and he just knows this stuff. Probably has a whole file on him. So who do we get?"

"Jack-O-Lantern," Owsley said. "He fought the Hobgoblin and got clobbered."

"Perfect! So he hires the Foreigner, the Foreigner sends his men in to kill Ned, and they take his costume and equipment and leave him tied to a chair!"

"So Spidey doesn't unmask the Hobgoblin? He just dies without any final confrontation?"

"Exactly!" I said. "And the best thing about it is this: In the months between when the Spidey/Wolverine comic comes out and we do the reveal in *Amazing*, Ned will go from being the character everyone thinks is the Hobgoblin to the one guy everyone knows is *not* the Hobgoblin, because he'll already be dead! It's unprecedented! No one will ever see it coming!"

"It's stupid!" said Jim. "Everyone will hate it!"

"Right! That's why we'll catch everybody off guard! It would never occur to anyone that we would do something that insanely idiotic!"

Owsley sighed and then signed off on it, and that was the story I wrote. I was right on both counts. Absolutely no one suspected that Ned was the Hobgoblin and the fans deliriously hated it because it so completely deviated from comic book norms. That was, until Roger Stern eventually came back and did his own version of the Hobgoblin and revealed him to be Roderick Kingsley, a third-rate character that had fans going, "Who? What? It was him? That's stupid; I liked Peter David's version better."

Owsley's recollection of that time was that he was insanely hard on me, mostly to satisfy editorial directives from higher up. I don't remember it that way. For me it was an entertaining time, playing with Marvel's characters that I had grown up reading.

I remember one time being in Jim's office, and Tom DeFalco told me that the problem with my writing was that I wasn't paying attention to the big picture. That it was necessary to provide only the illusion of change, but not do anything that would have a huge, long-term impact. "For instance," he said, "I could do this great story where I kill off Jonah Jameson. He's dying after Spidey defeats the villain that mortally wounded him, and as he's dying Spidey reveals his identity and there's this terrific scene where they forgive each other and then Jonah's gone. But what do we do next issue?"

Without hesitation I said, "Well, I'd have the Kingpin buy the *Daily Bugle*."

Tom blinked. "What?"

"The Kingpin buys the paper!" I said with growing excitement. "And the staff is outraged, and they say they're not going to work with this criminal. And the Kingpin has this big meeting and says, 'Look, I am a businessman, pure and simple. All I care about is that the paper continues to make money. I intend to have no involvement with the day to day production of the paper whatsoever. I have no biases that I'm going to foist on you, which is more than you can say about my predecessor. Furthermore, I've been looking over your healthcare, and I'm frankly stunned. Huge premiums and deductibles. Also you have no dental. That's all going to change. You'll be paying much less a month and have dental. Freelancers as well. So I'm hoping you'll all stay.' And now the *Bugle* goes nuts, because half the staff is like, 'But he's the Kingpin!' and the other half is going, 'But health care! And dental!' And Peter's torn because it means health care coverage for Aunt May, but on the other hand, it's the Kingpin! And maybe half of them can go on strike and Peter has to figure out which side he's on! Oh my God, this would be great! Jim! Jim, let's kill off Jonah!"

And the whole time poor Tom is saying that I'm totally missing the point while Jim appears to be mulling the idea over. I wasn't able to talk him into it but boy, that would have been a great story. And who knows, maybe later we could have had Doctor Strange bring him back.

Whatever. It didn't matter because soon after that, Owsley fired me off the title. The explanation he gave me, and I really did understand it, was that he was trying to save his job because Jim Shooter, the editor-in-chief, was supposedly irritated that this direct sales guy was still writing our lead character, or maybe he just didn't like my stories, or maybe he didn't like the stories *because* I was the direct sales guy.

(Here's how malleable the passage of time is. A couple of months ago I ran into Owz at a convention and he asked me, with a completely straight face, "Why did you leave Spider-Man?" I stared at him incredulously and said, "You fired me off the book!" His eyes widened in shock. "I did? No, I didn't." "Yes, you did!" This is one of the tricks of human memory; it's wholly unreliable. But trust me, he did fire me.)

In any event, I was devastated. I had done my best and felt I had lost the title through no fault of my own. Sales had been going up on the book, the fans generally liked my writing. I did everything right and had lost the title anyway.

Shortly after Jim delivered the news, Carol walked into my office. Whatever else she came in about she immediately forgot because she said, "What's wrong?" I told her.

Now you have to understand that Carol wasn't thrilled about me taking on a writing assignment. She was perfectly content with the division between editorial and sales and was worried that if there was conflict between the two, I might wind up taking the other side. But when she saw how upset I was, she immediately said, "Let's go out to lunch." And she took me out and she sat there trying to come up with a way to get me back onto the title. Because that's the kind of woman she was; if it meant that much to me, she was on board with trying to get the job back. I told her not to worry about it, that there really wasn't anything she could do, and if she did try to interfere it would likely be bad for her politically.

So I figured that was the end of my writing at Marvel.

Then one day, Bob Harass walked into my office and said, "I'd like to talk to you about a writing project."

I knew exactly what to say. "Can you come back at 5 so I'm not discussing editorial stuff while I'm working in sales?" If I'd learned anything from the Owsley experience, it was to keep editorial as separate from direct sales as possible so no one could possibly conflate the two.

Bob came back at 5 and told me, "I need someone to write the Hulk."

"And you're coming to me?" I said slowly. "Editorial hates me as a writer."

"There's no one else."

I stared at him. "What do you mean?"

"I'm taking Al Milgrom off the book. I wasn't wild with the plans he had."

"What plans did he have?"

"Well, he wanted to do a series of stories in which two characters were going to discuss things the Hulk did, and he'd have a series of adventures in which he learned a lesson by the end of the issue. And the two characters were a talking donkey and a sentient patch of land, and they were named Smart Ass and Wise Acre."

I started to laugh and then realized he wasn't kidding. Al was and is a terrific guy, but sometimes he thought far too much outside the box. "Uh, okay, I see the problem with that. But dialogue is my strong suit, and I'm not sure I can do much with a character whose dialogue is, like, ten words."

"Oh, no, that's not the Hulk right now. Al changed him back to the original gray Hulk and he's perfectly articulate. Rick Jones is the green Hulk now."

"Holy crap," I said. "I shouldn't have stopped reading the book."

"Anyway, like I said, wasn't wild about Wise Acre and Smart Ass. So I want someone else to write the title. And nobody wants to. No writers want to take it on, and I can't even find an editor who'd be willing to write it on the side. So if you come on the Hulk, no one's going to care because they all had the opportunity and passed. And you can write about whichever Hulk you'd want."

"Well, it would be the gray Hulk. Rick Jones shouldn't be a Hulk. He should be the one normal guy in the Marvel Universe." This of course was decades before A-Bomb. "I would probably rid Rick of being the Hulk as fast as possible."

"Fine," said Bob. "Whatever you want to do. Are you on board?"

"I'm still not sure what I'd do with it. I'll commit to six issues to start. How's that?"

"Okay!" said Bob. "Let me show you the artist I want to have do it."

I went with him to his office and he started pulling out pages from the issue preceding the one I'd start with. He also produced an issue of *Infinity Inc.* from DC Comics. "He's a young guy and I think he's got a lot of potential. I wanted to put him on a different title, but the writer didn't want to work with him because he was so raw." I studied the issue of *Infinity Inc.* and immediately saw what Bob was talking about. The kid had some weaknesses in storytelling, and he was hiding it by turning the pages into twisty turny puzzles with panels tilted in all kinds of directions. It didn't remotely conform to Marvel's more standard style of page layout. I studied the Hulk pages and I saw body stiffness and uninspired storytelling, but I still felt there was something there.

"Now if you don't want to work with him, I'll find someone else," said Bob.

"No, no.... I think you're right. I think there's something there. Yeah, I'll work with him."

Which was how Todd McFarlane wound up staying on *The Incredible Hulk*. Which later led to his run on *Spider-Man*, and then his own *Spider-Man* title, and a lot of other stuff I'll get into later.

I still wasn't sure where I'd go with the Hulk and started reading up on tons of back issues. In my reading, I came upon an issue that established that Bruce Banner's father had abused him as a child. It was written by Bill Mantlo, although Barry Windsor-Smith states that he came up with the story originally. In any event, that triggered something for me. Typically, people who suffered from Multiple Personality Disorder had been abused as children. MPD was their way of coping with it; their minds splintered as a coping mechanism to protect their inner self. I thought, *My God, that's perfect. Whenever Bruce has tried to rid himself of the Hulk, he's always done it from the outside in, trying to address the Gamma rays. But the problem isn't the Gamma rays; it's Bruce himself. Bruce is an MPD. The Hulk is simply another aspect of Bruce, but it's entirely possible that even if he'd never been caught in the Gamma Bomb explosion, he'd still have developed another Hulkish identity. This is the story of a man caught in an inner conflict that has existed ever since he was a kid. We've never actually seen a healthy Bruce Banner in this book. I should do a series of stories that features Bruce in mental battle with the Hulk, and then eventually have him treated the same way that genuine MPDs are treated: I'll have him hypnotized so that his personalities are merged, and he'll be the Hulk with Banner's merged brain!*

And that's how I wound up writing the Hulk.

I embarked on the series and at first there was no movement in sales. But Todd's improving artwork, plus the guest shot of Wolverine in issue #340 (which I arranged to keep Todd happy because he really wanted to draw Wolverine) caused sales to begin to skyrocket.

Twelve years later, I was fired off the book. But by that time, I was a full-time writer.

Becoming a Full-Time Writer

Writing was going well. At that point, my run on *Incredible Hulk* was not generating any pushback from editorial and I was becoming more comfortable on the series.

Meanwhile my novel-writing career was improving. Sharon Jarvis had found a publisher for *Knight Life*, the great folks at Ace Books with editor Ginjer Buchanan. I was already working on a second novel entitled *Howling Mad*, which was an inversion of the classic werewolf legend. Instead of a man being bitten by a werewolf and transformed into a wolf, I had my hero be a wolf that is bitten by a werewolf and transformed into a human being. I subtitled it, "A Tale of Relenting Horror" since the horror let up every so often. So between the comics and the novels, finances were on pretty solid ground.

I started to consider the possibility of becoming a writer full time. The idea was attractive to me. The major thing would be that I would be at home with my two daughters: the older, Shana, and the younger, Guinevere, whom we called Jenny at the time but later decided she wanted to be called Gwen. Shana was five and Gwen a mere one, so Gwen would never know a time when Daddy wasn't there for her. Meanwhile it would provide my wife, Myra, the opportunity to go out and pursue her own career.

I haven't mentioned Myra much until now because the marriage ended in divorce, she's remarried, and frankly I didn't want to leave myself open to lawsuits. The fact is, though, that she was indeed responsible for much of my early success, and she also contributed greatly to the development of *Space Cases*, which I will cover in a later chapter. So enabling Myra to open up her career opportunities after having raised the kids for five years seemed to me the perfect concept.

Still, before I made the decision to go full time, I needed to know if I would be able to pick up additional comic book work from DC, the other major New York–based publisher. I was in a delicate position, however. I was Marvel Comics' direct sales manager by that point. If I approached DC and asked them for work, that would be unethical, so I had to proceed very delicately.

This was in the days before email, so I called Bob Greenberger. Bob, the guy who had hired me to write the *Comics Scene* article that launched my sales career, was now an editor at DC. I phoned him up and said, "I need to ask you a very carefully phrased question. If I became a full-time writer, would DC be interested in hiring my writing services?"

"Why don't you come over for lunch and we can discuss it?" he said.

I took him up on it and went over to meet him for lunch. I think there was someone else there with him. Maybe editor Mike Gold, but I don't recall for sure. Even during the lunch, we all phrased the conversation very carefully. That *if* I became a writer, then the projects that we were discussing would be made available to me.

The first project they did/did not offer me was a *Phantom* limited series scheduled to be penciled by Joe Orlando. If I became a full-time writer, I already had one project at DC with more assured to be on the way.

(I had a great amount of fun writing that, and I even got to meet Falk. He wound up autographing the original artwork from the cover of the first issue to me. It turned out, though, that he didn't like my story because I had the Phantom shooting his guns at bad guys, wounding them, rather than just shooting their own weapons out of their hands. I had no idea that was a policy of the Phantom's; Falk had certainly not made that explicit in any of the material I'd read. I wish he'd just told me that when I was first writing it; I would have been happy to accommodate his wishes. But the bottom line is that human beings are not psychic. I couldn't do what someone wanted me to if they didn't bother to tell me ahead of time.)

So I finally went to Carol and told her that I was giving her two weeks notice; that I was going to become a full time writer.

I was worried that she would be angry with me, that I was "defecting" to editorial. But if she was at all angry, she certainly managed to keep it to herself. Instead she congratulated me on my new career and promised to throw me a celebratory lunch on my last day.

Which indeed she did. She, my assistants Sandy Schechter and Fred Baumann and I all went out to lunch. I even remember that she wore a skirt that day, simply because she always wore jeans and I had never seen her legs or even her ankles. So she sported a denim skirt to accommodate me.

My last day at Marvel was June 5, 1987. I remember it exactly because I was at Shea Stadium where Marvel was doing a promotional bit having a costumed Spider-Man marrying Mary Jane on the pitcher's mound, with the vows being read by Stan Lee. Why do I remember it so vividly? Because I wrote the vows. It was one of my last actions as Direct Sales Manager. Carol oversaw the coordination of it and she asked me to write what Stan Lee was going to say. The only line I remember was, "With this ring, I thee web."

What I most remember was that there were a bunch of fans sitting behind me who would not shut up. They were yammering loudly to each other, drowning out the so-so audio feed, and finally I couldn't stand it anymore. I turned and said, "Would you guys be quiet? I want to hear this!" Defiantly one of them said, "Why?!" I replied, "Because I wrote it!"

Instantly their attitudes changed. "Really?" asked one. "Yes," I said. They then promptly shut up and listened to the entire thing, so that was nice.

Over the next years, I worked on a number of other projects as well. I'd like to discuss three of them here.

X-Factor

I was invited to take over the comic series *X-Factor* and I was very excited. "I get to write the original X-Men!" I chortled.

"Actually, no," said the editor. "It's going to be a whole new team. It's Havok, Polaris, Guido..."

"Who the hell is Guido?!" I said.

"He's Lila Cheney's bodyguard."

I remembered who she was but couldn't place him at all. "Who else?" I said tentatively.

"Jamie Madrox..."

"Oh, for Christ's sake," I said. The general take on him at the time was that Madrox was a boring guy whose power was to transform into a lot of boring guys. Obviously, I had not given him a good deal of thought at the time. "Anyone else?"

"Wolfsbane."

At this I perked up a bit. As I mentioned, I had given her the name and so always felt closer to her. I liked the notion of being able to write her and so I said okay.

"Oh, and Quicksilver."

Quicksilver. Oy.

Understand that I hate speedster characters. The problem with them is that if you play them realistically, they're unbeatable. There is no defense against superspeed. Captain Cold shouldn't be able to say, "It's the Flash!" and swing up his gun because the moment that the Flash is close enough to be spotted, it's game over. By the time Cold is able to bring his gun to bear, the Flash has already gotten there, grabbed him, and dragged him to prison, period. The only speedster I never had a problem with was Impulse, because he's the original ADD boy. He could be running into battle and then get distracted by a kid playing a video game, so he wasn't an issue.

But this crew sounded for the most part like a bunch of losers. Nevertheless, it was an assignment being offered, so okay, I'd do it.

I was also given a special request. John Byrne had done a story in *The Thing #3* which revealed that Lockjaw, the Inhumans' dog, was actually a mutated humanoid Inhuman perfectly capable of speech. He winds up talking to Quicksilver, which is why Pietro decides not to expose his daughter to the Terrigen mists. While I read the story and just kind of shrugged, the editors hated the story because it basically made the Inhumans look like assholes for treating him like a dog for decades. I was asked to undo it. So I came up with the simplest fix I could. I revealed it to be a practical joke played on Quicksilver by Karnak and Gorgon. Hardly my most brilliant retcon, but it was quick, simple, and got the job done. I've no doubt that John added it to the list of things he hates me for doing, but in this case I was really just following instructions.

I decided that with this whack-job collection of characters, I might as well take a humorous approach to the material. I started early on when X-Factor held its first press conference and the press asks what Guido's code name is. I had no frickin' idea what to call him, and finally tossed in a bit where a little kid says, "He must be the strong guy! Every group has a strong guy!" Which, when you think about it, is pretty much true. So he dubbed himself Strong Guy. I reasoned that it wasn't inherently any more stupid than Superman.

I threw in all kinds of jokes. I had them encounter a Scots villain and when Havok points at his X belt buckle and says, "Do you know what this symbol means?" the guy replies, "No parking?" Havok says, "What?" And Rahne has to admit that actually, yes, in Scotland that's the exact symbol for no parking. Later I had a villain mistakenly call them X-Force and Guido corrects him by saying that no, the difference between X-Factor and X-Force is that there are no X-Factor action figures. What's hilarious is that eventually there was an X-Factor figure released: it was Guido and the package was labeled "Strong Guy."

But the issue that everyone remembers is *X-Factor #87*.

The other X-books were being written by Chris Claremont, and Chris had a very distinct style. He wrote lengthy thought balloons in which we were always informed of every damned thing that was going through the characters' minds. For instance, Storm would walk into a room and she'd think, "This room is so small ... it's reminding me of when I was a child and my home was destroyed, burying me under rocks and giving me a permanent case of claustrophobia, goddess, I have to open a window right now!" Which actually never happened but you get the idea.

I tended not to do that. I had the characters say things that were not necessarily what they were really thinking and allowed the readers to try and figure things out. This, as it turned out, was the wrong approach. Fan letters declared that the characters were one-note and not really thought out, which annoyed the crap out of me. I thought, "I have to do something about this." So what I decided to do was have an entire issue where the characters did nothing but talk about themselves. I had just had them finish a rough outing and figured that, since they're a government agency, the government might well require them to sit down with a psychiatrist and talk about their experiences. The doctor would of course be Doc Samson because he was pretty much the only shrink in the Marvel Universe (just like Marc Spector was the only cab driver). I figured that this way I could have them explain themselves to the fans' satisfaction.

It worked beautifully. The greatest beneficiary of the story was Quicksilver. Ever since Pietro was introduced, he's been kind of an asshole. Doc even asks about PMS, or Pietro Maximoff Syndrome.

Quicksilver then basically asks, "Have you ever stood in line at a banking machine behind someone who doesn't know how to use it?" As he's talking, he's rapidly assembling a jigsaw puzzle that Doc had been struggling with. "Or wanted to buy stamps at a post office and the fellow in front of you wants to know every single way he can send his package to Istanbul? Or gotten some counter idiot at Burger King who can't understand 'Whopper, no pickles'?" When Doc admits to it, Pietro asks him how that makes him feel. "Impatient? Irritated? A little angry sometimes." To which Quicksilver then says, "Precisely. Because your life is being slowed to a crawl by the inabilities or the inconvenient behavior of others. It's not a rational or considerate attitude to have, but there it is. Now imagine, Doctor, that everyone you work with, everywhere you go, your entire world, is filled with people who can't work cash machines. I venture to say, Doctor, that you too would suffer from PMS. Get the picture?" He holds up the completed puzzle—a picture of a snail—and says, "Not so puzzling now, is it."

We were flooded with letters when that issue came out. Fans said that they had always hated Quicksilver until this issue came out, and now they totally got him and understood him. It was wonderful.

Flash forward to years later and Evan Peters, playing Quicksilver in the upcoming X-movies, was asked about his character during a panel at the San Diego Comic-Con. Peters said, "Well, have you ever been stuck behind someone at an ATM who didn't know how to use it?" Thank God I wasn't there because I would have been on my feet saying, "Dude! I wrote that!"

But all was not well on the book. I was on it only twenty issues and half the time it seemed that I had to stop what I was doing to write issues that tied into a crossover. It was annoying as hell. The best-selling issue was a fight between Cable and Wolverine, neither of whom were regulars in the book. It just made me nuts.

Then I had this great issue that was an abortion story. I thought it was brilliant. Doctors develop tests to determine whether a fetus has the mutant gene and, if so, the mothers can opt to have the child aborted. It also featured the revelation that Polaris had had an abortion in her youth, which shocked the anti-abortion sensibilities of Rahne. The editors loved it, it was all set to go.

And then Northstar announced that he was gay.

This had been a subtle thing for a number of years, but in 1992 he came out. It was a big story, a huge story.

Here's where it goes off the rails.

Some huge shopping chain—Target, Walmarts, one of those—informed Marvel that they were not going to carry *any* mutant action figures because they didn't want angry parents returning any other characters they thought were gay, as they were already doing with the Northstar action figures. Yes, you read that right. Angry parents were returning gay action figures. In the modern age, where gay weddings are no big deal, it may be hard to imagine that people were that insensitive only a few decades ago. Then again, considering people boycotted the live action *Beauty and the Beast* because LeFou danced with a man for three seconds, anything is possible.

So the word came down from on high: no controversial stories anywhere in Marvel, period. Which knocked my abortion story all to hell. Rather than abortion, they made it about people learning their children were mutants and considered having the X-gene extracted, which made NO sense at all. You can't just remove genes; it's absurd. And chunks of the story got rewritten.

Meanwhile I had been doing stories where Rahne is more and more hung up on Havok. I wanted to do a reveal where she's walking down the street and all these dogs start barking furiously as she passes, and she comes to the stunned realization that she's in heat. That got killed, too, the sequence completely rewritten with dogs barking for no reason, and that's when I quit the book. One of the few times I ever resigned from a series.

Here was the second time:

Spider-Man 2099

Marvel approached a number of writers, including me, about the new 2099 line. It was intended to be the definitive far future of the Marvel Universe (before that whole concept got tossed aside). This particular group of writers was approached about coming up with the identity and back story of Spider-Man 2099. We were given a few specifics. He was going to be a lab tech working at this megacompany called Alchemax, and an accident would transform him into the titular character. We were to come up with everything else: his identity, supporting cast, how his powers worked. Everything.

I got to work.

The first thing I decided was that he would definitely not be a descendant of Peter Parker. That was way too obvious. What I decided to do was zig everywhere that Stan Lee and Steve Ditko zagged.

Peter Parker was basically a WASP. I decided to give my hero mixed ethnicity which, considering the way the world is currently going, seemed the right thing to do for a hundred years hence. I picked two ethnicities that did not seem to go together. I made him half Irish and half Mexican. The Mexican part was perfect because that explained why he happened to have a costume lying around. He had worn it during the Day of the Dead festival and kept it around. I dubbed him "Miguel" after my friend, actor Miguel Ferrer, and "O'Hara" because it was a common Irish name.

Peter was an orphan. Miguel would have a mother.

Peter was an only child. Miguel would have a brother.

Peter was a teenager with no idea how to approach women. Miguel would be in his mid-twenties and have a fiancée.

Peter's powers basically worked with no explanation at all. We never did explain how the hell he sticks to walls (static electricity? Magic?) His spider sense didn't track because what spider has a psychic sense that danger is approaching? Why didn't Peter have biological webbing? I went in the opposite direction. I gave him talons like real spiders have which not only would enable him to climb walls but also could be used in combat situations. I gave him biological web shooters a decade before Tobey Maguire had them in the first Spidey film. I gave him fangs with poison as real spiders had. And I replaced his spider sense with accelerated vision that warned him when something was incoming. I also endeavored to emulate parachute spiders by giving him webbing on his back, made from anti-gravity material that enabled him to glide so that he'd have a different means of locomotion.

I worked out the details of his origin and sent it off to Marvel.

A few days later I got a call from Joey Cavalieri, who was going to be editing the 2099 series. He told me he loved my pitch. For starters, he said it was the only one that didn't feature the S-Man (the nickname I came up with) as being a descendant of Peter Parker. He asked if I would be interested in writing the series, and naturally I said yes. Marvel paid me a bonus of a few thousand dollars, which in retrospect was probably chump change, but it was much appreciated anyway.

That's how I wound up some weeks later at the first creator meeting for the 2099 line. The best was that Stan Lee, who was going to be writing *Ravage*, was sitting directly to my left. How cool is that?

After the initial overall discussions of the books, we broke up into smaller groups. I will always remember sitting with my artist, Rick Leonardi, as we developed S-Man's costume. I told Rick what I wanted and he improved upon it and the character came to life on his drawing pad. I wish to God I'd thought to ask him for the drawing because if I had, it would have had a place of honor above my desk.

I have signed more copies of the first issue of that title than any other book I've ever written. Why? Because we sold over a million copies. I was astounded. Shocked. In the Golden Age of comics, a million wasn't a big deal. But in the 1990s, if you sold a quarter million you were a huge deal. So over a million copies? Holy crap.

I sailed along on the series, and then for some reason, Marvel decided to fire Joey. I was stunned. Joey was the heart and soul of 2099 and I quickly decided that if Joey was gone, I was gone too. Pretty much all of the other creators felt similarly and likewise departed. Two issues later Marvel cancelled the entire 2099 line. Quite the comedown from a million copies.

But the character absolutely refused to die. The rest of the 2099 characters have mostly vanished, but Miguel remains. First, he appeared in a video game. Then they produced an entire video game which co-starred him and Peter Parker, and the game was written by yours truly.

Then Steve Wacker, a Marvel editor, transitioned to the West Coast but wrote a farewell letter that ran in the Spidey books and he mentioned that a 2099 book was in the works. For once fandom united and said, as one, "We will definitely buy a Spidey 2099 book as long as Peter David is writing it." The truth is that someone else was slated to write it, but in this day and age of splintered opinions, when fandom speaks as one, Marvel listens. So the editor contacted me and asked if I'd be interested in writing Spidey 2099 again. I said, "Sure." She said, "Okay, we need a five page story by Friday (this was on a Wednesday) to run in *Spider-Man #700*, and we need the script for issue #1 by the middle of next week." I said, "When is the book coming out." She said, "July." Stunned, I said, "But it's May already!" She replied, "I know. You're really late."

So welcome to comics, kids.

DC vs. Marvel

Remember the kid who called and asked who would win in a race, Superman or the Silver Surfer? He was hardly alone. Fans incessantly argued the superiority of their respective favorite characters. Superman vs. Hulk. Captain America vs. Batman. Aquaman vs. Namor, and on and on and on. It seemed a pointless discussion because the question could never be resolved.

Except it was, when Marvel and DC decided to do a four issue crossover miniseries.

Let me tell you for a moment about Mark Gruenwald and Mike Carlin.

Mark was an editor and Mike was his assistant, and their office was a demented funhouse. One time they closed their door for an entire day and all we heard was hammering and sawing. The next day the door was opened and we saw that Mark and Mike had created wooden platforms and raised their desks two feet into the air, so you always had to look up at them when you came into the room. They were literally brothers in everything but blood.

Mike eventually moved over to DC and became an editor there, so when it was decided that there should be a crossover, Mike and Mark were naturally the guys to oversee the editing. And they brought in two writers who were reasonably familiar with both sides of the casting. One of them was Ron Marz. The other was me.

We all gathered in neutral territory: Mark Gruenwald's lovely apartment in New York City. There we hammered out the basics of the plot. Two cosmic brothers, the creators or overseers of two universes, were in combat with each other. They conscripted their respective superheroes to battle to decide which one was better.

Now I honestly don't recall who came up with the fundamental concept. It might have been me because I remember doing something very similar in one of the *Photon* novels. Or it's possible that we all worked it up, or maybe Mark and Mike had that fundamental underpinning already in place, because we were really symbolizing their relationship. Whatever the issue behind the background, there were two other aspects in place. The first was that the fans would vote for the battles in issue #3, and Issue #4 would focus on the results of a merged universe before then concluding the series.

We also knew that in issue #2, we were going to have an assortment of battles that we were going to decide. The wins would be evenly split so that, no matter how the fans decided, neither company would lose across the board. Since a battle between any of these duos could realistically go for tons of pages, we came up with the idea of following wrestling rules. If one of the heroes was pinned or immobilized for three seconds, that was it: they lost.

There were two things I wanted to put in that didn't happen.

First, I wanted to have a sequence where Darkseid faces Thanos. One of them says, "So ... it begins." The other says, "Bring it on." And then they both stand there, staring at each other. Every so often we cut back to the scene and we see nothing happening except the two of them standing, staring. And at the end, Thanos—with no explanation whatsoever—collapses. The notion was that their battle was so cosmic that it was happening on another plane entirely. But we didn't do that.

The second was my idea for a crossover character: merge Snapper Carr and Rick Jones into Snapper Jones, Professional Sidekick. I was ready to write it. Couldn't convince them. Dammit.

The major problem to sort out, though, was how to write it. Ron and I initially tried to switch off on the first issue, but Mark and Mike didn't like it. The fundamental problem was that our writing styles were too different, and it didn't read smoothly at all. So Ron and I got on the phone to hash it out and I suggested we just each write two entire issues.

"Who does which ones?" said Ron.

I said, "Well, honestly, I wanted to do two and four."

Ron sounded stunned. "Really? Because I want to do one and three!"

I knew why I wanted to do two and four. I had no interest in doing the first issue because it was mainly introduction. And in three we had the fans voting, and I was sure that the votes would present some annoying results. (I'm sorry, guys, Wolverine doesn't beat Lobo. Lobo can go head to head with Superman and Wolverine just can't.) In issue #2, on the other hand, I would get to write the battles that we had come up with, including Aquaman beating Namor ... which I had begged for since I was writing *Aquaman* at the time. And issue #4 was the big finish. I suppose Ron wanted #1 and #3 because they were the most heavily

Me, Stan "the Man" Lee and writer/artist Colleen Doran at the New York Comic Con, promoting the autobiography *Amazing! Fantastic! Incredible!*

publicized issues, which was true. That was fine with me. He could have the aggravation that I wanted to avoid.

And I was right, it really was aggravating. It was certainly more work, because when Ron was writing it, we didn't have the fan voting results yet, so he had to write every battle twice. There was artwork for both outcomes. I got to avoid that.

DC vs. Marvel was easily one of the most creatively fulfilling projects I ever had the opportunity to work on. It brought me back to the core of my fandom as four adults sat in a room arguing about who would beat whom.

Comic book writing never gets better than that.

The Kids

When I was writing *X-Factor* in the 21st century, Marvel Comics had mandated the inclusion of an introduction page. Basically, editorial was remembering one of the truisms of comics, which is that you have to assume that every issue fans pick up is somebody's first comic book. So you have to make everything crystal clear as you're writing and make sure that anyone who is a first timer is going to understand what the hell the story is about.

Most of the books had the intro sheets done by the folks in editorial, but I was offered the chance to write the intro pages for *X-Factor*. I was fine with that, but naturally I had that aspect of my ego that made me feel competitive with all the other intro pages. I wanted to do something that would make ours memorable. So on each page, after I summarized what had happened in the book, I would then close out with some commentary about something that had happened in my personal life. Typically it would be about one of my daughters. I'd write about some accomplishment that they had made, some achievement they had performed. Maybe Caroline had gotten all A's. Or Shana had opened a brand-new screen at the movie theater owned by her and her husband. Whatever it was.

To my astonishment, people loved it. I lost track of how many times people would come up to me and tell me that their favorite thing was reading about my family updates. The insecure part of me worried that I wasn't doing well enough with the stories I was writing if the little three line blurb about my family was the aspect they most enjoyed, but really they were just trying to be flattering, I'd suspect. I'd hope.

I'm going to take that oft repeated interest to stop talking about my career for a chapter and instead talk about my girls. I have four daughters. I'd often claim that if I had a fifth daughter, I would mount my own production of *Fiddler on the Roof*. I had the first three with my first wife, Myra and the fourth with my last wife, Kathleen. You know, I should really discuss my wives, too.

Myra

I'm going to be nice. I mean, the fact is that she left me after twenty years of marriage and broke my heart, and yeah, she did some crap to me. But it's not like I was Mister Perfect Husband, either. It takes two people to bust a marriage.

So I will simply say this:

We met at a *Star Trek* convention. We fell in love and I wound up moving to New York City, where she lived, so I could be near her. We got married and produced three children. We had our ups and downs, but she very much contributed to the growth of my career and, on her good days, was a valued partner and supporter. As did I, she remarried and I hope her life goes well. Whatever ill will I harbored for her is long ago burned away and I'm convinced that we are both happier apart than we were together.

But we did have good times.

Shana

First children have it the worst. I would know, being a first child. The first kid is the one you make all your mistakes with. It didn't help that Shana was (1) incredibly bright and (2) always knew what she wanted and never hesitated to demand it. And if you stood in her way, God help you. There was one time where I

This is why I love New York City. Kath and I were eating at a restaurant near Lincoln Center called P.J. Clarke's, and they had a black and white picture on the wall that looked like a very young Fyvush Finkel. But I didn't know for sure. Then we went to see a concert version of *Company* and who did we run into coming out? Fyvush Finkel, who was able to confirm it was indeed him.

came home from work and found Myra seated on the floor, sobbing, and Shana (who was maybe a year old at the time) running around in a diaper. I asked Myra what happened. She told me Shana hadn't wanted to wear clothes that day and the poor woman had spent the entire day just trying to get her dressed, an undertaking that had failed spectacularly.

Shana's grandparents hated her name. "Shana" means "beautiful" in Yiddish and that appalled her maternal grandparents (mine had all passed away by that point) because they both felt it was tempting the evil eye. The evil eye in Judaism is sort of a free-floating curse that cuts down Jews who are stupid enough to undertake one of the endeavors that could cause it to notice. If you wish someone good fortune, you then say "poo poo poo" and/or spit three times to ward the evil eye off. You never name a child after someone living because that means you're wishing for the senior possessor of the name to die. Being a member of the 21st century, of course, I never believed in that. Then again, when my good friend Bob Greenberger named his new son Robbie, I wanted to warn him against it. But I held my tongue. Twenty years later, poor Robbie passed away from leukemia and part of me has always blamed myself for not saying anything. Stupid, I know, but superstition dies hard.

But her name was Shana and we stuck with that. She was mostly named after my paternal grandmother, Hela, whose Hebrew name was Shanedel.

When we first brought her home, I carried her to the newly erected changing table that was situated in the living room of our small one-bedroom apartment. She was wearing a cap on her head, and when I removed the cap, my eyes widened in horror. When she'd left the hospital, she had a head of fine blondish hair. Now she was bald. All the hair was in the cap. I did the only thing I could think of: I put the cap back on her head and rubbed it quickly, hoping that static electricity would cause the hair to reattach. Then if Myra took off the hat and the hair once again fell off, I could blame her. That didn't work very well.

It was impossible to get Shana to take a nap. Put her down in her crib and she would cry and scream, no matter how tired she was. We discovered that the only thing that could get her to fall asleep was if she was riding around in her car seat. If she needed to nap, we'd strap her into her car seat and drive around the block and she'd pass out. Eventually we didn't even need to do that. The moment she was belted in, she'd conk out. I'd sit in the car and read a book until she woke up.

One day when Shana was aged four, she came to me with a copy of the book of *The Wizard of Oz*. "I read this book, Daddy," she said.

Certainly she was no stranger to being read to. Myra and I read to her constantly. But I knew she couldn't actually read and I told her so.

"Yes, I can," she insisted. "I read this book."

"You couldn't have."

"I did."

Not wanting to prolong the discussion, I flipped a few pages in and said, "What happened to Toto when the house was lifted into the air?"

Immediately she replied, "Once Toto got too near the open trap door and fell in; and at first the little girl thought she had lost him. But soon she saw one of his ears sticking up through the hole, for the strong pressure of the air was keeping him up so that he could not fall."

I couldn't believe it. She had stumbled slightly over the word "pressure" but other than that it was word for word what Baum had written. "Holy crap," I said. Somehow, in a way that to this day I could not explain, Shana taught herself to read.

God, what a mess that turned out to be.

Because when Shana began school, it was a fiasco.

Why? Because the big thing they focus on in elementary school is teaching kids how to read. Since she was ahead of every kid in the class, she was bored out of her mind, and bored kids become problem kids. Why pay any attention to the teacher when she's not telling you anything you don't already know?

The teacher understood it but the principal did not. I was brought in to speak with him; I don't recall Myra being there. Maybe she was at work. But Shana was sitting in a chair outside his office as we spoke to figure out how to address Shana's boredom. I told him the problem was that she could read and so was bored.

"She can't know how to read," he said.

"Shana, come in here, please," I said. She trotted in and I took a copy of *The New York Times* off the principal's desk and pointing to an article at random, I said, "Read this."

She proceeded to do so, and aside from tripping over the name "Zbigniew Brzezinski," she read it flawlessly. I will always treasure the dropped jaw of that principal as I turned to him and said, "You see the problem."

She subsequently took a test to see if she could get into the gifted program. To my shock, she was rejected. Why? Because they felt she couldn't draw geometric shapes accurately enough. Yes, you read that right. A five-year-old child whose hand-motor skills weren't on par with some other kids was refused entry into the gifted program.

We took her out of the school and enrolled her in a Yeshiva. That worked out great because she didn't have the slightest idea how to read Hebrew, and she loved learning something new. When we eventually moved out to Long Island, she was old enough and all the kids knew how to read, so we put her back in public school and she did fine.

I'll never forget one night when she was about six. She had been a right royal brat that day. She left Myra in pieces and when I put her to bed, she said, "Read me something new, Daddy! Read me something new!"

So I read Edgar Allan Poe's "The Tell Tale Heart."

I look back on that now and am appalled by my actions. Yes, she had been a little horror show during her waking hours, but nevertheless she was six. What in the name of God was I thinking when I inflicted one of most horrifying stories onto the brain of a child who is about to go to sleep? Nevertheless, with the idea firmly set in my demented mind, I blew through that story at full gusto. When I got to the end, I raised my voice in a crescendo and howled, "I admit the deed!—tear up the planks! Here, here!—It is the beating of his hideous heart!"

Then I dropped my voice to normal, conversational tone and whispered, "Good night, honey."

She was lying there, her eyes wide in shock. Clearly, she was petrified. And I, thorough bastard that I am, congratulated myself on avenging Myra's rotten day.

And what happened? The next day she wanted to read Poe. Anything by Poe. It fueled an interest in the author that she carries to this day. In the book *Fearless*, I describe the adventures of a little girl named Mary who is, as the title suggests, fearless, and I had her mother do the exact same thing that I did in order to try and instill some sense of fear into her. It works as well as my attempt did.

I'll never forget one Earth Day when Myra and I were walking around in Central Park with Shana, who I was carrying in a backpack. Her sharp hearing brought a familiar song to her ears. "Puff! Puff!" Shana cried out, and we strained to hear what she had picked up. It was definitely the familiar song, and then Myra and I suddenly realized who was singing it. We sprinted to the bandshell and sure enough, there were Peter, Paul and Mary singing their best-known tune.

We also took her down to Disney World when she was around two. Unfortunately she was not at an age where she appreciated the costumed characters. She'd never seen anything like them, and she was clearly terrified of them, always hiding her eyes whenever one came near. Toward the end of the day, however, Pluto came sauntering by and was immediately enamored of the cute little girl who was too frightened to look at him. We explained the problem and Pluto took—and this is no exaggeration—ten minutes to do nothing but interact and play with Shana. By the end of the ten minutes she was absolutely enamored of Pluto. He had completely turned around her fear of the Disney characters. Later on, we went into the Emporium, which is basically souvenir central. Shana promptly climbed out of her stroller, made a beeline for the stuffed toys, wrapped her arms around a plush Pluto, and went back to her stroller with it. She flopped down, hugged it to herself, and smiled. Myra and I exchanged looks and I shrugged and said, "I guess we're getting her Pluto."

When Shana turned twelve, she was seriously contemplating becoming an actress. To that end, we sent her that summer to an acting camp in Long Island called Usdan. She had a great time there, but some of it was overshadowed because she developed an intense dislike for one girl in particular. She couldn't stand her. She said the girl was arrogant, incredibly full of herself, and convinced that she was going to become a movie star. The girl's name was Neta-Lee Hershleg, although by that point she was already going by the stage name she had chosen: Natalie Portman. Boy, did she despise Natalie Portman, who wound up going on to some small fame and, oh yeah, won an Oscar.

As she grew older and became a teenager, Shana displayed a wicked sense of humor. One time I did an author appearance at a nearby (now long gone) Borders Books, and I brought the family along. Shana hovered near the outskirts of the crowd, and speaking with her younger sister, Gwen, murmured things that were perfectly understandable if my daughter was saying them and remarkably creepy for anyone else.

Such as:

"I know where he lives. Sometimes I just stand outside his house. Or I'll walk up the steps as if I was going to go in. I think about him sitting on the edge of my bed, kissing me goodnight or singing songs to me." Stuff like that. Gwen told me how anyone who was in earshot looked at her with confusion and fear. They were sure I had picked up some kind of weird stalker.

Eventually Shana grew up and married a young man named Tim Massett. Together they own the Sun-Ray Cinema in Jacksonville, Florida. If I lived in Jacksonville, I'd be there every week because they always run great shows. Also serve great pizza.

Gwen

Raising Shana prepared me for a second daughter who was relentlessly demanding and would never go to sleep. I could not have been more wrong.

Gwen was born on New Year's Day. The drive to the hospital was insane. We drove down Northern Boulevard in Queens, which is typically stop and go traffic. Not that day. There were literally no cars. I wound up treating red lights like stop signs. I would stop, look both ways, and if there were no cars coming, I would go through the light. I figured the worst that would happen would be that a cop would pull us over and when he saw my pregnant, in-labor wife, he'd give us a police escort. Nope. Drove the whole day and never encountered a single police officer.

Gwen's full name was Guinevere Corey David. "Corey" was taken from a Harry Chapin song titled "Corey's Coming." Guinevere was obviously based on the Camelot queen. We were going to call her Jenny, which is Arthur's nickname for her in the stage show of *Camelot*, but when she grew older she insisted she didn't want to be called Jenny anymore, but instead "Gwen," and we have honored her request.

Gwen was an extremely intelligent little girl. She watched what Shana did that got her in trouble and then did the exact opposite. Not only did she always go straight to sleep if we settled her for a nap, but when she got older and could go up the stairs herself, I would just say, "Jenny, nap time" and she'd say, "Okay" and march up the stairs. Five minutes later, she was unconscious. It was wonderful.

My drives with her would oftentimes prove interesting.

One time I was driving along, and I had a can of Coke in the cup holder next to me. Gwen, aged about eight at the time, was seated next to me in the passenger seat. At a red light I picked up the can and sipped from it. Immediately she grew alarmed and said sharply, "Daddy! You're not supposed to drink and drive!" I laughed so hard I nearly snorted up the soda. "This is Coca-Cola, honey," I said. She shook her head and said, "They taught us in school that drinking while you drive is bad." Whereupon I had to explain to her that the sort of drinking involved in that situation was alcohol.

See, neither Myra nor I drank. I have always had zero tolerance for alcohol. I am, as of this writing, sixty-three years old and I have never been drunk. Ever. Because if I drink alcohol, I immediately wind up going to sleep unless I consume it very, very slowly. If you drink it as slowly as I do, it is physically impossible to drink too much. So Gwen was unfamiliar with alcohol. One time when she was little she found a six pack of beer shoved into the back of a cabinet. She immediately was concerned that Myra and I were alcoholics, because she learned that alcoholics hide their liquor so that no one will know they're drinking it. Naturally that wasn't the case. It was a six-pack left over from a New Year's Eve party we'd thrown where we stocked up on a few six packs in case any of our guests wanted some beer.

So I was able to assure her with confidence that we aren't alcoholics.

Another time we were driving through New York City and were stopped at a red light. A shabbily dressed individual was working his way down through the stopped cars, knocking on their windows. Gwen asked, "What's he doing?" I said, "He's asking people for money." She looked at the large pile of change that was next to my seat (which I kept for tolls—this was long before E-Z Pass) and said without hesitation, "Well, we should give him some." I realized she was correct. If I had money, why not give it to the guy to help him out?

I took her to the movies one time when she was in her early teens. She desperately wanted to see Baz Luhrmann's production of *Romeo and Juliet*. So I'm sitting there watching it with her, and the film is reaching its climax. Romeo has come to the tomb where he is about to drink poison.

And I suddenly heard two girls seated behind me whispering, "Watch, she's going to wake up just before he drinks it."

I was incredulous. They had no more clue of what was going to happen than a Shakespearean audience would have had in the late sixteenth century.

So Romeo drinks the poison and—I have to admit this was a nice touch—Juliet wakes up just after he drank it. He looks at her with shock, realizing that he's just performed a major balls-up, and then dies.

Juliet then reaches for his dagger. And the same two girls are now muttering, "She's going to *stab* him, too?"

Which of course she doesn't do. She stabs herself. For never was there a tale of more woe, etc., etc.

Then the credits started to roll, and it wasn't just the two girls. There was a number of teens in the theater and *all* of them were shocked to see that Leonardo DiCaprio and Claire Danes had died. They were all muttering their disappointment with open incredulity, sure that Danes and DiCaprio would triumph over all odds and live happily ever after.

I couldn't stand it. I stood up, turned around, and shouted at all the teens, "What part of the opening speech did you *not get*?! 'A pair of star-crossed lovers take their lives.' It was right at the start of the film. They had it there twice! First they printed the text and then they had a newscaster broadcast it! Putting aside that they're obviously not teaching you anything in school, how could you possibly have missed the text that was shown and then repeated?!"

That might have been the last time that Gwen ever went with me to a movie.

When Gwen was seventeen, we were driving up to Montreal, Canada, for a "Simpsons Live" show. We stopped along the way at a rest stop and Gwen pointed out a box with a sign on it that read, "Win Ben

Stein's Vacation." Playing off the then-popular *Win Ben Stein's Money* TV gameshow—now notable mostly because it was the first time we met Jimmy Kimmel—it was exactly what it said. Contestants were invited to answer a series of fairly easy trivia questions and drop it in the box. First prize was a vacation for two to Mexico. Gwen filled out the questions and inserted her entry.

Several months later I got a phone call from some woman who asked me if Gwen was there. When I said no, she began talking about a vacation. I figured she was a saleswoman and started to tell her we weren't interested. I was about to hang up when she mentioned Ben Stein and suddenly the contest came snapping back to me.

By that time, Gwen had moved up to Boston to live with Shana. Shana was attending Berklee University and Gwen wanted to attend a Massachusetts University, which would be substantially cheaper if she had lived in the state for a year. We drove up to visit with them, me carrying the envelope from Comedy Central with all the info. When we got all settled in, I said casually, "Hey Gwen, remember the Win Ben Stein's Vacation contest? Well, it turns out you won a prize. The technical term for it is, 'Grand Prize.'" Gwen and Shana let out startled shrieks of joy in discovering they were getting a free vacation to Mexico.

Once, while in college, Gwen was taking an art history class. The teacher said, "Today we're going to be discussing art during the time of the Spanish Inquisition. What can anyone tell me about it?" Gwen's hand shot up and she immediately said, "It was unexpected." The teacher laughed. None of the other students did; they didn't get it and had never heard of Monty Python. At least I trained my kids correctly.

Gwen eventually met a sweet young man named Heath Mayhew and they got married. She currently works in the library of a major art museum in Montreal, and several years ago she gave me my second grandson, Orson.

Ariel

I wanted to name our third child Ariel if it was a girl because I absolutely loved the Disney *Little Mermaid*. Myra did not embrace the idea. "What, and if it's a boy, we'll name him Pinocchio?" she asked disdainfully. But some weeks later, the doctor did a sonogram that revealed our child was going to be a girl. And Myra whispered, "Hi, Ariel." I blinked in surprise. "Ariel?" Myra shrugged. I guess the name grew on her. We gave her the middle name of "Leela," after the Doctor Who companion.

Moments after she was born, the nurse said, "Oh my God. Look at those dimples!" It was true. She had been alive less than a minute and in that time, she stopped crying and was *smiling*, dimples on either cheek.

Ariel was a relentlessly sweet child. Unfortunately, she was the only one of the first three that I didn't manage to get into a guest spot on my TV series *Space Cases*. I'll be writing about it at greater length later, but I want to recount one Christmas story I'll always remember.

The Montreal producers were holding a Christmas party for the cast and crew, and they wanted me to be Santa Claus. I agreed to it and the makeup people did a fantastic job. This wasn't just Peter wearing a white wig. They made up my face to age me dramatically but also gave me rosy red cheeks and white eyebrows. I didn't recognize myself, and the costume they got me was top notch. Real boots and everything. I strode into the party with a big bag of gifts. Five-year-old Ariel was staring up at me with rapture. I turned to her and in my faked, deep voice I said, "I know you! You're..." I paused a moment as if recalling, and then said, "Ariel!"

She gasped, her eyes wide in shock. That was it. I had to be Santa because how else could a total stranger have walked in and identified a random girl? I gave her a present, which was a little bear that she had been oo'ing and aah'ing over in a store a couple of days earlier. The best thing was that, when I returned to the party some minutes later, devoid of makeup, she ran up to me and said, "Daddy, where were you?! Santa was here and you didn't get to see him!" I felt like George Reeves in the old *Superman* series. "Gee, Lois, I'm sorry I missed Superman! Again!"

When Ariel was six, I took her to Broadway to see a production of *Grease*. At that point in time, Lucy Lawless was performing as Rizzo, and Ariel was a huge fan of *Xena, Warrior Princess*. So I took her to a matinee. After that we did the stage door Johnny thing and waited outside so Ariel could meet her and get something autographed. But we stood there for an hour and then the stage manager (or whomever) came out and announced that Lawless would not be coming out. That she was tired and was resting up for the evening performance. Well, Ariel was crushed. She'd loved the show and loved Lawless in it but was incredibly disappointed not to have met her.

Flash forward twenty years. I was backstage at the Atlanta Dragon Con convention, preparing to go on stage to deliver that year's Julie Award (named after Julie Schwartz) for achievement in various forms of entertainment. And who should be backstage but Lucy Lawless, sitting in a wheelchair because she had sprained her ankle after chasing after a group of Xena cosplayers to get their picture.

Well, I told her about the *Grease* incident, and she suggested I call Ariel. I did and she answered. Wondering if she actually still recalled the incident, I said, "Remember when I took you to see Lucy Lawless in *Grease*?" Without hesitation she said, "Yes, and we waited for her to come out and she never did." I said, "Oh good. Someone wants to talk to you." I handed the phone over to Lucy, who said, "Hi, Ariel, this is Lucy Lawless," and she proceeded to apologize for having let Ariel stand outside without meeting her. They chatted for a few minutes and then Lucy handed the phone back. I said, "Satisfied?" A stunned Ariel said, "That was Lucy Lawless!" The next day I swung by Lucy's table and got an autographed picture for Ariel. Only took twenty years.

Ariel became quite a formidable bowler as she grew older. She joined her high school's bowling team and that year they even won the local championship. I'll never forget one game where she was competing. She opened on her first three frames, and came over to me and said, "Any advice?" I said, "Have you tried not sucking?" She became so infuriated that she went back to her team and proceeded to throw nothing but strikes for the rest of the game.

She was also enamored of the *Twilight* books. One time I brought her to a local Barnes & Noble where there was a big publishing party for the next book in the series. There was a line of girls standing outside. I sighed and said, "I wonder what I could write that would cause that many girls to show up." Ariel suggested I read the first book so I could see for myself what the author had done. It seemed a reasonable recommendation.

So I read it. Then I came back to her and said, "Okay, I read it. There's a problem: I can't write this badly." She didn't speak to me for a week.

Dragon Con really worked out for Ariel. Her birthday runs over that weekend, so she's always the birthday girl. One year she had a birthday lunch with Ted Raimi, who played the decidedly unheroic Joxur the Mighty on *Xena*. Another year the actors who played the Weasely twins both kissed her on the cheek. But to my mind, the best was one year when I was MCing the Saturday night awards dinner. I had just about wrapped up and was about to say goodnight when, to my shock, my cell phone rang. I didn't have the slightest idea who it could be because pretty much everyone I knew was there. I answered the phone. It was Myra. "Hi," she said, "I was calling to wish Ariel a happy birthday."

I said, "Well, you've got some kind of timing. I'm on stage at the Dragon Con awards dinner." Then I turned to the audience. "It's my ex-wife, Myra. Everyone say 'Hi, Myra.'"

Over a hundred voices chorused together, "*Hi, Myra.*"

Ariel leaped up from the table and ran over to me. I tossed her the phone and then said to the crowd, "I don't think I can top that. Good night, everyone." People were sure that someone else had called me for the sake of a joke. Nope.

When Ariel grew up, she went to college to become an elementary school teacher, a job she continues to do to this day. She also gave me my first grandchild. She said he was going to be named Anthony, after his father, and Jack, after the Americanized nickname that my father adopted. The moment she told me that, I said, "Oh! So he's A.J." The nickname immediately stuck.

Several years later she had a second child, a daughter, named Leliana.

I'm not going to discuss the man she had them with because I don't need to worry about being sued for libel. Yes, truth is the ultimate defense, but I don't need the court grief.

I am also going to mention something now that is kind of relevant to my kids, but is also a bit of a sidetrip. It's relevant to Ariel because this happened only a couple of days after we brought Ariel home.

I will always remember Myra sitting on a chair in the living room and my answering the phone. It was a friend of mine, Steve Saffel, whom I had met while working at Marvel. We chatted about a couple of things and then it turned out he had buried the lead of the conversation:

Carol Kalish had died.

You know how, in movies and on TV, characters drop a telephone upon getting shocking news? That's what happened here. My hand went numb and the phone slipped out of my fingers. I couldn't believe it. She had collapsed in the streets of New York City. She'd been rushed to a hospital where she returned to consciousness, stated she didn't feel well, and then died. A pulmonary embolism. She was thirty-six years old. Thirty goddamn six years old. Mark Twain stated that if God existed, we must be forced to the conclusion that he is a malign thug. Further proof of *that* assertion.

If it had happened a week earlier, I can assure you that Ariel would have been named Carol instead. But we weren't going to change Ariel's name even though the ink was scarcely dry on the birth certificate.

As it turned out, I would have a chance to rectify that.

Caroline

Caroline was never supposed to exist. I thought Myra and I would stay married forever and since Myra got her tubes tied after Ariel's birth, I was pretty sure that was it.

Life can throw you some curves.

I'll talk about Kathleen in greater detail later on, but I'll say this: We agreed that we were not going to go to extreme measures to have a child. We would leave it up to the fates. If we conceived a child, great. If we didn't, then nature didn't want it to happen.

Well, we did.

When Caroline was born, the nurse took her over to have her footprints placed on her birthing form. She let out a startled gasp and Kath, who was barely keeping her head screwed on, said, "What is it? What's wrong?!"

The nurse laughed. "Oh, nothing's wrong. She's just got huge feet."

She did. There were two squares on the paper for the prints to be laid down; her toes extended above the edge and her heels were over the bottom. I knew immediately that she was going to be the tallest of my daughters. As of this point she's seventeen and I was correct. A couple more years and she'll be taller than me.

We named her Caroline as a tribute to Carol Kalish, to whom I owed so much in the comics industry. Originally I was going to name her Carol, but Shana suggested Caroline and I decided I liked that name better.

Because of Kathleen's work schedule, we didn't have the time to go to a birthing class. Having gone through it three times, I was reasonably sure there was nothing more they could teach me, but Kath was a first-time mother and I figured she could benefit. So we hired a birthing coach to do a crash lesson for us. We scheduled her to show up on the first Saturday after Kathleen began her maternal leave from work. We had no idea that she was going to go into labor Wednesday and have the baby Thursday. With everything that happened, I clean forgot to cancel the meeting. I'll always remember answering the door Saturday morning and she was standing there with several bags full of giveaway stuff. I said, "Oh crap! I totally forgot about you! Uhm … there's been a change in plans." I gestured for her to enter and pointed to the couch. Kath was sitting there with a two-day old Caroline in her arms. The woman roared with laughter. I offered to pay her the fee for her time, but she declined. She handed us the bags of giveaway stuff, went over what it was and how to use them, and wished us luck with her.

One time I was lying on the bed and the infant Caroline was sleeping on my chest. The top of her little head was just under my chin, and her feet were touching my belt. I had likewise dozed off.

Then Caroline began to slide off my chest. If she'd fallen to the left, she would have tumbled right out of bed onto the hardwood floor.

I *instantly* woke up and caught her. She never even stirred as I slid her back into position and moved a couple of feet further onto the

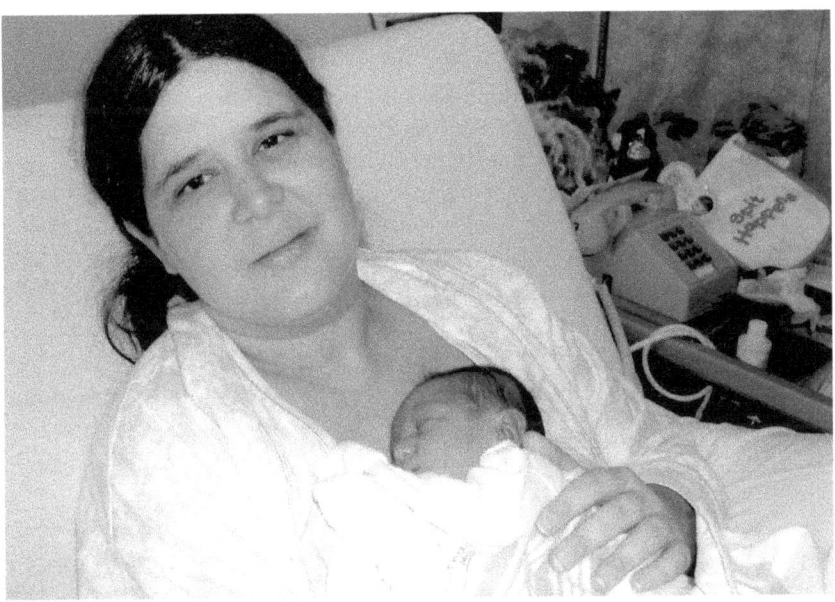

My favorite picture of Kathleen, about an hour or so after having given birth to Caroline.

bed so that, if she did wind up sliding off, she would simply land on the bed.

Caroline never learned to crawl. She would either roll or she would skid along on her diapered buttocks. We had a large plastic corral set up in the middle of the living room. At nine months of age, one day she pulled herself to standing, stared at the far end of the corral, and then walked across to it with complete confidence. I was stunned.

Now I should emphasize that when you're a new parent, your child taking her first steps is cause for excitement. Get the video camera, alert the grandparents, that sort of thing. When it's the fourth, you respond completely differently. I called, "Kath! She's walking! We're screwed!" Why screwed? Because we hadn't baby proofed the house since the rolling child couldn't reach high up. Now we had to quickly prep the house to account for her brand-new accentuated reach.

What was interesting was that she had a mother who was new to the process and was as frightened and concerned as any other new mom. But her dad had done this three times already and had no new-parent jitters.

Kath was constantly concerned that Caroline was ill. If the kid sneezed once, Kath would think she had a cold. If she took her temperature and it read normal, she'd think the thermometer was broken.

She would incessantly voice her concerns over Caroline's health to her mother, Helen, who is an RN. Helen would invariably say the same thing: "What does Peter say?" Kath would reply, "He says she's fine," whereupon Helen would respond, "Then she's fine. Listen to Peter."

I told Kath over and over that if Caroline were genuinely sick, she'd know it. Then one day, when Caroline was about nine months old, Kathleen came downstairs and said with one hundred percent conviction, "She's sick." I went upstairs and walked to her crib. I knew it even before I put my hand to her forehead. The poor kid was lying there in a daze, her face flush. The heat of her rising temperature was radiating off her. Without hesitation I said, "Yeah, she's sick." My hand on her forehead indicated to me about 102 Fahrenheit. She recovered, but it was not a fun time.

When she was four years old, we took her to Disney World, and it was a very memorable trip.

We have a friend down there named Graham Murphy, formerly of the Adventurers Club, a marvelous place that Disney foolishly closed down some years ago. But Graham was still a Disney employee, so we had some ins. At the time, there was a Disney princess show that was being held in front of the Magic Castle. Graham had a small role in it but said if we came around the back, he could get us in to meet one of the princesses backstage. So we took him up on it and met at the appointed place backstage.

Well, it turned out, Graham had lied. Because *all* the princesses were there, with their princes right beside them, plus the fairy godmother.

Now of course I knew we were meeting a group of actors in costume, but nevertheless my breath was taken away by this living manifestation of Disney magic.

Caroline, on the other hand, was overloaded. Kathleen was holding her and she turned her face away from the princesses. If she could have climbed back into the womb, she would have done so.

Cinderella's fairy godmother immediately took point. She saw that Caroline was clutching a plush Simba and engaged her on that basis. Caroline loved talking about her plush Simba and within minutes she was eagerly chatting with all of the princesses.

The meet and greet went on for another couple of minutes, and then we let ourselves out while the princesses retired to rest up for the next show.

Caroline then immediately marched to a souvenir store in Fantasy Land and went straight over to a rack of princess dresses. She made it quite clear that she wanted to be Cinderella and we had zero choice but to accommodate her. Minutes later she was attired in a Cinderella dress and she then went over to a different shelf where they had pink and blue crowns. She insisted on a pink one, even though I strongly suggested a blue crown would go better with the ensemble. No, she wouldn't have it, so a pink crown it was.

We then brought her around to the front of the castle so she could see the show. There were two other little girls there close to her in age, one dressed as Jasmine, the other as Belle. The three of them bonded instantly over their mutual love for princesses.

Then the show started.

The princess came sweeping onto the stage, and Cinderella spotted Caroline almost within seconds. The young lady was obviously thrilled and delighted that Caroline had chosen her to model herself on. She gestured over several of the other princess and they all saw Caroline and began waving to her.

Well, naturally the other girls assumed they were waving at all three of them, when the fact was that they were basking in Caroline's reflected glory. But I wasn't about to tell them that. By the way, it should be noted that one of the girls was African American and the other was Hispanic. So please don't tell me that bias against ethnicities is ingrained into human beings. As the song goes, "You've got to be taught."

Later that day poor Caroline was worn out, so we went back to our hotel. Caroline immediately fell asleep but Ariel still wanted to do some other things in the Magic Kingdom, so she and Kathleen took off on a bus back to the park.

Caroline woke up about an hour later and she marched straight over to a full-size mirror on the closet door. She stood there and stared at it for a long moment, and then announced, "I need a boo cwown!"

Apparently during her nap, her fashion sense had kicked in and she had realized that a pink crown just did *not* go with a blue dress. She firmly set her little hands on her waist and repeated, "I need a boo cwown!"

I immediately responded, "Yes, Verucah," a name that meant nothing to her, but Willy Wonka fans would get it. I then pulled out my cell phone and called her mother in the park. "Our daughter has a message for you," I said, and handed the phone to Caroline.

"I need a boocwown," she said, getting so tired of repeating it that she hurried her pronunciation, which made it even harder for Kath to understand since she was surrounded by so much ambient noise. She told Caroline to put Daddy back on, which she did.

"What is a boocwown?" she asked.

"Blue crown. She realized pink didn't go with her dress and she wants a blue one instead."

"Ooh," she said, comprehending.

So Caroline got her blue crown and she insisted on giving the pink one to her friend Katie across the street. Katie had massive Lego blocks designed to become a castle, and the two crowned little girls made them into a castle while chortling with glee.

She has easily traveled to more places than pretty much any kid in town. Australia, New Zealand, Las Vegas, Los Angeles, Phoenix, Canada, and on and on. I'll always remember visiting Hobbiton some years ago, and by that I mean the actual place where *Lord of the Rings* was filmed. It's a working sheep farm but people come all the time to visit it and go on tours.

The older she got, the more interested she became in cosplaying. And her mother being a seamstress made it way easier. When she was eight years old, for instance, Kathleen made her a great costume of Astrid from *How to Train Your Dragon*. That year at Dragon Con, George Perez and I hosted the costume contest. I brought Caroline dressed as Astrid, armed with a papier-mâché battle axe, on stage to serve as our personal guard. Of course nothing untoward happened

Caroline visiting the genuine Hobbiton. It was built on a functioning sheep ranch and they still do daily tours. Make a *lot* of money doing so. The town even has a statue of Gollum in the town square.

until a guy came out as an oversized, roaring dragon. The dragon began to stomp toward us in a threatening manner, and I immediately said into the microphone, "Get him, Astrid."

I had unleashed the whirlwind on the poor SOB. Caroline went straight at him, swinging her battleaxe in a way that seemed to suggest it was very real and could have done serious harm to the costume. Neither was true, but with his head and vision blocked or obscured by the outfit, he had no way of discerning it. As the audience roared its approval, the dragon immediately backed up as fast as he could, making it clear he wanted no truck with the attacking Viking girl. She would have chased him off the stage if I hadn't called to her, "Okay, Astrid, I think he gets the idea! Come on back!" It remains one of my favorite recollections.

Caroline is also, by any measure, the smartest of the four girls. I don't say that to diminish the other three or to proudly boast. I'm saying that from the beginning of Middle School through to her freshman year in high school, she has gotten almost all A's. She got B's in seventh grade in math; otherwise she's been nothing but perfect. It's phenomenal. I never got all A's in a single year of my academics.

For the longest time, she declared that she wanted to grow up to be president. But she has also vacillated over becoming an attorney, or a veterinarian, or perhaps a lawyer who specializes in animal rights cases, and currently she's leaning toward animation. Whatever she decides to do, I'm sure she'll be great at it.

So that's my kids.

Kathleen Gets Her Own Chapter

It only seems fair, really. She's lived her life so much in the public eye as a result of being my wife, so I figure she deserves to have her own chapter about our relationship.

It's interesting that I met both my wives at conventions. Myra was at a New York *Star Trek* convention. Kathleen, on the other hand, was at the Atlanta Fantasy Fair.

I should provide a bit of backstory first.

As I mentioned earlier, Bob Greenberger, Mike Friedman and I had just conspired to create a long-standing show that we were going to produce at a Trek convention called "Shore Leave" in Maryland. We were going to ape the famed TV series *Mystery Science Theater 3000* by doing "Mystery Trekkie Theater 3000." We were going to produce a *Star Trek* episode on the screen, sit behind the screen so that our shadows would be cast onto the picture, and snark on it for an hour. It wound up becoming insanely popular and we did it for twenty years before retiring it in 2017.

The thing was, I wanted there to be a puppet involved, just as Joel Hodgson did with the robots of Tom Servo and Crow. I wasn't sure what kind of puppet, but I figured I'd know it when I saw it.

So that year I was attending the Atlanta Fantasy and while walking around the dealer's room, I spotted the puppet that I knew I had to have for the sketch.

It was a Muppet-esque version of a Klingon.

The person who had built it wasn't at the table at that moment, but I bought it from the young lady who was watching the table on her behalf. She told me that the puppet came with a free half hour lesson on how to operate it. I said fine and left my name with her.

Word of the purchase spread to the people running the convention, and when Kathleen returned to the table, they told her with great excitement that Peter David had purchased the puppet. Kathleen said fine, and when I returned to the table some time later, she gave me a crash course on how to operate it.

She seemed nice.

That evening when she went home, she lay down in her bed and glanced up at her shelf of books. Her gaze fell upon several *Star Trek* novels and she saw the bylines. "Oh, *that* Peter David," she said.

Kathleen O'Shea was born on an easy-to-remember birthday: September 9, 1963. That's 9/9/63, and since six plus three is nine, that's 9/9/9. Kind of an upside-down sign of the beast.

She was the first child born to Don and Helen O'Shea. Donald was (and still is) a physicist who specialized in dealing with lasers. Helen was a college teacher and a registered nurse. Over the years they would produce three more children: Sean, Patrick and Sheila.

Kathleen was a puppeteer by talents, and a stage manager by training, a graduate of the renowned Yale School of Drama. She did some of whatever she could to pay the bills, including working at a local comic book store and working shows at the Atlanta Museum of Puppetry.

I saw Kathleen many times over the years, especially when I would attend conventions in Atlanta. Our friendship blossomed and as time passed, I slowly began to think of Kathleen as more than a friend. I realized I was becoming attracted to her. But I said nothing about it because I was married and I was not about to cheat on my wife.

Then Myra filed for divorce and I came to the realization that I no longer had to bottle up my feelings about Kathleen.

I was attending Dragon Con that year, the convention that had arisen over the years and eventually drove Atlanta Fantasy Fair out of business. I had wanted to approach her about my feelings toward her, but there was never a moment during the convention that the two of us were alone. Finally, I was at the last panel of the con I was attending, featuring Joe Straczynski and Michael O'Hare talking about *Babylon 5*. I was seated toward the back and Kath was next to me. My departure time was drawing near because I had an airplane home to catch. So I leaned over and said to her quickly in a low voice, "I've been wanting to tell you this. Myra is filing for divorce. My marriage is over and I wanted you to know that for a long time I've been thinking about you as more than just a friend and I'd like to pursue a relationship with you, and if you just want to remain friends, that's fine, too, just think about it and let me know, okay, bye."

Her jaw dropped and she couldn't even begin to frame an answer for me before I sprinted out of the room.

Over the next months we communicated constantly on computers, messaging with each other (this was before you could text each other on cell phones). We grew closer and closer. She came up to New York for our first date: the Marvel Comics Christmas party. The date, which was actually a long weekend, went very well, and eventually she decided to move up to New York to be with me. She packed up her pick-up truck which she had nicknamed Gandalf the Gray and made the fourteen-hour drive up to New York.

My three daughters really took to her. Originally Kath was going to find her own apartment and live separately, but the girls begged me to let her move in, and I finally agreed to it. Kath slept in my bedroom and I bunked on the pull-out couch down in my office.

Kathleen settled into our lives. She got a job as an editor at Del Rey books and in that way became known to a number of science fiction writers who loved working with her. She also participated in production of the *Star Wars* novels.

Sometimes this resulted in amusing incidents. At one point, for instance, they wanted to do a book that was set much later in Luke's career. They needed a visual reference, and Kath asked if I could call Mark and ask for a recent headshot. I called up Mark's wife, Marilou, and asked her to send us one for cover reference, which she immediately did. I gave it to Kath and she in turn gave it to the artist, who meticulously used it for reference. But when they sent the cover off to Lucasfilm, the folks there didn't want to approve it. They said the rendering of the older Luke Skywalker wasn't remotely right. When Del Rey informed them that the picture had been done off Mark's headshot, Lucasfilm wisely backed off.

And after three years, with my first marriage dead and gone, I decided I wanted to marry Kathleen.

It was not something I did lightly, and certainly not without some degree of trepidation. The dissolution of my marriage to Myra had left me with—shall we say—trust issues. I'm sure anyone who's been through a busted relationship ... which is probably just about everybody reading this ... can relate. Nevertheless, it felt good, it felt right, and it felt like it was time. But how to do it? I only knew that I wanted to do something stylish, because I felt she deserved it. And I also knew that I wanted as many of my children as possible to be present when I did it, because it was going to affect them as well. If they were going to share in her being their stepmother (something I knew they supported since I'd spoken to each of them about it individually), they should also get to share in the emotionality of the moment rather than Kathleen and I just coming back from a dinner and our saying, "Guess what?" Only one place seemed suitable:

Disney World.

We were going to Disney World anyway on a family vacation at the beginning of September: The first one in three years, and the first family sojourn to the Mouse House since the marriage had fallen apart. Shana was flying down from college to join us, so we'd all be together, staying in one of those cool family-sized cabins at Fort Wilderness. The question then became: Where at the Park? One popular place was the restaurant inside the Castle; it's such a popular venue for popping the question that there's a whole department in Disney that helps stage proposals there. But if there was one thing I'd learned, it was that relationships weren't storybook, weren't flights of fancy. They were more of ... an adventure. And that's when it hit me:

The Adventurer's Club.

To use the official Disney description, the Adventurer's Club—situated on the popular night spot Pleasure Island—is "an interactive entertainment experience in a setting reminiscent of the fictional 1930's gentleman adventurer clubs, as depicted in Hollywood films of that era.... Think of the AC as a theater that is presenting a play. In ordinary theaters, the audience is seated while the action continuously unfolds on the stage in front of them over a fixed, limited period of time. The AC, however...(has) the action sporadically occur all around you, even to the extent of your functioning as an extra in the play. At the AC you are a visitor to the Adventurers Club, circa 1935, and are treated as such by the resident cast of characters." The cast includes "Fletcher Hodges, the slightly off-center Club curator," "Graves the Loyal Club Butler," and others. But two other characters, found in the club's man salon, are Babylonia and the Colonel. Babylonia is a gigantic talking goddess mask, and the Colonel is a 1930s–style British Raj–style officer. Both of them are puppets.

It was perfect. The plan leaped from my brow fully formed, scaring the cats and knocking over the furniture: I, the writer, would write a script for one of the puppets, who would then propose to the puppeteer in the Main Salon at the AC ... provided I could get the folks at the AC to go along with it.

A few calls to Disney put me together with a fellow named Bill Shepherd, the Adventurers Club stage manager. I explained exactly what I wanted to do, and sent him the copy for what I'd want the Colonel (it was quickly decided that he would be the more appropriate conveyor of the proposal) to say:

"You're here in the Adventurer's Club, Kathleen, so you must be an adventurous girl. Tell you what, Kathleen: I'm going to invite you to take part in an adventure right now. You see, the rather round fellow you've been dating for the past three years—Peter—is standing next to you with an engagement ring. And Peter's hoping that you will accept this proposal of joining in the adventure of marriage, and become a wife to him and a stepmother to his three daughters—preferably not an evil stepmother, because we all know where that leads. What say you, Kathleen?"

Of course, if she said no, I'd look like the king schmuck of the Universe. But then again, writing full time for years has certainly prepared me for that feeling.

Shepherd set the whole thing up. The question of course was when. I worked out an itinerary of our stay at the Park one evening and casually said to Kathleen, "How about we hit Pleasure Island on the 3rd [of September], say, around ... oh..." "Ten p.m.," suggested Kathleen. "That sounds fine," I said, and gleefully informed Shepherd of exactly when we'd be there. He had to know the time so that the Club "members" could work the proposal deftly into the evening's activities without throwing the normal schedule off. I was told to touch base with "Fletcher Hodges" as soon as I arrived in order to put the thing into motion. "He'll be wearing a pith helmet and a grass skirt; he should be easy to spot," Shepherd assured me. Everything was in place.

Now—here was the slight wrinkle in the cunning plan.

My sister Beth and her husband Rande had decided to go down to Disney World for a second honeymoon. They were arriving early on the 3rd. Beth had not told me of this impromptu plan, because what she had concocted with Kathleen was that they would meet up with us at the Adventurers Club to surprise me. So now we had two siblings both trying to arrange surprises, with Kath the coconspirator of one and the target of another. Naturally, we wound up working at cross-purposes to one another.

The morning of the 3rd, while we were all walking around at Universal (you *must* do the Spider-Man ride) Kathleen got a call on her cellphone. She said "Unh huh," and "okay, sure," a couple of times, hung up, turned to us and said, "That was Sheila [Kathleen's sister]. Had to ask me something." We shrugged and thought no more of it. But in point of fact, it had been Beth calling to say, "Y'know ... why don't we make it nine o'clock instead? Ten might be a little late for us." Kathleen said no problem, waited an hour or so (so we wouldn't associate what she was saying with the phone call) and then said, "How about we go to the Adventurers Club at nine tonight instead of ten? Because I don't know how much energy I'll have left by the end of the day."

Well, now I was screwed. If I said, "No, no, we have to stick to 10 o'clock," it would sound suspicious. So I said the only thing I could say: "Sure. That sounds fine. Nine it is." Fortunately, since it was hot out, the sweat on my brow seemed perfectly understandable. But inwardly I was panicking, because we were going to arrive an hour early and the whole thing was in danger of being thrown out of whack. Ten o'clock was the time, all was in place, the puppeteer who operated the Colonel was ready to go. For all I knew he wouldn't even be around an hour earlier. I had to find a way to alert the folks at the AC that there was a change in plans ... except I had no direct line for the Adventurers Club (and there wouldn't be anyone there during the daytime anyway), Bill Shepherd had the day off so he wasn't around, and besides, I was never alone. The girls or Kathleen were with me at all times. This was, after all, about family togetherness. So I had to find a way to ditch my loved ones long enough to wend my way through the Disney phone chain and connect directly with the AC to alert them. And somewhere, at that moment, Beth and Rande were gleefully rubbing their hands together, anticipating the look on my face when I saw them that evening, not realizing that their good-heartedness had just thrown my cunning plan out of whack.

By 6 p.m. Kathleen, Gwen, Shana, Ariel and I had returned to the cabin at Fort Wilderness, preparing to go out to dinner at a restaurant at the Grand Floridian, and I still had been unable to break away and inform the AC of the change in plans. Still, I couldn't resist one moment of personal whimsy: Kathleen, in prepping to go out, said, "Should I wear my hair up or down?" "Down," I said. "I mean, I think it looks better that way, and I'd want you to look your best tonight." "Why?" she asked, curious at my phrasing. "Because," I said suavely, "I'm positive that when we're in the Adventurer's Club, every eye will be on you." "Flatterer," she said.

Meantime, we'd been informed that a package was waiting for us at the Fort Wilderness Trading Post. We knew what it was: It was stuff we'd bought in the park the day before that we'd had shipped to FW so we wouldn't have to schlep it around. The thought was that we'd hop in the car, swing by the Trading Post, pick up the package and head out.

That's when I came up with my new cunning plan. Complaining of stomach pains, I went into the bathroom, shut the door ... and proceeded to make loud retching noises. It wasn't that difficult: My stomach was in knots anyway. I came out and said that something we'd had at lunch disagreed with me. "Tell you what," I said, looking wan, "why don't you guys go on ahead to the Trading Post ... give me a few minutes to pull myself together ... come back and pick me up."

Immediately solicitous, Shana said, "Why don't they go and I'll stay here and keep you company." "Me too!" Ariel piped up.

Desperate beyond measure, I shouted, "Will you just friggin' go and leave me alone for a few minutes?!?"

"What a grouch," sniffed Shana, and off they went. The instant I heard the car pull out I was on the phone. First, I couldn't get an operator. Then when I finally did, the operator rang the AC. No answer. She tried another number there. Still no answer. Third number. No answer. I kept an eye on the window, getting more frantic. One last number—and a bartender at the AC picked up just as I saw the car coming back. The message I gave him must have sounded incoherent: "Tell Fletcher that the guy Bill Shepherd told him will be showing up with the proposal thing with the Colonel will be there at nine instead of ten!"

"Which Fletcher?" said the bartender. "Different people play Fletcher on different nights; what if the Fletcher that Bill Shepherd spoke to called in sick and the guy playing him tonight doesn't know what you're talking about?"

"Great. Thanks. Something else for me to worry about," I said crankily. "Just do the best you can, okay?" And I hung up an instant before the car honked for me, grabbed the engagement ring out of the shoe that I'd smuggled it down in, shoved it in my pocket and ran out the door.

At the restaurant were all sorts of nice-looking dishes … none of which I could reasonably have since I'd just "thrown up" minutes before, so naturally I had to stick with something mild. I wound up ordering mac and cheese off the kid's menu. Everyone at dinner was very solicitous of me, probably because I looked like a nervous wreck, which I was. What if the whole thing fell apart? What if she said no? Geez, what if she said yes? Was I ready for this, really? Three years, which had seemed so long to be together, suddenly seemed like "only" three years. My guess is that if Kath hadn't known Beth and Rande were expecting to meet us there, she would have suggested we cancel the evening excursion entirely, because I was a mess.

We got to the Adventurer's Club at five minutes to the appointed hour. "Fletcher Hodges," the club's curator and my contact, was standing by the door acting as greeter. We entered, me bringing up the rear, and I said in a low voice, "My name's Peter…. Bill Shepherd said I should touch base with you…"

Immediately he replied, "Yes, I know, everything's ready." I breathed a sigh of relief and then I said, in a slightly louder voice, "Could you tell me where the men's room is?"

Fletcher immediately said jauntily and loudly, "The men's room? Certainly! Why, I'll show you there myself!" And off we marched, getting a very strange look from Gwen. Once we rounded a corner, Fletcher pulled me through a "cast only" door. The first thing he said was, "My name is Graham Murphy and I am a huge fan of your writing. In fact, everyone in the club is."

I let out a deep sigh of relief. I can honestly say that never in my life had I been thrilled to meet a fan. (Actually, as it so happened, I had met Graham several years earlier when he'd had me sign some stuff at a convention. Didn't remember it, obviously.) Immediately all my concerns vanished; if fans of mine were handling it, it was all going to be fine.

We locked down the final details. At 9:05 the Adventurers members were going to embark on their radio broadcast (don't ask) in the library. That let out at 9:25 into the Main Salon, where the Colonel was, and that's when the Colonel would involve Kathleen in the discussion leading to the proposal. Kath wouldn't suspect anything at first, because the Colonel habitually busted on people in the crowd, so she wouldn't wonder why he was singling her out; she'd just chalk it to luck of the draw.

The radio show was in particularly fine form. Even my tough-to-impress teenagers were roaring with laughter. I was feeling more relaxed with each passing moment. We emerged into the Main Salon and the Colonel, on cue, came to life. He verbally fenced with the crowd for a moment or two, looked over in our direction and said, "Hello, young lady, what's your name?"

Immediately Gwen piped up, "Gwen!" I felt a momentary return of panic: If the Colonel wasn't paying attention to the names, or had limited vision, I was going to wind up proposing to my fifteen-year-old daughter. Without missing a beat, the Colonel said, "Hello, Gwen, and who's the young woman next to you?" "Kathleen," she replied. "Kathleen! My, you're a tall drink of water, aren't you!" said the Colonel. He started to banter with her and then went into the scripted material. My heart was racing. I reached into my pocket, ready to pull out the engagement ring on cue.

And then a low voice said, almost in my ear, "Hey, aren't you Peter David? I'm a big fan!" I thought, *Oh, geez, not now!* I turned and Beth was standing there, grinning. Rande was just behind her. I blinked like an owl in a spotlight, and suddenly my attention was divided. On the one hand my mind was racing with questions as to what my sister and her husband were doing hundreds of miles from home, and on the other hand the Colonel was fast approaching the point at which he would say, *You see, the rather round fellow you've been dating for the past three years—Peter—is standing next to you with an engagement ring.* If I was talking to Beth instead of holding the open box in my hand, everything would come unraveled. So I grabbed her by the side of the head, pulled her ear toward me and whispered, "Just listen!"

I switched my attention back to the moment just as the Colonel was saying "rather round fellow" and pulled the box from my pocket, flipping it open like Captain Kirk would a communicator. By this point the throng of about a hundred people suddenly realized something genuine, as opposed to staged, was going on and became totally caught up in it. When the light hit the ring, people started "awwwiiing" or reacting with similar comments of surprise. Tears worked their way down Kathleen's cheek as the dime dropped. Shana immediately startled yelling, "Out of the way!" as she swung her camera up and began snapping pictures. Gwen was grinning. Ariel was incandescent. Fletcher, on a balcony overhead, was videotaping it. There were more photograph records of this than the JFK assassination. The Colonel continued, "And Peter's hoping that you will accept this proposal of joining in the adventure of marriage, and become a wife to him and a stepmother to his three daughters—preferably not an evil stepmother, because we all know where that leads," and then arrived at the one moment that was completely out of my hands: "What say you, Kathleen?"

Well, she said yes, and everyone cheered, and the manager of the Adventurer's Club brought out a bottle of champagne (the good stuff) compliments of the AC, which we promptly cracked open. It was a good thing Beth and Rande were there because they helped us drink the champagne. And then Kath ran off to call her folks while I managed to get my pulse down to something normal. And when she came back, I put my arms around her and said, "Told you every eye in the Adventurer's Club would be on you."

So that's how Kathleen and I got engaged. Indeed, the engagement was such a huge success and so well received that Disney added a proposal package that could be enacted at the Adventurers Club. I understand they pretty much just repurposed my script, except in those instances you had to pay Disney $300 for the privilege. So no, they didn't pay me for the script reuse, but on the other hand they didn't charge me for it as they would have if we'd done it at the Magic Castle, so I saw it as a wash.

The huge tragedy of the thing was that some years later, Disney shut down the Adventurer's Club; indeed, every club on Pleasure Island got the boot. I believe to this day it remains one of the dumbest decisions they have ever made. But we wound up becoming good friends with Graham, and also Karl Ockstadt, who gave voice to the Colonel. It was a friendship that blossomed even deeper when I had a stroke down in Florida. More on that later.

We chose a wedding date of May 26 the following year. We decided that we would get married down in Atlanta because more of the people who would be attending lived in that area. Kath wanted to get married in the nondenominational chapel of Emory University, where both her parents taught. At least she *said* it was nondenominational, although I

Me, Caroline and Warren Spector, the creator of the videogame *Epic Mickey*, for which I did the comic book adaption.

couldn't help but notice the ten-foot-high cross on the side wall. A priest was going to perform the ceremony, but we were going to be married under a *chuppah*, a canopy that Jewish couples stand under during the ceremony. I also was going to step on a glass at the end. The last time I had done so, the glass skidded out from under my shoe, which I decided later was a bad omen when the marriage dissolved. So I was determined to crush the little bugger on the first attempt.

Harlan Ellison was going to be my best man. We also wanted George Takei to come. As I recounted earlier, we approached him while he was in Long Island and got him to agree to attend since he was going to be down there for a convention anyway.

I then contacted Bill Mumy, told him we were getting married in Atlanta that weekend, and urged him to contact the convention organizers and say he wanted to come. That way his airfare and hotel would be covered. Bill did just that and consequently both Bill and George were able to attend.

At the Farpoint convention before the marriage, I introduced Kath to Andreas Katsulas, the wonderful *Babylon 5* actor. Andreas immediately said, "I want to speak to you" and, to my astonishment, whisked her away. He proceeded to grill her about how she felt about me, and then his concluding question was, "Does he make you laugh?" "Yes," she said. "Do you make him laugh?" "I try to." He finally smiled then and said, "Then you can get married." God, I miss Andreas.

We rented a party bus to take all of the guests from the hotel in which they were staying, the Atlanta Hyatt, to Emory University. I decided, since it was a morning excursion, that we would provide Krispy Kreme Donuts for everyone attending. Bob Greenberger accompanied me to a local Krispy Kreme. We walked in and I told the counter girl that we wanted three-dozen donuts. I saw her inwardly wincing; she figured it would take forever because I'd want three of this and four of that. So when she said, "What do you want?" I said, "I don't care. I don't care if you give me three-dozen of the same donut. Just give me whatever you want. One caution: I don't want anything filled." I didn't want people to worry that jam or Boston Kreme was going to drip onto their clothes. "Other than that, I leave it in your hands." Well! The look of relief on the young lady's face was palpable. What promised to be an endless endeavor was transformed into a very quick job.

The ceremony itself went without a hitch, and I managed to crush the glass with no problem. The party was held at a place called the Shakespeare Tavern, and we had a fantastic time.

Harlan gave the best man speech, and it naturally went right off the rails. One of Kathleen's aunts had zero sense of humor, and she wasn't laughing at anything Harlan said. And Ellison, who had a spider sense for detecting party poops, focused much of his act on her, desperately trying to get her to laugh. She never so much as cracked a smile. She also then refused to talk to Kathleen's mom for several years, which was fine because Helen couldn't stand her.

After the party we retired to our hotel room and then later hung out in the hotel bar with a few of our friends. Kath sat there with her head on my shoulder, and Glenn Hauman said, "You can tell she's a new bride." His wife, Brandy, immediately said, "Right, because she's still got that new bride smell." That sent everyone at the table into hysterics and became the punchline for the rest of the evening.

We honeymooned on the *Disney Magic* cruise ship, and by "we" I mean Kathleen and I and all three girls. Bringing the kids was Kath's idea. Her contention was that we were starting a new family, and what kind of message would we be sending if three fifths of the family was left behind. Of course, our cabin was on the opposite end of the boat from the girls' cabin. We're not stupid.

I will say that a number of my friends didn't entirely trust Kath at first. They were concerned that she was just some fan who was looking

My favorite photograph of (from left) Shana, Gwen and Ariel, frolicking in the pool on the *Disney Magic*—our honeymoon cruise ship.

to elevate herself in the world of fandom by hooking up with a popular writer. But the more they came to know her, the more they liked and trusted her. In fact, at this point, if we ever broke up, the majority of my friends would likely side with her rather than me.

And whatever distrust the few remaining friends had for her vanished when she became pregnant. Once she joined the sisterhood of mothers that was that; she was one of the crowd.

I'll never forget when she went to the obstetrician toward the beginning of her ninth month. It was a Wednesday and the doctor began his internal examination. He was saying, "From this point on, you'll be coming in every week so..." His voice trailed off as he poked around and said, "You're seventy percent effaced and four centimeters dilated. You're in labor!"

"I am?" Kath said in surprise. "I thought those were Braxton-Hicks."

"Nooo, they're real. You're having this baby within twenty-four hours."

"Dammit!" I said. "It's my bowling night! Kath, you promised you wouldn't go into labor on my bowling night!"

The pains were not yet coming five minutes apart, so it wasn't time to take her to the hospital. Naturally, because I'm an idiot, I went bowling. But my mind was elsewhere, obviously, and I bowled for crap, so I stopped after one game and hurried home to be by her side, which is where I should have been in the first place.

When we left for the hospital, I made sure to leave late enough that we would arrive after midnight. Here's the thing a lot of people don't know about hospitals: If you arrive even five minutes before midnight, you get charged for an entire day. Which, to my mind, sucks. But that's the way they reckon it, so if you ever have to go to a hospital, try your best to go after midnight.

We were brought to a birthing room where there was a small couch against the wall. As the night and labor wore on, I tried to lie down on the couch as best I could, figuring at least it was an improvement over the plastic chairs I sat in during the births of my previous three children. Then a nurse walked in, looked at me oddly, and said, "You know that folds out, right?"

She was correct. The couch was also a fold-out bed. Kathleen doubtless never fully rested during the birth, but at least I was able to get some sleep.

To try and distract her, I would read newspaper articles. For some reason she fixated on one article about the Rockefeller Center Christmas tree. She kept wanting to hear it. I must have read it a hundred times over the next hours.

Caroline was born at 2:58 p.m. on December 5. Meanwhile we had a snowstorm. When I went out to the car to drive home, it was covered with snow. After a dangerous drive home, I was reunited with Ariel who immediately wanted to get back to the hospital to see her stepmom and brand-new baby sister. I told her no way; I'd been lucky to get back home in one piece and I was not going to tempt fate and the icy roads to head back. I brought her the next day once the streets were plowed.

In the intervening years, Kath has been a wonderful mother and wonderful wife. She is as supportive as any mate could possibly be. Nothing ever seems to faze her, probably because of her stage manager training. No matter what emergency comes up, she is able to handle it.

That was certainly evidenced when I had a stroke.

Worst Trip to Disney Ever

It was December of 2012. We had been up to Atlanta to visit Kath's parents and family during Christmas, as we customarily did. We had then driven south to Jacksonville, Florida, and had dropped Caroline off with big sister Shana. Caroline loved spending time with Shana, who happily put her to work in her movie theater, which Caroline loved even more. She has a desperate need to feel useful. That's just the way her mind works.

That left Kathleen, Ariel and myself to go off to Disney where we intended to spend a few days before driving back home. We checked in at the Coronado Springs hotel. We always stay on property when we go to Disney because my wonderful Disney employee status (since Disney purchased Marvel) gets us discounts of up to fifty percent. So all the convenience of staying on property while all the financial advantage of staying at a cheaper hotel off property. God, I love working for Disney.

On December 29, things started going wrong with me.

My vision began to blur. I began to slur my words. I had no idea what my problem was and was willing to write it off to exhaustion because I had both been driving a lot and also working late at night. I also began to feel weak in my right knee, which I chalked up to my recurring osteoarthritis.

Around 2 a.m. in the morning, I woke up because I had to urinate. I got out of bed and collapsed to the ground. My right leg was no longer functioning.

Immediately I screamed in alarm and Kathleen whisked me off to get help.

Kidding.

I was so damned stupid that I continued to figure the osteoarthritis was wreaking havoc with me. I crawled to the bathroom, hauled myself to standing, thanks to the handy handicap railings on the wall, peed, and then made my way back to bed by leaning on cabinets and the bed itself for support. Then I went back to sleep.

By the time I awoke in the morning, my leg seemed somewhat functional, but I still had to lean on stuff to stay upright. Furthermore, my vision was more blurred than the day before and my slurring was more pronounced. Kathleen immediately called her mother, the registered nurse, and ran my symptoms past her.

You must understand that Helen O'Shea is southern gentility. She never uses profanity.

When Kath told her my symptoms, Helen said, "Have him stick his tongue out."

Kath had me do so. My tongue canted over to the left. When Kath told her what happened, these were Helen's exact words:

"He's having a stroke. Get him the fuck to a hospital."

Now I must admit something here: I had no idea what a stroke was.

I mean, I knew it was bad to have one. That it could permanently cripple you or kill you. But I wasn't sure what caused it, or what it felt like. And there are plenty of people out there who share that ignorance. I've had many fans ask me, "What did it feel like having a stroke? Did it hurt?" The answer is: Absolutely not. It's not like having a heart attack, where the railroad spike being driven into your chest lets you know what's happening. A stroke doesn't feel like anything. There was no pain at all, unless you count when I fell.

Leaning on Ariel, I limped out to the hotel lobby. We had been scheduled to pack and check out that day, but that wasn't going to happen: Kath was going to drive me over to the nearest hospital which was called—right hand to God—Celebration Hospital. Anywhere within five miles of Disney has a Disneyesque name.

So I made my way to the front desk and told them, "We're supposed to check out today, but it seems I'm having a stroke, so we have to go to the hospital. So if you could give us a late check out..."

"Don't worry about it," said the guy behind the desk. "Get to the hospital." So Kath drove me over.

I figured that when we got to the emergency room, we'd have to sit there for three or four hours until they got around to us. Turns out, no. They bring you *right in* when a possible stroke is in play.

Here's why: There's some medication that, if you receive it within four hours of the symptoms presenting, greatly lessens the impact, minimizing it so much that oftentimes you don't even have to stay overnight.

Unfortunately, that was a no-go for me since my symptoms had hit me something like sixteen hours earlier.

The first thing they did was take my blood pressure. Keep in mind that a normal BP is 120 over 80.

Mine was literally double that: 240 over 160.

They checked me in immediately, threw me onto a gurney. And as they did so, the right half of my body shut down. It's as if it was saying, "Oh good, you're somewhere they can take care of you, now we're getting down to business." I could no longer move my right leg or right arm. They were dead. It also turned out my right kidney had shut down. If the left one had shut down as well, Kath might be writing my biography right now and would likely be sobbing over this chapter.

After that, my memory is *very* spotty. I am told that's not unusual. It is normal for the brain to refuse to hold onto memories of a traumatic incident. Car crashes, physical assaults, horrendous line waiting at SDCC ... we tend to block these things out. So it was with me.

Kathleen contacted Shana, told her what happened and made her swear not to tell Caroline. Shana readily agreed to that. I think she just didn't want to deal with Caroline's reaction, and who could blame her? Caroline had been having a sleepover at the house of a friend, Jenny, and when Caroline spoke to Shana later in the day asking when she'd be picked up (since she was expecting to meet us at the theater) Shana said actually she was going to get to stay at Jenny's for another day. "What's wrong?" asked Caroline. "Nothing," Shana immediately said, assuring her that it was just a mild change in plans, and she shouldn't be at all concerned.

Kath then called Karl, the man who had been voicing the Colonel an eternity ago when he had proposed to her on my behalf. We'd retained close friendships with both Karl and Graham, and that relationship had never been more valuable than when we were in dire distress. Karl offered his home's guest room to Kath, to stay in for as long as she needed to, an offer for which she was eternally grateful. She remained at the hospital while they ran me through a battery of tests, none of which I remember. They were sure that I was having a heart attack as well because of my elevated BP, but no, my heart was ticking along just fine.

They finally decided that another hospital with the decidedly unDisneyesque name of Florida Hospital was better suited to deal with my condition. If I ever wanted to check "Riding in an ambulance" off my bucket list, this was my opportunity as they hauled me into an ambulance and sent me riding over to the other hospital. I'm told by Ariel (who was riding along with me) that I was cracking jokes and entertaining the crew. I'm sure I was, but again, no recollection.

They brought me into Florida hospital, checked me in, and began pumping medications into me to bring down my BP. They also brought me around for tests.

Finally, they were able to ascertain that yes, it was indeed a stroke which had occurred in the pons section of my brain, which is a 0.89-inch part of the brain stem.

The doctors were not tremendously supportive. They told Kathleen that she might have some "tough decisions" to make in the future. What that meant was that they were concerned I'd have another stroke, wind up brain dead and she'd have to decide to pull the plug. Furthermore, they told her that 85 percent of people who had the kind of stroke I had died. Only one percent has what is called a full recovery. Effectively they were saying my life was over and it was only a matter of whether I lived to be a vegetable or died in bed.

She didn't tell me any of this. Thank God.

By the time she finally got around to getting to the front desk at the Coronado Springs to check out, with bags all packed, it was six o'clock. They could easily have charged us for another day. Instead they charged us absolutely nothing additional. I've always appreciated that, although I never want to stay there again because of all the negative memories associated with it. But it was a great hotel.

Kath went to get Caroline. Caroline was beginning to get antsy because she knew that in a couple of days she was supposed to start school and she was afraid she would miss it and get in trouble. So Kathleen went to pick her up and once Kathleen had her in the car, she said, "Something happened to your father."

Caroline said, "Oh my God. Is he dead?"

"No. He's had a stroke, and the doctors aren't sure how he's going to recover."

At which point Caroline began to sob. She cried for about fifteen minutes, then ate part of an oversized Tootsie Roll she had bought and, wisely, fell asleep.

Meanwhile, word was starting to get out. My editor at Marvel had called my phone to ask me about rewrites on an issue of *X-Factor*. Kath took the call and explained exactly what had happened. Within literally seconds Dave Bogart called. Dave is the talent manager at Marvel, and he called Kathleen to get a full update on my condition and also promise her that Marvel's medical plan would be one hundred percent behind me. Which they were. They assigned a caseworker to work with her and oversee all my needs.

Since word was moving through Marvel, I decided it would be wise to go public. On my website I posted the following on December 30:

> We were in Florida when I lost control of the right side of my body. I cannot see properly and I cannot move my right arm or leg. We are currently getting the extent of the damage sorted out and will report as further details become clarified.

Rich Johnston told me that within fifteen minutes of that going up he got six emails from people going, "Have you heard?!" Sixteen minutes after it went up, he reported it on his website, "Bleeding Cool News." Within seconds of him putting it up there, it went viral. The news of my stroke was everywhere, in every language. Tibetan monks were praying for me, for God's sake, and that is no joke. To this day, if you enter "Peter David" and "stroke" on Google, you'll get over 34,000 hits.

The Internet was one hundred percent behind me, except for one schmuck who tweeted that he was glad to hear it and hoped I'd drown in my own feces, which got him pummeled on Twitter. The Heroes Initiative also helped tremendously. People were asking where they could send donations to in order to help with our financial situation, and we instructed them to send it to HI, who gathered a fund for me and sent us the money. They also sent funds from their own coffers to help with medical care.

Before we posted it, Kath called my sister Beth and told her what happened, and asked Beth to inform my brother and parents, which she did. My parents were stunned. The notion of their son suffering a stroke—the possibility that I could pass away before them—was shocking. That's always how it feels to a parent when a child's life is threatened. It goes against the natural order. You have children, they care for you in old age and then you die and they go on with their lives. The prospect of losing me was horrific to them.

Overall, I spent ten days in that hospital, and I have exactly one clear memory of my stay there.

It was New Year's Eve. Everybody was in my hospital room watching the ball descend in New York City on television. Ariel was holding my right hand. And just as the ball touched down, my right hand curled around Ariel's. It was the first movement on the right side of my body in two days. It could not have been better timed. It was my body telling me that hope was not lost.

At the end of my hospital stay, with my BP down to a much steadier 120 over 80, it was time to move me to a rehabilitation center so that I could work on learning to walk again. Shana suggested that I be brought to Brooks Rehabilitation Hospital in Jacksonville, so that I would be in her back yard and she could serve as my on-site representative. That seemed like a nifty idea, and so I was brought in sort of a mini-ambulance to Jacksonville.

When I first began therapy, I was told that I would be there for eight weeks and very likely leave in a wheelchair.

I refused to accept that. I apologize right now to everyone who is in a wheelchair reading this, but to me it would be a sign of weakness. The wheelchair wouldn't be the boon that would enable me to get around. It would be the punishment for failing to push my body enough that I could walk again. If I'd broken my spine, that would be one thing. But being deprived of my mobility by a section of my brain less than an inch long? No freaking way.

Two women named Ali and Sarah took point in my training. There are videos floating around my website that show me endeavoring to walk again, with my right leg bandaged up, leaning on a railing that ran down the hallway as I attempted to make my way down it.

I even introduced a running gag.

As my recovery progressed, Ali started putting me on a treadmill. One of the challenges of the treadmill was to step over random objects that they would toss onto it. At one point they threw a rubber chicken onto it. I stepped squarely on it.

"No, Peter, you're supposed to step over it," Ali reminded me.

"Right, got it, sorry," I said.

The next time the chicken showed up, I squashed it under foot.

"Ooookay," said Ali.

Whenever that damned chicken showed up, I would always bring my foot down upon it with as much ferocity as I could. Indeed, one time when I stepped over it, they reminded me I'd forgotten to step on it.

There was one day that completely sucked. Kath called to tell me that Gordon Lee had passed away. He'd had a stroke.

I'd know Gordon for several decades. He was a comic book retailer in Rome, Georgia. When his store had been targeted for selling books that accurately depicted a nude Picasso living in a sweltering loft apartment in Paris, he contacted me and asked for the help of the Comic Book Legal Defense Fund. I informed the CBLDF and we voted unanimously to take his case. It cost us a fortune, but we succeeded in defending him.

And now he was dead, from the same thing that had attempted to take me out. So I was kind of a mess for the entirety of the day. Ali and Sarah both understood and didn't go too hard on me that day.

As time progressed, they both expressed great satisfaction with my progress. My original release date of eight weeks was scaled back to six. Not only that, but my walking was improving. Instead of departing in a wheelchair, it looked like I was going to be walking out on a cane.

Toward the end of my stay there, Stephen King's assistant contacted me.

His assistant said that Steve was down in Florida and wanted to come up to visit me. That surprised me since I thought he never wandered south of Maine, so I said, "Sure."

Stephen King with Kathleen, visiting me at the recovery center in Jacksonville after my stroke.

I figured he was nearby. He actually drove five hours to see me. I was stunned.

The great thing was that he signed in at the visitor's station. As he sat and chatted with me, various employees passing by would glance in and frown, clearly sure that they knew this guy from someplace. So they would go to check the visitors' log in, which meant that every so often we would hear a delirious squeal of excitement as they saw who it was.

It made sense that Steve could relate to what I was going through because everyone knows that he had experienced pretty much the same thing after being hit by a van.

What was interesting was that we had finished up the original *Dark Tower* comic book and I said to Steve, utterly truthfully, "Fans keep asking me when we're going to do Roland finding his Ka-Tet. They wanted to see Eddie and Susannah."

"Really?" said Steve. "We should do that then."

Some weeks later I got a call from my editor who said, "*Dark Tower* is back!" So, y'know, thank God I had a stroke.

But it gets better.

We were scheduled to leave on a Delta flight out of Orlando that

Saturday. The problem was that there was a massive snowstorm in the New York/New Jersey area.

That evening I got an email from Steve's assistant again. It said, "Steve is worried about your getting home. He'd like to have his private plane fly you back."

I wrote back and said that wasn't necessary, we had tickets on Delta. But now I was beginning to worry that our flight might be cancelled. So I called Delta.

I got a recording that said, "We have very busy phone lines because of the snow storm. If you would like, we can call you back in (pause) two hours."

It was 8 p.m. That made sense to me. They'd call back by 10. That was certainly preferable to sitting on hold for two hours. So I touched one for yes, hung up and waited.

Ten o'clock came and went. Eleven came and went. I fell asleep.

My phone rang at four in the morning. Groggy, I picked it up and a cheerful recording said, "You are the next person we're going to speak to!"

Half an hour of Muzak later, I hung up.

Meanwhile I'd gotten another email from Steve's assistant, assuring me that Steve's plane wasn't a twin-engine puddle jumper, but a genuine business class airplane. At that point my confidence in Delta had fallen precipitously and I wrote back and said, "Sure! Count us in!"

Saturday morning, I called Delta again and this time got through to them. They were thrilled to take our cancellation because they had indeed wound up cancelling a number of flights and were insanely overbooked. They probably had our seats assigned before I hung up.

We went to the private field where Steve's plane was waiting. It was gorgeous. We had our own stewardess. I cannot recommend highly enough having your own stewardess. My first major test was getting up the stairway to the plane, but I managed okay.

They had a couch that converted into a bed. It was glorious. I lay down on it and covered myself with this incredibly warm brown blanket. I ate some of the great food that they had packed in and then fell asleep. We landed, not in JFK or New York, but at a small private airfield that was a mere twenty minutes from the house. By that point I had so fallen in love with the blanket that I asked if I could keep it. "Sure," said the stewardess. Seven years later, it's still on my bed. We call it the Stephen King blanket.

It should be noted that our plane departed at 3 p.m. and got in about 5:30. Meanwhile the Delta flight we'd cancelled was also scheduled to leave at 3 p.m. Actual take off time? 9 p.m. So I definitely made the right call.

The following weekend was a convention called Farpoint, a Trek convention in the Maryland area that we always attended. My original check-out date had been the same weekend as the convention, but their moving forward of my departure meant I had a week to settle in. It was really going to come down to how I was feeling that weekend.

When Friday rolled around, I decided that I was up for it. Kathleen contacted the convention committee. They prepared our hotel rooms but agreed to keep it hushed up in case I changed my mind and insisted I couldn't manage it. We didn't want to disappoint anybody.

We drove down and our timing could not have been better. The only people who knew I might be showing up were the convention committee, Bob Greenberger and Glenn Hauman. The convention was right in the middle of their opening ceremonies and they were even having an auction for money to help me. Leaning on the cane, I walked slowly up the stairs to the backstage area. A great musical group called the Boogie Knights had just finished—or hell, maybe they were right in the middle of—their set, and then the convention guy who was the emcee of the evening, took the mike and said, "Ladies and gentlemen, I'd like to welcome onto the stage a very special guest: Peter David."

I heard a mild chuckle from the audience, probably assuming that one of my friends was going to take the stage in a Peter David disguise. But the moment I made my entrance, the place went wild. They leaped to their feet and banged their hands together. It was the longest ovation I have ever gotten in my life. It went on for at least a full minute if not longer, and if that doesn't seem like a long time to you, try doing it. Even convention guests Lee Arenberg (Pintel in *Pirates of the Caribbean* and Grumpy on *Once Upon a Time*) and Felicia Day joined in the ovation.

I just stood there, beaming, having never felt such an overwhelming display of welcome. Was it worth having the stroke to get it? Good lord, no. But it was glorious nevertheless.

And here's a coda: Kathleen may well have saved at least one life.

She took point on my website and wrote about me for weeks. One of the things she beat herself up for (and does to this day) was that she didn't ask me to stick my tongue out. Had she done so when I was first feeling the symptoms, it would have canted in one direction or another, and she could have brought me straight to a hospital and vastly minimized the effects. So she put a warning out that if you're with someone who is starting to slur their speech and their eyesight is troubled, make them stick out their tongues. One day she got an email from a guy whose wife seemed to be having strange symptoms. He had her stick out her tongue, and when it canted, he brought her straight to the ER even though she was objecting she felt fine. No, she didn't feel fine: She was having a stroke. They were able to administer the medication that reduced the condition to an inconvenience, and he profoundly thanked Kathleen for telling him what to look for.

I guess it's always possible to find benefits in tragedy if you're just willing to look for it.

Star Trek I
The Fandom Menace

Star Trek has been such a huge part of my life for so long, it's hard to believe I wasn't there when it started.

But I wasn't, because NBC scheduled it at times that my parents wanted to watch another program. In those days, we didn't have DVRs, nor did we see the need for having more than one television in the house, or even one in color (my father was suspicious of them, believing they projected damaging x-rays or something). So I was pretty much out of luck during the mid-to-late 1960s when the show was first being played to America and pretty much no one except Bjo Trimble and a cascade of fans were watching.

When I entered middle school, however, I met someone who turned me onto *Star Trek*. His name was Keith.

Keith was a great guy. Soft-spoken and friendly, always happy to listen. We talked about all kinds of things. We became the best of friends.

And kids began derisively calling us "faggots."

Now there's something you have to understand: I led a very shielded life when it came to things outside of the standard realm of being a young white Jew. You know the whole "talk" dads are supposed to have with their sons about sex? Never had that. Learned about it in a course in school.

So when we were referred to as faggots, I didn't have the slightest idea what they were talking about. Neither did Keith who apparently was raised in the same sort of bubble I was, except he was Methodist.

Eventually we wound up going to the school library, cracked open the dictionary and looked up "faggot." What was the definition? *A bundle of wood tied together for burning.*

Keith and I shrugged. They were calling us bundles of wood? It made no sense, but okay, fine, whatever. It meant nothing to us.

A year or so later, I found another dictionary and this had something in addition: *Slang term for homosexual.*

I thought, "Okay." Another term that meant nothing to me. I looked up "homosexual." *A person sexually attracted to someone of his or her own sex.*

Huh?

I know it may be extremely difficult to believe that I was in eighth grade and didn't know about the existence of homosexuality, but it's true. Remember that at the time homosexuality was considered to be a mental disorder. Hell, *at the time*? The World Health Organization didn't remove it from its list of disorders until 1992.

I told Keith and he was as stunned as I was. Neither of us could fathom it. We were just friends. We talked about attracting girls, an occupation that both of us had zero luck with. And because of that, the other idiot kids thought we were having sex *together*? I had only the slightest understanding of how straight sex worked, much less homosexual.

We entered high school lonely and depressed, surrounded by kids who despised us. But at least we had each other.

Then Keith and his family moved away, and I was pretty much alone.

I was attending Verona High School and was relentlessly pounded upon. I was attacked in the boy's shower room during Phys Ed. The word "FAG" was painted on my locker. It was a horror show. This was long before the days of trying to convince kids they shouldn't kill themselves because things would get better later in life. There were a number of occasions where I sat in the kitchen with a steak knife to my wrist, trying to muster the will to just end it all.

One kid who made it his priority to torment me was named Gil. With an adult perspective, I look back on it and speculate that deep down Gil had his own homosexual urges and was acting out against me. Or he was just an ass. Either way, he loved to make fun of me or try to shove me around whenever he had the opportunity.

That wound up stopping, though, for a terrific reason.

One day we were coming in from gym. I had stepped into the hallway that led to the locker room, Gil was right behind me at the door, and he called, "Hey Peter! Heads up!"

I turned just in time to see Gil hurl a soccer ball at my head.

Now there's something about me I haven't mentioned yet. I have fast reflexes. *Very* fast. When I eventually took driving education, the teacher had each of us in the class sit in this device in which we kept our foot on the gas pedal while a light on the dashboard in front of us glowed green. At some point it would flip to red at which time you hit the brake. My reaction time: one quarter of a second. The teacher was so stunned he had me take it again and got the same result. He said that was a school record for that device.

So even though Gil was the goalie for the soccer team and was reasonably sure he could hit me with a ball while standing two feet away, neither he nor I were aware of how fast I could respond to imminent danger.

What it came down to is this: Gil threw the ball. I ducked.

So instead of hitting me, the ball hit the wall behind where my head had been. Was there anything else on the wall? Why yes, there was. What was there? Funny you should ask.

A fire alarm.

The ball struck with sufficient velocity to shatter the glass and hit the button. Instantly fire sirens sounded throughout the high school.

My jaw dropped open. It may well have been the first time in my life that I said, "Holy shit." All the blood drained out of Gil's face. The coach immediately burst out of the locker room door, saw a stunned me and a petrified Gil standing there, and put two and two together with remarkable speed. "What did you do?" he demanded.

I know there is a schoolboy code where you don't rat out another student, but there's nothing that requires you to defend a guy who treated you like crap for as long as you had known him. I pointed at Gil and said as succinctly as I could, "Gil threw a ball at my head, I ducked it, it hit the alarm." There was no way in hell I was sharing responsibility in this fiasco.

The coach shifted his gaze to Gil, who nodded forlornly. I'll give Gil credit for one thing. He didn't try to shift responsibility over to me. Didn't claim I'd thrown the ball first and then Gil threw it back. He flatly conceded my short story: Unprovoked, he'd thrown a ball at my head, not counting on my having the ability to get out of its way.

In the distance, we heard the bells of the fire truck rolling toward us. There was only one good thing coming out of it: all the naked girls sprinting out of the girls' locker room, wrapped in towels and nothing else. I watched them running from the school and realized I was grinning widely with deep longing in my eyes. If anything could have done away with the Peter-David-is-gay mantra, the look on my face would certainly have accomplished it.

Eventually I was brought into the coach's office, in front of the other coach and the fire chief. I explained in slightly greater detail what had happened, assured them that I had done nothing to provoke it, and was simply acting in self defense not to get a hard-thrown soccer ball slammed against my head. They then sent me out and brought in Gil, and I assume he told them the truth. After that he never bothered me again, or spoke to me, or even looked my way, so I have to assume the coach came down on him like a ton of bricks and warned him that if he ever did anything to attack me again, he would be ... I dunno ... put on permanent detention. Thrown off the soccer team. Expelled. Whatever it was, it caused him to keep the hell away from me. So at that point pretty much *everyone* kept away from me.

There was exactly one bright moment in my Verona High School life, however.

William Shatner, the captain himself, was to appear in a road production of *Period of Adjustment* by Tennessee Williams. It was going to be running at Playhouse in the Mall, a New Jersey theater managed by a friend of my father's named Robert Ludlum.

Yes, *that* Robert Ludlum.

I desperately wanted to interview Shatner for the school newspaper, and my dad arranged it through Ludlum. Ludlum said that I could interview him for ten minutes after the show.

Now, I know there are all sorts of stories about how Shatner was mean to this guy or nasty to that guy. All I can tell you is that when I, a fourteen-year-old boy interviewed him after he'd gotten off stage and was probably tired, he was so patient. So sweet. I listened to the audio tape I'd made and was horrified how amateurish and nervous I sounded, and Shatner never condescended to me, never talked down. He was relentlessly nice. Ten minutes? He talked to me for forty-five minutes. It was fantastic.

A week later my interview with Shatner ran in the school newspaper, and for the first time ever, girls were suddenly interested in me.

"Peter, you interviewed William Shatner?!"

"How did you meet William Shatner?"

"A play? How many tickets did you get?"

"Are you going again? I would love to go with you."

"Here's my phone number. Call me if you can take me along."

The one bright spot in my entire school life at Verona was thanks to Shatner. Otherwise it was hell.

Then a miracle occurred. My father's newspaper, the *Newark News*, folded. We wound up moving to Fort Washington, Pennsylvania, where I was able to begin a new life at Upper Dublin High School without anyone having heard of Keith. I flourished there, began seriously pursuing writing (under the guidance of a teacher, Adria Mednitsky), even got a girlfriend. It was heaven.

There was one *Star Trek* incident from Upper Dublin High School.

When I was a teenager, my father arranged with his friend, Robert Ludlum, who was managing a theater in New Jersey, for me to interview William Shatner after he performed in a production of *Period of Adjustment*.

At one point, my English teacher was preparing to teach us about *Paradise Lost*. In discussing it, she said, "My favorite line from it has always been, 'It is better to rule in Hell…'" Then her voice faltered and she said with uncertainty, "Wait, is that how that line goes?"

Immediately I said, "Yes, that's right." Other kids guffawed because they figured I was clowning around. How the hell would I know a single line from an incredibly old book they'd never heard of? Then to their shock, I continued, "'It is better to rule in hell than serve in heaven.' Lucifer says it when he's exiled by God."

"That's right!" she said brightly. "Very good, Peter."

The kids stared at me in mute astonishment. I had given them the impression that I was such a genius, I read John Milton in my spare time.

Certainly not. I remembered the exchange from the *Star Trek* episode "Space Seed." But I sure as hell wasn't going to admit that to them.

Some years later, when I was going to be getting married (for the first time), I decided to reconnect with Keith and have him be my best man. I hadn't seen him in about eight years.

He showed up at the wedding.

I saw him for the first time with an older and more experienced mind.

He was gay. Unquestionably gay. We're talking *Sean-Hayes-as-Jack-McFarland-on-Will & Grace*-level gay. Every classic stereotype of gayness that existed, that was Keith. What had been screamingly obvious to every other kid in school, if not the universe, was finally obvious to me as well. Suddenly my entire adolescence made sense. Which isn't to say I forgave the kids who tormented me: they were still all assholes. But I finally got why they all thought I was gay. I was Keith's best friend, and Keith was clearly gay, so they just figured I was gay as well.

A couple years later, Keith called me up and said he had something to tell me. "Your best man ... your junior high buddy ... is gay."

"Yeah, I know," I said. I told him I'd figured it out at the wedding.

Haven't spoken to him in a few decades, although we occasionally correspond on email. My understanding is that he and his partner—or maybe husband, I don't recall—run a real estate company on the West coast.

All of that was in the future, of course.

In this instance, we were still in middle school and the class was doing the Scholastic Book Club. Keith pointed out to me book three of the James Blish novelizations of *Star Trek* episodes. "You should get that," said Keith. "It's really good."

So I took his word for it and sent for it. It showed up a few weeks later and I began reading.

I blew through it so fast that I went to the one bookstore in Verona (which closed shortly after I moved away, I suspect because I was likely the only customer) and found books one and two. By the time I was finished, I was thoroughly into *Star Trek*.

Astoundingly, I was still so damned thick that I didn't realize these were novelized episodes. I thought they were original *Star Trek* stories. I learned of my mistake when I saw "Who Mourns for Adonais" and realized that I knew everything that was going to happen. Furthermore, the short story had an ending cut from the script: McCoy reports to Kirk that Carolyn Palamas is pregnant with Apollo's child. Decades later, that child's grandson would be Mark McHenry of the starship *Excalibur* (which I'll discuss in greater detail later).

By that point, *Star Trek* was now airing in syndication, and that was where I began to get serious about the series.

Now at that time I was still on my own when it came to fandom. Verona was only a memory, but I was unaware of the existence of *Star Trek* fandom ... or any fandom, really. That ignorance changed when, in early 1972, *TV Guide* ran an article about the first *Star Trek* convention that had been held in New York City.

I read about it and was astounded. I hadn't heard anything about it, but plenty of people had. The organizers were expecting five hundred people and three thousand showed up. Gene Roddenberry and Isaac Asimov had both attended. It sounded wonderful and I had completely missed it because I wasn't hooked into any fandoms.

The following year, however, things changed.

My father knew an attorney. I don't recall his first name, but his last name was Kitty. Mr. Kitty had a son, Steve, a couple years older than me, and Steve was planning to attend the next *Star Trek* convention. I was invited to come along. My notoriously protective father was okay with allowing his seventeen-year-old son to go to New York on his own because he figured Steve would be watching over me.

The next thing I knew, I was off to the second *Star Trek* convention.

Now you have to remember that it had only been a few years earlier that I had been alone in the world, with no friends because everyone thought I was gay. Also my interest in science fiction in general and *Star Trek* in particular further served to isolate me because no one in Verona that I knew of cared about that stuff. Yet now I was surrounded by thousands of people who had the same interests I did. It was glorious. I have little recollections of specifics at the convention other than having a wonderful time.

Oh. And I remember Yeoman Rand's room number.

They had a major trivia contest during the convention, and one of the questions that people were hotly debating was, "What was Yeoman Rand's room number?"

Nowadays conventions typically run episodes on a TV screen in small rooms. Back then, way before such things existed or were even dreamt of, they had 35 mm films of episodes that they ran in the ballroom. Saturday night, after the trivia contest answers had been handed in, they ran the episode "Enemy Within." That's the one where Kirk splits into good and evil halves. In one scene the evil Kirk is swaggering down a corridor, drinking, and then he looks to his left and smiles fearfully. The camera whip pans over to reveal a door with the following emblazoned on it: Yeoman Janice Rand. 3C-46.

Two thirds of the audience howled in fury and one third cheered. I was in the former.

Decades later, *Saturday Night Live* did a sketch lampooning Star Trek fandom, and it began with fans debating the trivia quiz answers. One of them said, "What did you put for Yeoman Rand's room number?" The other says something like 2D-70. The fans snicker and he says, "Why are you laughing?" And I said, "Because it's 3C-46, asshole," and then moaned because I still remembered it after all that time. I swear, when I die, it'll be like in *Citizen Kane*. I'll be sitting there with a drink, mutter "3C-46" and croak, and others will be investigating what that could possibly mean.

Steve and I remained friends, and a couple years later there was going to be a *Star Trek* convention in Philadelphia. Either Steve or I came up with an idea for a sketch to do during the costume masquerade.

Remember "Who's on First?" Of course you do. The acclaimed Abbott and Costello sketch that hinged on the notion that Abbott was trying to explain to Costello the names of the players on his baseball team: Who's on first, What's on second, Idon'tknow is on third, and so on.

The notion was that we would give it a *Star Trek* spin and make it, "Who's on the bridge, What's in sickbay, Idon'tknow is in engineering." We rewrote the entire sketch, right down to making it a battle against the Klingons rather than a triple play at the end. I would be Kirk and Steve would be Spock.

My father, who remember came here to be an actor, served as our director. He was especially useful in dialing me back, pointing out that what makes the sketch funny is Costello's slow burn. He starts out calm, but his anger gradually escalates until he's shouting in fury. I was starting off too angry, too fast, so it gave me nowhere to go emotionally. My dad explained how to do it right.

Flash forward to the masquerade and we take the stage, my father sitting in the audience; one of the few times he attended a convention. We launched into the sketch, and Steve began to talk about the oddly named crewmembers who had just started duty on the *Enterprise*. Steve-as-Spock said, "We've got Who on the bridge, What in sickbay, and Idon'tknow in engineering."

The audience moaned. They began to boo. Why? Because their thinking was, "Oh, God, this is just some old vaudeville schtick that everybody knows."

I saw panic in Steve's eyes. The concept of failing in front of my father nearly paralyzed me as well. But I kept going, and Steve had so drilled the material into himself that his responses were automatic.

And very slowly, the audience began to laugh.

Because they thought they knew the sketch, but they didn't really. Sure, they knew the opening set up lines, but they didn't know the infinite twists that Abbott and Costello had in the routine. My descent into confusion matched Costello's and the longer we went, the more the audience got into it.

"So what's the name of the man on the bridge?"

"No, What's the name of the man in sickbay."

"I'm not asking you who's in sickbay!"

"Who's on the bridge."

"I don't know!"

"He's in engineering."

No matter how I tried to rephrase it, it always came back to that exchange, with the last line eventually shortened to just "Engineering." The audience became so much a part of the sketch that when we reached that point they began chorusing "Engineering!" with me.

The sketch was a huge success and I wouldn't be surprised if people who were there will read this and go, "Oh my God, that was Peter David?!"

Furthermore, I found out about where fandom existed in the Philly area. I joined the editorial staff of a fanzine called *Space-Time Continuum*, run by an extraordinarily eccentric woman named Alice Eve LaVelle, or just A.E. as she went by back then. The quarterly fan publication was edited by another woman named Sandy Weisman. A third woman involved was Sara Paul, a librarian who became my unofficial big sister. Back in those days, we didn't have access to the many printing options that exist nowadays. We printed every issue with a Gestetner mimeograph printer. To this day I swear I still have ink under my fingernails from that damned thing.

Eventually A.E. and Sandy wanted out, so they fobbed the fanzine over to me and my former girlfriend/then friend Wendy "Wedge" Goldstein. I'll never forget the assembling parties we would have where we'd print the stencils up (praying that we wouldn't tear one along the way) and then assemble, staple, and put them in envelopes to send to our two hundred subscribers. It was my first experience with writing *Star Trek* fan fiction, including producing my favorite, a Gary Seven/Questor team up.

I never dreamed I'd wind up writing fanfic professionally.

Harlan

This chapter was going to be entitled "*Star Trek II:* First Contact," but I received a call the other day that blew it right out of my mind.

It was Susan Ellison, the wife of Harlan Ellison. For those who don't know her, she is a fiftyish British woman with short blonde hair and the patient temperament to allow her to remain married to Harlan longer than all his preceding wives combined.

"I wanted to tell you this before you spoke to Shana," she said, which made no sense to me at all. She continued, "Shana had an appointment to come visit with Harlan today and I totally forgot about it."

I was unaware that Shana was even in California, but I very much doubted that Shana would call me to complain that she had slipped Susan's mind.

"She got here," Susan went on, "and with all the police..."

Police?! I thought.

She apparently realized that she had buried the lead: "Harlan died last night."

I was stunned and yet somehow not. The fact was that since he had had a stroke, Harlan had effectively been bed-ridden for two years. He'd get out of bed twice a week for one hour to work with a physical therapist, but you can't recover from a stroke by exercising two times a week.

Indeed, some years before that, I'd been chatting with Harlan on the phone. I asked him how he was doing. His response: "I'm dying."

"What?" I said, stunned. He sounded so blasé about it. "What's happened?"

He rattled off a list of ailments which were, individually, irritating. In fact, they were typical conditions encountered when aging. But none of them was remotely life threatening. I thought he'd been diagnosed with cancer or something. "Is that it? Harlan, none of those will kill you."

"But my body's winding down. I can feel it. And I'm not upset by it; I'm ready for it."

"I wish you wouldn't talk like that," I said. "It's really upsetting."

"Yeah, everybody I told that to has said the same thing. What's wrong with all of you?"

The conversation inspired me to write a short story entitled, "Bronsky's Dates with Death." In the tale, an elderly man named Bronsky is just like Harlan, saying he isn't afraid to die, he's totally fine with it, bring it on. He's so excessive about it that Death itself comes to him and tells him to knock it off because he's giving Death performance anxiety. I mailed it off to the *Magazine of Fantasy and Science Fiction*, and two weeks later I got a contract and check back in the mail. So that was nice. Eventually it was reprinted by Random House, and you can find it here: *http://a1018.g.akamai.net/f/1018/19022/1d/randomhouse1.download.akamai.com/19022/pdf/July_2011_Peter_David.pdf.*

That story was written eight years ago and yet he held on for all that time. The stroke, however, was finally what knocked him out. When I was working at the recovery center in Jacksonville to return to what I had been before the stroke, the folks there often praised me for my determination. "Many people give up," I was told repeatedly, "and your ability to recover comes entirely from your determination." Harlan turned out to be one of the stroke victims who gave up. Considering he was sure he was dying years earlier, it became a self-fulfilling prophecy.

Yet the concept that Harlan died peacefully in his sleep was still a lot for me to process. I always figured Harlan would go down attempting to thwart a bank robbery. Or intercepting a bullet aimed at a famed writer or politician. Or flying off some curvy mountain road racing against some young asshole who thought he was hot stuff. Something like that. Quietly? In his sleep? Really? Someone online commented that it was probably better that he was sleeping when Death came for him, for if he'd been awake, "there would likely have been a ruckus."

When did I first meet Harlan? I remember that quite clearly. It was 1974, at Discon II, the World Science Fiction Convention held in Washington, D.C. I was eighteen (almost) and my father arranged for me to get press credentials for it so that I could cover the convention for the *Philadelphia Bulletin*, the (now defunct) newspaper he was working for at the time.

I was standing in the room that was the base of operations and doubled as the press room. I was talking with the convention press liaison, going over my list of guests that I was hoping to have the chance to speak with. "And Roger Zelazny, and Harlan Ellison," I concluded.

Before she could respond, a voice bellowed "Coming through!" and a short dervish of a man sprinted through the room, shoving me to one side as he sped past. I caught myself on a chair and said, "Who the hell *was that*?!" The others in the room laughed, as if almost being knocked

My wedding day. From left to right: Rozana O'Shea (Kath's sister in law), Mary Aileen Buss (maid of honor), Kath, me, Ariel, Harlan, Sheila O'Shea (Kath's sister), and my dad, Gunter David.

on one's ass was a commonplace occurrence, and they said, "That was Harlan Ellison."

Flash forward to 1987. I was attending the San Diego Comic-Con and noticed a number of people schlepping a sizable book entitled *The Essential Ellison*. Out of curiosity I asked each of those toting it around, "Could you have lived without that book?" Every fan said with certainty, "No."

Some months later I was required to do a list of holiday suggestions for *Comic Buyers Guide*. Remembering what had happened at SDCC, I recounted the experience and said that I believed *The Essential Ellison* was a must-have for fans.

The day after the issue came out, I came home and played the messages on my answering machine. To my utter shock, there was a message from Harlan, thanking me profusely for the plug and proposing marriage. I had no idea how in the world he had gotten my phone number. I guess he called Maggie Thompson, the editor of CBG, and asked her.

Over the next few years we developed a steady friendship.

And then in 1994, something happened.

Harlan called me, distraught. A group of people, led by professional douche Charles Platt (aided by Fantagraphics head Gary Groth), had begun a group called "Enemies of Ellison." He faxed me over an anonymous flier announcing that the group was formed to accommodate a very special selection of people: "[T]hose who have been named as enemies by Mr. Ellison and have been maligned, harassed or assaulted purely because (in most cases) they spoke the truth, or expressed skepticism re [sic] his reputation, craft, or self-promotional hype…"

To become a full member of EOE, you had to come up with nasty anecdotes about Harlan and send them $14, for which you would receive a bi-monthly free newsletter. How something can be considered "free" when you've paid them $14, I couldn't really fathom. Furthermore, members could contribute to a book called "Harlan Ellison as We Knew Him." This was described as a memorial book. So basically, a group of anonymous goons (their names were only revealed later) were going to wait until Harlan died and then publish a slam book, which contributors would not be paid for but would be allowed to buy copies of for a princely twenty-five percent off.

I read the fax and became furious. Was Harlan a perfect individual? God no, but who is? (Okay *maybe* Fred Rogers.) Some of his public escapades had reached the level of legendary. But this attack was so cowardly, so vicious, that I resolved it would not stand.

Fortunately, I had a vehicle to do so: *But I Digress*, my weekly column in *CBG*.

Yes, I had a weekly column. Some fan—to this day, I have no idea who—wrote into the *Comic Buyers Guide* magazine and suggested that *CBG* begins a weekly opinion column produced by yours truly. Rather than give me a heads up, Don and Maggie just ran the letter, said "It sounds good to us. Peter?" and left it there. I found out about it when my phone started ringing off the hook from people asking me if I was going to do it. I wound up taking them up on it and thus *But I Digress* was born. It became the most popular column in the paper. I would talk about whatever was going on in my mind and it wound up leading to some serious dust-ups that I will discuss in a later chapter. I continued it right up until the last issue of *CBG* came out in 2013.

And this instance with Harlan seemed a perfect opportunity to make use of it.

Boy, did I lay into those guys.

After first ripping the anonymous schemers for their cowardice and mendacity, I announced I was going to launch a counter group called Friends of Ellison, or FOE. To become a member, all you had to do was send me a letter recounting some positive story about Harlan. Then for no money at all, you would receive a free FOE membership pin. And I'll tell you, these were damned nice pins. Silver with red printing, decorated with our logo, two and a half inches wide (I know, because I just measured one). I also ran some of the letters in *But I Digress*, from such luminaries as Robert Bloch and Julie Schwartz.

Enemies of Ellison fought back. First, they sent around another flier revealing their names. They also changed their name to Victims of Ellison, presumably to make people feel sorry for them. No one did. I received over a hundred letters, and they got somewhere around three. They ended up folding up their tents and retiring the group without carrying out any of their threats.

Harlan was ecstatic. He said that he had told a number of his friends about it and they had all advised him to suck it up, to ignore it because all the guys really wanted was attention and anything he did to try and strike back would simply give them what they desired. My being willing to fight back against them apparently elevated me in the status of Friends of Ellison.

Whenever I was in Los Angeles, I always had to make sure to let Harlan know I was in his backyard because if I didn't, some how he'd find out, call my hotel, and demand to know when I was going to come over to visit the famed Ellison Wonderland.

Coolest house in the world. His workplace was up a curved set of stairs. He kept his assorted Hugo awards stacked there, along with such unique items as a note from Dorothy Parker praising his writing. He had an array of movie paraphernalia, ranging from the silver statue of Gonzo wielding a plunger from his truck in *The Muppet Movie* to the jade skull from *The Phantom*. To get into the main room, you had to pass through a shrunken doorway like something out of *Alice in Wonderland*.

Being a friend of Harlan's always forced you to think fast. For instance, there was the incident with the guava paste.

What is guava paste, you ask? The Internet describes it as a very thick puree of guava fruit and sugar.

Harlan, Neil Gaiman and I were attending a convention called Madcon, held in Madison, Wisconsin. On Saturday evening there was a special dinner where each of the guests sat at a table with a group of fans who had paid money to be seated with them.

So since these fans had shelled out money to enjoy my company, I felt that I needed to do something that would make it worth their while.

Harlan had brought guava paste. When it was time for dessert, Harlan was going around with his guava paste, spread on slices from a block of Philadelphia cream cheese. (The acquisition of the cream cheese was an event in itself because the hotel didn't have any on premises and some poor schmuck had to run to a supermarket to get him the required cheese.) He had served it to us first: Kath loved it, as did

Caroline. I nibbled on it and then quickly passed it off to Kathleen so Harlan wouldn't see that I didn't like it.

There was Harlan, now working his table to be followed by the rest of the room. Neil, meantime, was recounting tales of his career (I presume) and the fans at his table were eating it up.

Then there was my table, where the conversation was light and entertaining, but nothing that would sear its way into their brains and be recounted later with delight. I wanted to give them something memorable.

That was when a twisted idea seeped into my mind.

"Hey guys," I whispered, "how many of you remember the movie *Soylent Green*?" It was a silly question, of course. They were all science fiction fans. Naturally they recalled the Charlton Heston sci-fi thriller.

Quickly I outlined my plan. "Should I do it?" Their heads all bobbed as if they were bobble heads in a windstorm. My scheme seemed workable, but I felt as if it needed some sort of button.

With what I can only describe as psychic timing, this bald guy who had to be over six feet tall stepped up behind me. His name was Barney whom I would come to know better over the years. He said, "Mr. David, I just wanted to tell you what a big fan I am of your work."

There it was. The button to the bit. I quickly told Barney what I wanted to do and he readily agreed.

So I waited for another minute until I thought that Harlan was in perfect position, and then suddenly leaped to my feet, pointed at him accusingly, and shouted at the top of my lungs:

"Tell them! Let everybody know! It's people! Guava paste is *people*! It's *people*!"

When I first began to shout, people were looking on in shock. Harlan would later tell me that he thought that the pressure I had been undergoing during my divorce had caused me to flip. But once I got to the "Guava paste is people!" line, naturally they all got it.

And about ten seconds into my rant, Barney came charging up behind me as if he were security, or perhaps had been dispatched by the guava paste people because I was revealing the truth behind their product. He threw his arms around me, *lifted me off the ground,* and started hauling me toward an exit door as I continued to howl my "revelation."

The room was in hysterics. Harlan was stunned. Neil was laughing so hard that he literally almost fell out of his chair.

I "struggled" in Barney's grasp as he dragged me out of the room. I caught the edge of the door as he hauled me through it, pulled my face back into view, bellowed "*It's people!*" once more and then was yanked out of sight.

We waited for a few seconds and then Barney and I strolled back in, high fiving each other.

And Harlan frickin' Ellison dropped to his knees and salaamed me in the classic "I'm not worthy" routine from *Wayne's World*. That may have been one of the high points of my entire life. To this day, people still come up to me and swear they saw the guava paste bit. By my count, more people than were actually attending the banquet claimed to have been there.

That dinner was also worthwhile because Apropos of Nothing walked into my head that evening.

Before I came up with the guava paste bit, my mind was wandering and I found myself envisioning a king's court. In my vision, would-be knights were striding forward and introducing themselves. "I am William of Essex!" "I am Bedevere of the Southern Hinterlands!" And then in walked this young guy, lame of right leg and limping on a staff. His ears were slightly too large for his head, and he had a curly shock of red hair. And he bellowed, "I am Apropos, of.... Nothing." I made my way over to Harlan and said in a low voice, "What would you think if I wrote a book about a misfit knight called Apropos of Nothing?" Without hesitation, Harlan pronounced it the dumbest idea he had ever heard.

Four books later...

Harlan infiltrated our lives without any warning. There was one time that Kathleen and I were watching a Robin Williams concert on HBO. And he made a joke about the prospect of combining Easter and Groundhog's Day into one holiday where Jesus would emerge, see his shadow, and there would be another two thousand years of sin.

Kath's jaw dropped. "I told that joke to Harlan!" she said.

I immediately called Harlan and said, "Do you remember that Jesus joke that Kathleen told you?"

"Oh yeah," he said. "That was hilarious. That's why I remember it, because Kath's jokes usually aren't funny."

"Did you tell it to Robin Williams?" I knew Williams was a friend of his.

"Uh huh," said Harlan. "He thought it was hysterical."

I turned to Kath and said, "Congratulations. You've written for Robin Williams."

Although the best phone conversation I had with him was a few years later when I had badly injured my back, taking a tumble off a treadmill at the gym. I had shattered a disk in my spine. In two days I was going in for an operation to have it fixed, but at that point in time I was in complete agony. No amount of painkillers could do anything to ease my aching back. So the doctor put me on a morphine derivative. It did nothing to ease the pain, but it made me so loopy that I didn't care about it.

For some reason that made sense to my warped mind, I called Harlan. "Yeah?" he said brusquely as he always did.

"Hey Harlan," I said. "I just wanted to say I love you, man. You know that, right? You're like a second father to me. You're so great."

I went on like that for God knows how long, and then Kathleen walked in and said, "Who are you talking to?"

"Harlan," I said.

He apparently heard her because he said, "Give the phone to Kathleen."

I obeyed and handed it to her.

"What is he on and why?" Harlan asked her.

She immediately told him. His response was to shout for Susan, who immediately got on the phone. Susan had had back surgery and knew what I was going through, and gave her plenty of advice as to what to watch out for and how to handle it.

Harlan concluded by saying, "Do yourself a favor. Unplug the phone."

After she got off the phone, she proceeded to do just that. Immediately I protested. I said, "I want to call somebody else!"

"Who do you need to call?" she asked.

"Myra," I said.

"What could you possibly have to say to Myra?"

I stuck my tongue out and blew a loud raspberry. To this day Ariel resents Kath for not letting me do that.

Just to relate another Harlan anecdote that had nothing to do with me:

There was once a writer who had a career as a journalist, but he wanted to break into writing science fiction. He was having no luck. His stories weren't selling and he wasn't sure what he was doing wrong. Finally he decided to call Harlan and maybe get some feedback from him. He found his number and rang him up.

"Yeah?" said Harlan.

The writer introduced himself and said, "I'm trying to become a science fiction writer and I'm not managing to sell any stories. So I was wondering—"

Harlan cut him off. "You want to know what's wrong with your stories? I'll tell you. You listening?"

"Yes."

"They suck," said Harlan. "Your stories aren't selling because they suck. Once they stop sucking, they'll sell. Got it?"

"Oookay."

"Good," said Harlan, and he hung up the phone.

That was J. Michael Straczynski's first encounter with Harlan. He went on to create *Babylon 5*, so he obviously got the hang of it.

The largest audience Harlan, Neil Gaiman and I ever had was at MIT, in which we did a production called the Three High Verbals. Harlan arranged it because, naturally. The three of us came to an agreement: we would each have fifteen minutes to ourselves, then as a group we would turn it over to the audience for questions and answers.

I'll never forget Harlan's pep talk before we went on.

"You better have your 'A' material ready. Only the best stuff," he said as we waited backstage. "You've only done conventions up until now, and that's like playing lounge acts compared to this. This is the main stage, the Big Time. Your introduction to the Big Leagues. If we pull this off, other schools around the country will ask us to speak there, so you don't want to screw this up."

I went first. I began my talk with the following line: "Hello, I am Peter David, or as I will henceforth be known, 'The fat guy who was the opening act for Neil Gaiman and Harlan Ellison.'" This got a big laugh since I was basically admitting that Neil and Harlan were far better known than I was.

My speech took fifteen minutes. Then Harlan came out.

Forty-five minutes.

I'd seen that coming.

He was followed by Neil, who hewed much closer to the fifteen-minute mark. Then we opened it for Q & A.

The Q & A consisted mostly of MIT students trying to show that they had as big *cajones* as Harlan. There was incessant dispute about copyright laws, and Harlan took the lead. In fact, at one point I attempted to interject a comment and Harlan cut me off by saying, "Hey, I work a single!" That was his standard line when someone from the audiences tries to interrupt him during a talk. I stared at him and I think he immediately realized he'd screwed up: He wasn't working a single this time. I had every right to offer an opinion. He didn't acknowledge it verbally, but he knew he'd messed up and didn't say it again.

We had a set on the stage: Three comfortable chairs and copies of some of our books. The Q & A progressed and, as could have been expected, Harlan dominated it. About fifteen minutes in, I noticed the books. One was *Sir Apropos of Nothing*, the other was *American Gods*. I picked up Neil's book, he picked up mine, and we proceeded to read them on stage. Harlan kept talking but the audience was starting to laugh. He knew he hadn't said anything funny, so he turned around to see what Neil and I were up to. As Harlan glowered at us, we looked up at each other and gave each other a thumbs up to let each other know we were impressed by our respective efforts.

The next morning, we assembled for breakfast in the hotel restaurant. The discussion was so convivial and interesting that we attracted the attention of two elderly women seated nearby. When they finished their breakfast, one of them came over to Harlan and asked if he was a film director, since Harlan had been regaling us with stories about various Hollywood stars.

Now Harlan could easily have said "No" and that would have ended it right there. But no. He had to obey the immortal improv rule of "Always say yes." So he said he was indeed a movie director, in town shooting a movie.

"What's it called?" she asked.

"*Flesh*," he said.

Neil and I stared at each other and mouthed *Flesh?*

The woman asked who was in it.

"Well, we've got Kevin Costner," said Harlan, "and what's-her-name from *The Talented Mr. Ripley*..."

"Cate Blanchett," Neil volunteered.

"Right, Cate," said Harlan.

I volunteered, "Because Gwyneth wasn't available."

"Yeah, right, we thought we had Gwyneth locked up, last minute conflict," said Harlan.

It was fun at first, but the damned woman wouldn't go away. She kept asking question after question: Who was the studio? Any interesting supporting actors? Was there going to be product placement? It just wasn't ending.

Finally, I whispered to Kath, "Give me your cellphone." She did so and I took it and seemed to be listening to it. Then I said, "Sir. It's for you. It's the set."

Harlan took it and immediately started talking to no one. I prayed it didn't ring or the bit was blown. He said briskly, "Yeah, yeah, Kevin, we just finished breakfast. We're on our way over."

"All right, then," said the old woman, "I'll be on my way."

Harlan nodded and then rolled his eyes and shouted, "Kevin, I've told you a hundred times, no applesauce!"

We all smiled and waved at the woman as Harlan continued to rant until finally Neil, who had the best angle, said, "Okay, she's gone."

We released a collective sigh of relief and Harlan congratulated me on my quick thinking to terminate what had started as a good joke but morphed into an endless improv.

Was it always fun and games with Harlan? No.

One time he and Susan came to New York for a convention called I–Con, and I volunteered to pick them up at the airport. There was some sort of snafu about the books that Harlan had brought to sell at the convention, and for some reason Harlan was squarely blaming Susan for it. He castigated her at the airport and continued to scold her in the car as I drove. Susan did nothing to defend herself but largely just sat there and took it. I made no comment on it, until Harlan made the mistake of asking me what I thought of Susan's alleged screw-ups.

"I don't know what Susan did or didn't do," I said, keeping my eyes fixed on the road, "but I think a husband doesn't chew out his wife in public. It's disrespectful."

Harlan got *very* quiet then. He remained silent for about five minutes, and anyone who knew him could tell you that a five-minute silence for Harlan is an eternity for somebody else.

Then, in a low voice, Harlan said, "Susan, Peter feels that I was being disrespectful to you. I'm very sorry for that." And that was the end of it; he didn't say another angry word to Susan for the rest of the weekend, at least not in public. Susan later told me that she was eternally grateful for that, because she said, "No one ever stands up to Harlan" and she was so pleased that I had shut him down without hesitation.

We also introduced Harlan to a game called "Balderdash" in which you are challenged to come up with definitions for obscure words. Harlan was sure that he would know all the words and was astounded that the majority of them were outside his vocabulary. He won the game, of course, but I'll always remember how thrilled he was to learn an abundance of new words that he could hurl.

In the 1990s, when I had a lot of money thanks to *Space Cases*, I attended a charity auction for an actor's fund. I acquired two things: a signed glove worn by Jack Nicholson as the Joker, and a dinner for four with William Goldman, author of—among other things—*The Princess Bride*.

It was a great auction. I was standing in the back of the room and when the bidding started on the objects I wanted, I pulled a trick that Steve Geppi does: I raised my paddle and didn't lower it. That way I was able to immediately jump over other bidders. The auctioneer even referred to me as "the Standing Bidder." People were craning their necks to see who the madman in the back of the room was who kept jumping over everyone else. When I won the glove, one gentleman leaned back and, indicating a man sitting nearby, said, "Mr. Max really wanted it, but he saw you were quite determined." I said, "*Peter* Max?" He nodded.

Holy crap. I outbid Peter Max. Jesus.

I also wound up meeting Kim Cermak, the wife of Art Garfunkel. She was there with both her husband (whom I met later) and her son, James, who appeared to be about four. I looked down at him and desperately tried to stifle my reaction.

"It's okay," said Kim, "you can laugh."

And I did. I burst out laughing, because if you ever wondered what a four-year-old Art Garfunkel looked like, that kid would have been the answer. He looked like his father right down to the hair. It was hilarious, and I suspect that she had grown accustomed to peoples' amused reactions to the child.

Once I had acquired the dinner with Goldman via the same method as I had the glove, I contacted Harlan and asked if he and Susan would like to fly out to New York and join us. He immediately took me up on it. On the appointed night, as we headed for Goldman's apartment, he assured me that this was going to be my night. That he was just going to sit and be quiet and let me lead the conversation.

I immediately shut that down. First of all, I knew that was BS. Harlan had many wonderful qualities, but self-control was not one of them. Second, I said, "Are you nuts? The whole point of this is so I can have two of my favorite authors face to face. I want to sit back and watch you guys interact." Which was of course exactly what happened. It was a terrific evening.

But honestly, aside from when he was the best man at my wedding, my best memory of Harlan is this:

Harlan was being given the Science Fiction Writers Association Grand Master award in 2006. The affair was being held at the Nebula Awards at the Mission Palm Hotel in Tempe, Arizona. He had been complaining that there wasn't going to be anyone there who really knew him. On the spur of the moment, I found a great fare to Arizona and decided to fly out for the ceremony. My plane was an hour late getting into the airport and I drove like a lunatic to the hotel, certain that I was going to miss it.

As it turned out, my timing could not have been better. I got there and saw Harlan sitting up on the stage, and he seemed dead to the world. Everyone, it turned out, wanted to get up and say something about him, and it was as if his mind had shut down. Actually, it looked as if someone had been slamming him in the face with a 2 × 4. If you'd ever wondered what it would be like to be at your own funeral, hearing people file up and say nice things about you, this was the answer. It was obvious what he was thinking: *Just give me the damned award so I can go to sleep.*

I made my way toward the stage and Susan spotted me. Her eyes opened wide in shock. She drew me over quickly and said, "We didn't know you were going to be here!"

The last time I was at Harlan's house while he was alive. Patton Oswalt (left) and Neil Gaiman were also visiting.

"Yeah, kind of last minute," I whispered.

Susan then made her way to the convention organizers, told them I was there and wanted a chance to speak. Which was great, because they had almost reached the end of their scheduled speakers. I walked up to the podium unannounced and started talking. I don't remember what I said, but I remember Harlan's reaction. His head snapped around, his eyes widened, and a smile split his face. As soon as I was done, he leaped out of his chair, came up and hugged me, and then immediately sang, "I dreamt one night I was on the boat to heaven." I promptly replied, "And by some chance I had brought my dice along!" And we launched into a rendition of "Sit Down, You're Rocking the Boat." The audience went nuts. Harlan, for the first time that evening, had come alive and they had finally gotten a glimpse of the man they were awarding.

I could go on about his later years. More about the stroke that felled him. About the time I swung by to visit him and Neil Gaiman and Patton Oswalt were there visiting as well.

But it's too unpleasant. That's not how I want to remember him.

And it's not how you should remember him either. What you should remember is something he once wrote:

"For a brief time, I was here. For a brief time, I mattered."*

---

*Since I completed this manuscript, Susan Ellison passed away as well. She was sixty years old and, to the best of my knowledge, in perfect health. One night she just went to sleep and didn't wake up, the same as Harlan. I'm honestly skeptical of the existence of heaven, but I sure hope it exists and they're keeping each other company.

Star Trek II
First Contact

You remember Bob Greenberger. The guy who assigned me the article for *Comics Scene* that wound up getting me a job at Marvel Comics. The one who, when I first explored the idea of becoming a full-time writer, offered me a gig on the Phantom.

The next assignment I received was that I was offered the chance to write DC's *Star Trek* comic. You need to understand how incredibly jazzed I was by the opportunity. As a teenager and even into my early twenties I had written *Star Trek* fan fiction. Now I was going to be able to continue to write it and actually get paid for it. Life didn't get better than that.

I wrote about a dozen issues of the comic, and then DC pulled the plug on it. It wasn't because of sales; they were actually pretty strong. It ceased publication because DC failed to renew the license with Paramount, and apparently Marvel came in with a stronger offer.

But hey, at least I'd had the chance to write a *Star Trek* comic. I'd had the opportunity to contribute to the vast tapestry that was the Trekverse, and I was satisfied with that.

Then Dave Stern, who was the editor of the *Star Trek* line of novels at Simon & Schuster/Pocket Books contacted me. He wanted to know if I'd be interested in going out to lunch. I can tell you that if you want to get a freelancer's interest, offer him free food. That's just the simple truth. We're pretty easily bought.

So we went out to lunch and Dave told me that he had loved my work on the *Star Trek* comic and wanted to know if I'd be interested in producing a Trek novel.

I saw this as a terrific opportunity. I had actually launched a major continued story in the comic that I was unable to complete because of its cancellation. This would be the ideal chance to conclude it. I said, "I have a great idea for an original series novel—"

Dave interrupted me. "I actually have all the original series novels I need. I've got, like, two years' worth. If, on the other hand, you could give me a Next Generation novel, and you could do it quickly, I could have it on the stands in six months."

"Did I say original series? I meant to say Next Generation," I said immediately.

Now understand that Next Generation was relatively new at that time. I'd watched the first episode and had not been especially blown away. When Q showed up, I said, "That's Trelane! They're rehashing 'The Squire of Gothos!'" (Little did I suspect that years later I would write a Trek novel called *Q-Squared* that connected the two.) I also wasn't thrilled about how they spent ten minutes recusing themselves to the battle bridge and finally, once they were there, Picard surrendered. That just pissed me off. If you're all assembling in the battle bridge, there should be a damned battle. If Picard's order had been that they should retire to the surrender bridge, I'd've been fine with him surrendering.

Honestly. Contrast that moment with "*The Wrath of Khan*" and the moment that the *Enterprise* has had the hell shot out of it by the *Reliant*. Uhura announces to Kirk that they have received a transmission from the *Reliant* offering terms of surrender. The moment she says it the entire bridge goes dead silent, as if she had just uttered a profanity. Kirk? Surrender? And when Kirk tells her to put the hail through, she says "*Captain?*" with incredulity, as if even entertaining the notion of surrender was anathema. If you want to know where Tim Allen's character got "Never give up, never surrender!" in *Galaxy Quest*, that's your answer.

I have likened Original Series versus Next Generation to being produced before and after the Vietnam War. Before Vietnam, America was confident in its superiority and was certain we always knew the right answer and how to handle everything. After Vietnam we were uncertain as a country, sick of war, weary of fighting and ready to talk things out. That was Kirk as opposed to Picard. Kirk saw the Prime Directive as the thing to quote before he then did whatever the hell he wanted. Picard was slavishly faithful to it. Imagine, if you will, the episode "Friday's Child," in which Kirk, Spock and McCoy intervene to help the widow of a slain chieftain who is pregnant with his heir. Their tribal law called for her to die and she was ready to do so, but Kirk said "No way" and stepped in. The Prime Directive dictated that he not interfere and he ignored it. If it had been Picard in that situation and he behaved consistently with his character, he would have stood there and let her be executed. Boom. End of story.

I also wasn't wild about the character of Wesley Crusher. Roddenberry had always sworn that if something wouldn't happen on a modern

Navy battleship, then it shouldn't happen on the *Enterprise*. I invite you to find a single battleship that would put a teenager with no training at the helm. Good luck with that.

Nevertheless, I had an opportunity in front of me. Dave sent me the bible for the TV series as well as several scripts for episodes that had not yet aired, and I got to work. The result was *Strike Zone*, and one of the main things I undertook was the task of trying to redeem Wesley Crusher. The character was so reviled by fandom that I did my best to make him as sympathetic as possible.

Strike Zone came out and did quite well. It launched my career as a Trek novelist. *Rock and a Hard Place* followed and was also well received. Not only that, but DC managed to get back the license to *Star Trek* and I was once again brought in to write the comic.

Here's where life began to get tricky.

There was a guy working for Gene Roddenberry named Richard. Richard was a former Star Trek fan who had managed to ingrain himself into Gene's world and position himself as the go-to guy for approvals on all Trek comic books and novels. It was strongly recommended to me that I get along with him, because if Richard didn't like you, he could make your life a living hell. I obediently got together with him for breakfast at a convention so we could meet and greet and get our working relationship off on the right foot.

Things were going okay until Richard told me that he thought the Gold Key Trek comics were the best comic book presentation of Trek ever.

I laughed in his face. I thought he was kidding.

He was serious. And he didn't like being laughed at. At all.

From that point on, Richard apparently made it his mission to try and drive me off the Trek reservation.

Some of his pronouncements were flatly insane. In one book I had Riker say, in reference to an unwanted task, that he would rather walk border patrol on the Neutral Zone in his underwear. Richard rejected it, stating, "It has not been established that our characters wear underwear."

Yes, you read that right.

I also introduced a recurring love interest for Kirk. Acknowledging his routine dismissal of the Prime Directive, I brought in a protocol officer named R.J. Blaise who would ride herd on him if he made a decision that ran contrary to General Order One. She and he became romantically involved, because of course. She was rejected by Richard, who insisted she be throw out of the comics and declared that—and these were his words—"Kirk is no longer interested in women."

Yes, you read that right.

Some rejections became majorly problematic. I wrote one book, *Vendetta*, which I refer to as the great big book of Borg. It has a disclaimer in the front that states, "The plot and background details of *Vendetta* are solely the author's interpretation of the universe of *Star Trek* and vary in some respects from the universe as created by Gene Roddenberry."

Why was that put in there? To appease Richard, because *Vendetta* featured a female Borg. And after approving the outline, I then wrote the book and Richard subsequently rejected it because he insisted there was no such thing as a female Borg.

This was years before Seven of Nine. This was years before the freaking Borg Queen.

Pocket Books was furious. Since he'd already signed off on the outline, Richard was double dipping. The book had already been sent out to typesetting, and the cover with a clearly female Borg had been printed. They informed him that it was too late to make changes that had already been approved, and the idiotic disclaimer was the compromise. To the best of my knowledge, it still appears in editions even though the universe finally caught up with me.

I wound up quitting the comic book after Richard rejected one story I'd written because he deemed it too violent since I had Kirk in an extended fight scene. The fight scene happened entirely off panel, with Spock and McCoy commenting on it. So a battle I did not show was deemed too violent. As an experiment, the next script I turned in, I used a pen name, and made sure it was more explicitly violent than the issue before. That one sailed through with no changes, which confirmed for me what I'd already figured out: if it had my name on it, Richard would look for ways to reject it. (Although to be fair, the pen name I used was Robert Bruce Banner. I made it sporting, figuring that Richard knew nothing outside of Star Trek. I was right.)

The most insane encounter came over the book *Q-In-Law*.

I should mention that Pocket wasn't really interested in *Q-In-Law*, in which Lwaxana Troi, Deanna's mother (played on the series by Majel Barrett) goes head to head with Q. But they really wanted me to write *Vendetta*, and I talked them into a two-book deal. I wrote *Q-In-Law* and the manuscript was sent off to Richard.

Usually Richard responded within two weeks.

A month went by. Two months went by.

Nothing.

Faxes (this was before email) went unresponded to.

I had turned in the manuscript in October. By February we had still heard nothing.

There was going to be a Creation Con in that month and Richard was attending, as was I. So during my presentation on stage, I read a section from *Q-In-Law*. It was the sequence where Q and Lwaxana are actually battling each other and the crowd was howling in hysterics. They loved it. And Richard was in the back of the ballroom, simmering as a thousand fans endorsed the book with their laughter and applause.

On Monday Pocket got an angry fax from Richard declaring that authors were not allowed to read from unapproved manuscripts ever again at conventions. And that furthermore *Q-In-Law* was most definitely not approved. That it was "an insult to Star Trek."

The editor was astounded and demanded to know what, specifically, was an insult.

Richard went radio silent again.

Now it was April. The book was supposed to ship in September and if it was delayed much longer, it was going to miss shipping.

I could only see one out.

There was another I-Con convention in Long Island that month, and Majel was going to be attending. I said to the editor, "Send me a clean copy of the manuscript and a copy of the cover." (The cover had been printed but the manuscript, still unapproved, hadn't been typeset.) I told him I was going to give a copy to Majel. I wasn't going to mention Richard stonewalling it; I would tell her that I was interested in getting her input on her character. Not unprecedented: Marina Sirtis had given me guidance on Deanna for my first Trek novel. The editor warned me: "If she hates it, we're dead." I said, "As it stands, we're dead anyway." So he did as I asked.

I went to the convention and walked up to her table. I introduced herself and handed her the package, telling her my cover story. She looked at the cover and she brightened considerably. "I'm on the cover! I haven't been on the cover of a Trek novel since 1990!" "You're very important in this book," I assured her. She told me she would read it on the flight home.

She was as good as her word and better.

Now understand that Pocket had some spies at Paramount, so we found out what happened next.

Majel bustled into the Trek offices on Monday, raving about this wonderful new novel called *Q-In-Law*. She extolled its virtues to anyone with a pulse. She endorsed turning it into an episode, an idea rejected by the Trek brass because since it was a book, they insisted it couldn't be adapted (right, because adapting books into TV shows [*M.A.S.H., The Flying Nun*] or movies [*Gone with the Wind, The Wizard of Oz*] was unprecedented.)

And she sashayed into Richard's office and said, "Richard! Have you read this wonderful new novel, *Q-In-Law*?"

And Richard, who had been stonewalling it for seven months, said, "Why no! But I'll get right on it!"

Then Majel called me and told me how much she loved it and cited all her favorite parts.

Meanwhile Pocket then received a four-page memo from Richard stating everything he wanted changed.

Ninety percent of it was stuff that Majel loved.

So I took great joy in going through that memo and writing repeatedly, "Nope. Majel loved that part. It stays." We made some minor changes but otherwise it sailed through.

The book was so well received that Pocket decided they wanted to do an audio and have both John deLancie and Majel read it. I adapted the script, shrinking it to a trim ninety minutes, and they did a terrific job.

But then Paramount contacted Pocket and said it couldn't be released. Their assertion was that Pocket had produced something beyond the scope of their license. They could only make audio books in which one actor is reading the book directly. Here we had two actors who, at certain points in the reading, interacted in character. Paramount asserted that this was no longer a reading; it was a dramatization, and that was an entirely different category to which Pocket did not have the rights.

Pocket's response was simple. "Fine. We'll rerecord it entirely with deLancie, and you guys can explain to Gene Roddenberry's widow why she was dropped from the recording."

Paramount came back and said, "Okay, you know what? Just don't do it again."

Then there was *Imzadi*. Likely my most popular novel, it details how Riker and Troi first meet.

This is how much of an impact it had.

I was taking Shana, who was about seventeen at the time, to a Tori Amos concert at Jones Beach. I was willing to go with her, but she insisted I don't stand anywhere near her so no one would think she was going with her dad because, y'know, ick.

We got to Jones Beach and we headed toward the venue, me following about ten paces behind so no one would know we were together. The plan went off the rails, though, because she ran into two female friends from her high school. They squealed in delight and ran toward each other, at which point I suddenly realized we had a problem. I had both our tickets. I couldn't go in without her. So I was going to have to wait for her. That wasn't going to look suspicious at all: some middle aged guy standing a distance from three teenage girls, trying not to be noticed.

Finally they asked her the question she really didn't want to get. How had she gotten all the way out to Jones Beach? She sighed and said, "My dad drove me. He's over there," and she pointed at me.

Their eyes lit on me.

They let out an excited squeal.

And they ran at me.

They ran. At me.

I stood there, paralyzed, bewildered, as these two teen girls came at me as if they were Rolling Stones groupies having spotted Mick Jagger. And they leaped on me, hugging me furiously. Shana looked on in shock, all the blood draining from her face and probably coagulating in her shoes.

"Uh, girls," I said uncomfortably. "What's…?"

"*Imzadi!*" they shrieked. "Chapter twenty-six! Chapter twenty-six!"

In case you're wondering, chapter twenty-six was the one in which Riker and Troi have sex for the first time.

Understand that from an explicit point of view, it most definitely was not. It was pure PG. If it had been a movie, the camera would have panned upward as they kissed and we would have dissolved to later as they lay there covered up. There was no descriptions of throbbing members and such. The average *Twilight* book in later years was doubtless more specific.

But these were slightly more innocent times, and as near as I could tell, this was the first sex scene these girls had ever read. Apparently, it had been a major turning point in their young lives.

You have to comprehend that I am the world's lousiest dirty old man. This is somewhat out of sequence, but the story relates to my point so I'll tell it here. Some years later I was hired to novelize the first Spider-Man movie, and editor Steve Saffel arranged for me to visit the set of the movie since they were filming in New York City. Remember the point right after he saves Mary Jane from the Goblin's attack (she's wearing this red kimono) and lands with her on a rooftop? I was on the rooftop.

My instructions were very explicit: don't talk to the actors. I'm just a guest there to watch.

It was cold and windy up on the roof, which made sense since it was February. I was wearing a long brown duster, watching them working with Tobey Maguire. And then a female voice said from behind me, "Your coat is going to catch on fire."

I looked down and saw that it was brushing up against a space heater. Immediately I stepped away from it and turned to the speaker to thank her for the warning.

It was Kirsten Dunst.

Remembering that I wasn't supposed to talk to anyone on the set, I just nodded and started to turn away. But she wouldn't hear of it. She was sitting there in her crew chair with a coat and she said, "No, wait, who are you? Come, talk to me."

Well, I figured that if she was giving me an open invitation, I was in the clear. So we chatted. At one point she mentioned that Mary Jane was Peter Parker's first great love. I said, "Well, technically, no, that would be Gwen Stacy. But she died."

"How did she die?" asked Kirsten.

"She was shoved off the 59th Street bridge by the Green Goblin."

Her jaw dropped. "That's what happens to me!"

That was news to me because they hadn't gotten me the script yet. "Do you survive?"

"Yes."

"Then you're one up on Gwen."

Later on, when I related to other guys that I had chatted with Kirsten Dunst, the reaction I got was uniformly the same: "My God, she's so hot! So sexy!"

Except the entire time I was speaking to her, was I thinking she was sexy? Was I picturing her naked or whatever? No. All I kept thinking was, "She would be such a good friend for Shana." Which she would have been because she's almost Shana's age.

So anyway...

Star Trek also aided me in getting some non-fiction assignments. Pocket had hired Jimmy Doohan, Mister Scott himself, to write an autobiography. But it seemed that what he was producing wasn't particularly publishable or usable. Writing is not the easiest endeavor in the world to undertake, and they decided that he needed help. They chose me to do it, and the next thing I knew I was flying out to Seattle, Washington, to spend a week interviewing Jimmy for his autobiography.

I knew that Jimmy was not enthused about the prospect. He was obviously frustrated that he couldn't do it himself and didn't understand why Pocket felt the need to bring in a writer to, y'know, do the writing. So when he came to the hotel and sat there, glowering at me suspiciously, I knew the first question was going to be hugely important. I couldn't just sit there and say, "Tell me about yourself." I had to bring a point of view to it that would supplement his own and enable us to build an entertaining narrative.

I turned on the recorder and said, "Tell me about the first time you saw a television."

It seemed a reasonable question. Television was the medium for which he had gained the most fame, and I knew that it had not existed when he was first born. I was certain he had to remember his first encounter with one, just as I remember vividly the first time I saw a color television. (In case you're wondering, it was at the 1964 World's Fair, in an exhibit called the House of the Future. What was playing on it? "The Adventures of Superman.")

Jimmy's face lit up. Immediately all his defensiveness dropped away. "The 1936 World's Fair," he said. He recalled two young girls, neighbors, who had gone with him, which in turn uncorked a flood of recollections about them, and we were off and running.

The one big problem was recounting his time on the show: he barely remembered any of it. We went through every episode that Scotty was on, and individual anecdotes were rare. He simply hadn't attached any importance to it at the time. Fortunately, I had a lifetime's worth of behind-the-scenes stories that I was able to incorporate to fill the gap, so if you read the book and like the tales of his time on the *Enterprise*, most of those were mine.

I was perfectly happy with how the book turned out. Unfortunately, time was not kind to Jimmy. I saw him a couple years later at a convention and brought a copy of the book to have him sign. He had no idea who I was. When I reminded him I'd written the book with him, he stared at me blankly. He could scarcely string two sentences together. I looked hopelessly at his caretaker who was with him and he said in a low voice, "And this is one of his good days." He died within a year or so after that.

Meanwhile, Richard was continuing to try and do whatever he could to scotch my Trek career. At one point, Pocket had a hole in its schedule, and they asked me to come up with an idea for an original Trek novel. I came up with three. I wrote them with three different typefaces, and in three different styles in terms of spacing, margins and indentations. One was great, one was good, and one was basically a rehash of previous episodes to make the other two look better. They were all sent to Richard with no names attached and he was told to choose one. We have it on reliable authority that he was sitting at his desk, holding one in each hand and with one on the desk in front of him, saying, "I know *one* of these is from Peter David."

Which one did he choose? You guessed it: the rehash. The weakest one. I wound up turning it into *The Rift*, which actually came out a lot better than the outline indicated.

What wound up killing Richard was that he lost sight of the fact that he was basking in Gene's glow. He had no power; it all stemmed from Roddenberry. So when Gene died in October of 1991, Arnold's cloak was ripped away. We eventually learned that Gene's body was practically still warm when Trek overseers marched into Richard's office, informed him that he was fired immediately, and the guards stood there and watched him pack up. Their job was to make sure that he did not abscond with anything Trek related that he could wind up selling on the open market. He was then escorted off the Paramount lot, and thus was Richard's tenure over *Star Trek* brought to an unceremonious and highly appreciated termination.

Approvals were then kicked over to someone else, a woman named Paula, who was much more even handed and much better to work with.

Then one day Trek editor John Ordover contacted me with a proposal. They were going to do something unprecedented: launch a new Trek series that was set on a wholly original starship. We were going to carry over a couple of characters who had been introduced in Next Gen—Elizabeth Shelby and Doctor Selar—but otherwise populate the books with all new characters. It was going to be called "Star Trek: New Frontier," and be set on a ship called the *Excalibur*.

John's concept stemmed from the dissolution of the Soviet Union. In our world, when the Soviet Union collapsed, there were some countries which had been at an uneasy peace with each other, but the USSR's downfall caused old enmities to reignite. John wanted to do that in space. He wanted to have a vast space empire collapse and planets within the realm begin going to war with each other. The *Excalibur* would be a starship sent to ride herd on the entire situation. John asked if I'd be interested in coming up with the crew and writing the series.

To be honest, Paramount didn't have much hope for it. They gave the go-ahead to do it but were sure that Trek fans wouldn't have any interest in investing themselves in a completely original Trek book series.

I was mostly inspired by the movie *Braveheart* in the creation of my captain. I came up with the concept of a young planetary warlord whom Picard discovers and convinces to go to Starfleet Academy. I gave him the name of M'k'n'zy of Calhoun, who would wind up taking on the name of Mackenzie Calhoun. He would be the first lead Trek captain to be an alien. I pulled several other characters out of a YA Worf-at-the-Academy series I'd written for Pocket several years earlier, and the "New Frontier" was off and running.

We benefited tremendously from fan backlash to *Star Trek: Voyager*. Many fans despised the Kate Mulgrew–led series, and the book fans would reply, "If you're interested in a really good new Trek series, you should be reading 'New Frontier.'"

Over the course of nearly twenty years we produced two dozen novels, not to mention some graphic novels as well. Fans still ask me about them to this day and want to know when the next one will be coming out.

I haven't the faintest idea if any more will ever be produced. Indeed, I've no clue if I'm ever going to write *Star Trek* again. The editor currently in charge has been making promises for several years, kept none of them, and has closed me out of *Star Trek* for reasons that have never been explained. I honestly don't know why. I've gone from being a *New York Times* bestselling Trek author to someone who can't get arrested. It's kind of a shame, but it was fun for the decades that it lasted.

And hey, at least I got Sulu's name on the big screen. That counts for something.

The Name of the Place Is Babylon 5

The fast answer to the obvious question "How did you wind up writing for *Babylon 5*?" is crushingly boring: Joe Straczynski asked me to. Nothing else about the experience, however, was remotely dull.

Joe approached me at the San Diego Comicon, telling me that he was a fan of my writing. If I say that in a tossed-off way, as if I don't think it's a big deal that Joe is a fan of my work, I certainly don't intend to. I am, frankly, always astounded when people who I think are amazing talents express admiration of my efforts. Anyway, he told me that B5 was in production and that they were going to be handling the writing of the first season in house. But if the show went to a second season, he wanted to bring me in to write an episode.

Months later, good as his word, Joe contacted me about scripting an episode.

He had something very specific in mind: An outing featuring Londo, his last humorous undertaking before his betrayal of G'Kar would set him on his path to darkness. Joe felt that, my forte being humor, such an episode would be suited to my particular, even peculiar, talents. The notion was simple. Londo's three wives, referred to in an earlier episode as Pestilence, Famine and Death (which was to be the title of the episode), show up on B5, cause problems, and Londo has to handle them. (Note the far-thinking and foreshadowing that was the hallmark of B5. Londo's referring to his wives as three of the four horsemen seemed to be merely a throwaway joke. But that left "war" unaccounted for. "War" turned out to be Londo himself, as his actions set the Narn/Centauri conflict into motion. Trust Joe Straczynski to lace even the most casual comment with meaning.)

There was a secondary storyline intended for the same episode involving a first contact story with an arrogant alien race that puts Sheridan and his crew through their paces.

So I wrote the first outline, breaking the story down into the B5 teaser and act structure. It was okay. Not great, but okay. Joe came back with comments on the outline. I implemented the changes, but I still felt that I was struggling. The wives weren't fully snapping into character, and I was having difficulties making the storyline with the aliens work, either plot-wise or thematically. Also, Joe kept telling me my outline was "too *Star Trek.*" I had no idea what he meant, and he didn't seem able to clarify it.

Joe must have conveyed my struggles to Harlan Ellison, our mutual friend and Joe's creative advisor on the show. Harlan suggested to me the Clare Booth Luce play *The Women* as good inspiration. I read the original play and also watched the 1939 film version.

Ellison was right. Londo's wives walked into my head as the final credits rolled, fully in character and extremely impatient with me that I had been making them too cartoony and too interchangeable rather than developing each as a unique personality.

I even realized what Joe had meant about "too *Star Trek.*" The wives explained it to me: I had worked too hard to leave the status quo of *B5* the same at the end of the script as it was at the beginning. Originally the wives, uniform in nature and attitude, showed up and caused hilarious problems and misunderstandings. At the end of the story, however, I had restored the status quo so that all the characters were perfectly reset in the sandbox, just like a typical *Star Trek* episode (or book, for that matter). But B5 was all about kicking over the sandbox, and my two drafts had failed in that endeavor. The wives needed to be at odds with each other, and there had to be some sort of permanent result as the outcome of their visit.

What did these women value above all else? Luce pointed the way: status. It was all about maintaining status. So I would have their status be threatened with Londo informing two of the three of them that he was going to divorce them. They would be fighting for their social survival, and oh, the claws would come out. And how they responded to this challenge would tell us about them, and how Londo responded in turn would tell us about him.

I considered naming all three wives in direct relation to their original apocalyptic descriptions but decided that was too cutesy. The lone holdover from that notion was Timov—"vomit" spelled backwards—with the idea that she was Famine and therefore an emotional bulimic, purging herself of any compassion. Daggair was a corruption of dagger, with the notion that she would stick it to you when your back was turned. I dubbed the youngest wife "Mariel," a variant on my then-youngest daughter Ariel, a name designed to sound sweet and angelic and hide her true deadly nature.

The next San Diego Comicon was coming up, and Joe said he wanted to have a sit down with me. Harlan would be there as well. I was thrilled, jazzed. I knew I had solved the problem with the wives storyline. I hadn't entirely worked out the alien B plot yet, but I was sure that kicking around ideas with Harlan and Joe would take care of that.

We sat down at the Hilton in the coffee shop and there Joe told me, with Harlan looking on, that he was spiking the story. Killing it. I was stunned. I tried to tell him that I knew what he wanted and he would be blown away by the next outline draft. He told me that, according to WGA rules, he couldn't have me write another outline. I said, "Fine, let me go straight to script." But it was a Catch-22: He wouldn't let me go to script until he had an outline he was satisfied with, and he wouldn't allow me to write it.

"I'll write a script on spec," I said desperately, but again he wouldn't hear of it. Harlan tried to assure me that they didn't think the less of me, and Joe told me that I'd have another chance down the line. I didn't believe him. I didn't think he was deliberately lying, but I figured that I had little to no shot after washing out so badly in my first attempts.

It was the worst San Diego convention I ever attended. It didn't matter how many people told me they loved my work; all I could do was dwell on my total failure with my script.

Worse, the wives had set up housekeeping in my head. They continued to harass me, excoriating me for my abysmal failure. They were insisting that I write their story, WGA rules be damned.

Unsure of how to proceed, I called Harlan and told him that I was thinking of writing the script anyway. "Absolutely not," said Ellison. "Look, Peter, you didn't get the job done this time. Everybody fails from time to time. Just live with it."

This was obviously not the answer I wanted. So I called my then-agent and asked her if I should go ahead and write it anyway.

"Absolutely not," she said.

So I called my friend and writing partner and *B5* cast member, Bill Mumy, and asked him.

"No freaking way," he said. "It's suicide."

They all made sense. They all knew much more about show business than I did. I knew that everything they said was right.

The thing was, none of them had the wives living in their head calling them names.

I wrote the script. It was the only way to shut the wives up.

Since I had nothing to lose, I dumped the entire alien storyline. Instead I decided to go with a thematic link: Women's problems. The wives would have to struggle with an impending divorce. I would also bring in Talia Winters' heretofore-unknown ex-husband and have her coping with the opposite notion: An ex-husband who seemed interested in having her back. Wanting a humorous C plot to cut to, I went for a comical woman's problem: Hair care.

My reasoning was simple: For a human woman who has had hair all her life, a bad hair day is an inconvenience. For an alien woman who suddenly has to cope with hair, it's more than a mere speed bump; it's a roadblock. I liked the notion of the ultra-competent Delenn finding herself flummoxed by something so trivial and being frustrated because of that very triviality. And the capper would be at the end, when Delenn would inform Ivanova, her hair consultant, that she was starting to get "these odd cramps."

It all came together and, redubbing the script "Soul Mates," I banged it out in no time.

So. What to do with it? I knew that the only thing that would be more monumentally stupid than having ignored Joe's warning not to write it (not to mention the reiteration of that mandate by Harlan, Bill and my agent) was to send it to Joe. The equivalent of willingly walking into the lion's den wearing a steak tuxedo.

Which was naturally what I did.

Fortunately, I had a cover story. I included a letter telling Joe that DC had approached me about writing a couple of issues of the comic, which was absolutely true. I said that since he had planned to kill the story anyway, the wives were now in play. So I'd written their story in script format for the artist's convenience. Since Joe would have to approve it anyway, I figured I would save some time by sending it to him first.

It was a pathetically transparent ploy, a staggeringly obvious "Hail Mary" pass, but at the time, I thought it was rather clever.

So Joe called me a week later, on September 23. I remember the date because it was my birthday. Joe said sternly, "Peter, I got your *package*."

"Okay. Did you read it?"

"Yes, I *read* it."

I wasn't wild with the way he was emphasizing certain words. He sounded really pissed off. Mumy's words about "suicide" came floating back to me. My voice went up to a higher register as I said, "Well, y'know, like I said in the letter, I was figuring it might work for the comic book and..."

"I don't want this in the comic book."

My heart sank. I'd rolled dice and come up snake eyes, and probably killed any remote chance of working for *B5* again. "Oh. You don't?"

"No. I want to produce it. It's going to be the eighth episode." (It actually aired seventh.)

I stood there for a moment, stunned, and then shouted, "You son of a bitch!" which is, of course, exactly what you want to say to a guy who's just bought your script.

I found out later that Joe had called Harlan and said, "Guess what Peter sent me." Harlan had moaned and apologized and said he'd told me not to do it, and he would talk to me about it, and Joe had said to him, "Actually, it's really good. I'm going to buy it," and Harlan had been stunned speechless for one of the few times in his life. Harlan told me he thought Joe had gone too easy on me in our phone conversation; if it had been up to Harlan, he would have strung me along for a week.

Joe used the first contact storyline himself in the later episode, "Acts of Sacrifice." It turned out to bear little resemblance to his original concept, so I took some solace in the notion that even Joe couldn't make it work the way he initially wanted to.

Joe invited me to come to the set and watch the episode being filmed. You have to realize that this is something of a rarity in television and film production, but B5 was a very writer-friendly environment and naturally I took him up on it.

The first cast member I encountered upon my arrival was Claudia. Now understand, I was a bit worried about how she and Mira were going to react to the C plot I'd developed for them. After all, I was taking two incredibly strong female characters and having them worrying about hair care and cramps. I will always remember Claudia's first words to me: "Thank you! Finally a script where we get to act like women!" That made me feel a lot better. I figured that, even if fans slammed it for that reason, I could take solace that Claudia was cool with it.

Mira was ... less so.

I first saw Mira when they were filming the scene where she's confronted with her unruly mane. I figured they would give her a wig or something. Nope. They distressed Mira's actual hair. During one take, while Mira was waving the hairbrush around in agitation, it snagged on her hair. It wasn't supposed to, and with a frustrated grunt, Mira yanked it clear without missing her line. The moment director John Flinn yelled "Cut," Mira and everyone else broke up. It was the last take of that scene, and the one they used on air.

So while they were setting up the cameras for the next shot, I was introduced to Mira. In her elegant voice, she said, "So ... you were the one who wrote the line about the cramps." She draped an arm around me and said, "Let me talk to you about this line."

Oh, did Mira Furlan hate the line about the cramps. Hated it, despised it with the fiery passion of a thousand suns. Whether she felt it demeaning to Delenn or just a cheap joke or was simply uncomfortable with the whole subject, I wasn't sure, but she asked me if there was any way to change it or, even better, dump it. Apparently, she'd been saying the same thing to Joe and getting nowhere, so she was hoping she could appeal to the new guy.

I assured her that it was not intended as a cheap joke, but instead as a major set up and development masquerading as a cheap joke. She looked suspicious. I continued, "It's going to start all sorts of fan speculation. Don't you see? They're going to begin wondering whether, if Delenn has developed the reproductive system of a human woman, she and Sheridan could wind up having a child. It's a set up for future stories."

The truth is, it was in fact nothing more than a cheap joke and everything I was saying to Mira was stuff I was making up on the fly. But I convinced her, or at least she allowed me to think I had convinced her, and if she seems on screen to sound really uncomfortable talking to Ivanova about the cramps, well, Mira is a brilliant actress, but that wasn't acting.

However it turned out that I was right. To this day, on the B5 wiki entry on the episode, you see the following:

> Though it at first glance might appear to be a comedic throwaway line, Delenn's final complaint may actually be the most important revelation of the entire episode. It implies that her transformation has given her a human reproductive system. Possibly that was even the point of the transformation; if indeed the change was made to bring humans and Minbari closer together, a child born of a human father and a Minbari mother might be considered a powerful link by some. Which, of course, begs the question: who does she intend the father to be, if this is what she has in mind? Sinclair seems an obvious choice, given the evidence that she believes him to be the reincarnation of a great Minbari soul.

So it turns out the stuff I said to placate Mira was pretty much spot on.

I was fascinated by the different acting styles of Bruce Boxleitner and Andreas Katsulas. Bruce would chat with the cast and crew while waiting for his takes, and would continue to do so right up until John said, "Action!" at which point Bruce would snap into character, do his lines, and the moment John said, "Cut," Bruce would go right back to whatever he was talking about before.

Andreas, on the other hand, was unapproachable. It wasn't that he was a snob or rude or anything. It was just that he would sit there in a Zen-like state, and the understanding was you didn't disturb Andreas. He was in his zone. On the set of a television series, people were constantly getting out of the ways of camera, scenery, tech guys, whatever.

But Andreas Katsulas was the immovable object, and everyone gave him a wide berth.

Jane Carr, a brilliant British actress, was cast as Timov. Jane had been best known for the TV series *Dear John*, in which she played a group therapy leader whose catch phrase about any difficulty a member was dealing with was a tentative, even hopeful, "Is it a sexual problem?" Except she pronounced it "SEK-soo-uhl." There was one scene wherein Londo is going to be sleeping with two of his wives simultaneously and invites Timov to join in. Timov says to him archly, "Do you truly expect me to join in your sexual Olympics?" The first time we shot it, Jane said, "SEK-soo-uhl Olympics." And Peter Jurasik, still in character as Londo, rumbled incredulously, "Did you say SEK-soo-ul?" It brought filming to a complete halt as everyone fell over laughing. Once everyone had composed themselves, the concern was that—if Jane said it that way—it would kick viewers right out of the scene because they'd say, "Oh, *that's* where I know her from! She's on *Dear John!*" Jane labored to say it with an American pronunciation, and she managed to do so. In watching the aired episode, if Timov sounds particularly disgusted by the concept, emoting "sexual" with great disdain, it's not disdain so much as it's Jane just trying to say it the way John Flinn wanted her to.

On the third day of shooting, Jane came up to me and said crisply, in a "we are not amused" tone, "Peter (she said it 'PEE-tuh,' like Betty Davis), it has been pointed out to me that Timov is Vomit spelled backwards. Were you aware of this?" I copped to it and explained the rationale, and she understood it, but I don't think she was thrilled.

Peter Squared: Peter Jurasik (Londo) and me.

I was startled the first day that I saw the call sheet, because on the list was actor Carel Struycken. That confused the hell out of me because only weeks before I'd been in Romania during the filming of a cowboys and aliens movie called *Oblivion* and Carel had a prominent role in that. The towering Carel is instantly recognizable as Lurch from the *Addams Family* films or the ominous giant in *Twin Peaks*.

Joe's first choice for Daggair was Sandra Bernhardt, but it fell through at the last minute, and instead Daggair was brilliantly realized by accomplished stage actress Lois Nettleton, who regaled us with tales of her time on Broadway. Mariel was actress Blair Valk, who had such long hair that they needed to thread it through a hole in her Centauri bald cap and have it hang down as a pony tail, a sort of Centauri fashion statement. We were filming around Halloween, and Blair kept her Centauri makeup on when answering the door for trick-or-treaters.

Rick Biggs ... what a tragedy that we lost him so young. At one point Rick as Doctor Franklin was stumbling over a line of medical dialogue. He blew it take after take, and I offered to rewrite the line so it would be less of a tongue twister. But Rick demurred, and eventually he got it right.

Andrea Thompson ... my God, what a beautiful woman. The TV screen doesn't begin to capture what a knockout she is in person. I was totally smitten. Bill Mumy had a drawing done up of me smiling stupidly at Andrea while she wound me around her little finger, and that wasn't far off the mark.

Talia's ex was played by Keith Szarabajka, well known later to Joss Whedon fans as the menacing "Holtz" on *Angel* and to fans of *Supernatural* as the prophet Donatello. Keith's portrayal of Matt Stoner was low voiced and menacing, and one confrontation scene he had with Jerry Doyle's Garibaldi so crackled with energy that John Flinn, rather than calling "Cut," exclaimed, "God, that was great!"

Flinn was a terrific guy. John Flinn III was a native Californian with the air and swagger of a Texan. He had served mostly as *B5*'s cinematographer and director of photography, and "Soul Mates" was only his second outing as the show's director. So he was under a lot of pressure (mostly from himself) to do a top-flight job.

But John's back was up against the wall when it came time to film the big banquet scene. Let's talk about that in depth a bit.

Weeks earlier, when I had been writing the teleplay, I was sitting in my office at 3 a.m. scripting the scene where Ivanova tells Sheriden that they have been invited to the Centauri equivalent of a Bar Mitzvah. I wanted all the guests to have some unifying theme, just as congregants at a Bar Mitzvah wear yamulkas. So I wrote Ivanova saying, "All guests must..." Then I stopped. I wanted something simple, just in case the script was ever filmed. I didn't want to say that all the guests had to wear something because then wardrobe would have to make a hundred of them. I looked down, trying to think of something, stared at my bare feet, and wrote, "All guests must be barefoot, to symbolize that on the road of life, you must tread carefully." (The latter half of the line was filmed but cut from broadcast.)

So there we were, eight weeks later, in a room filled with a hundred barefooted extras, all because I wasn't wearing slippers at three in the morning. One of the extras was me, because I had talked John into letting me have a cameo in my own episode. I'm actually visible in a couple of shots, talking to Delenn and Lennier in the background. We were adlibbing the notion that I was a convention organizer trying to convince Delenn to come to a *Babylon 5* convention.

The extras were, to put it mildly, not happy. "Who's the foot fetishist who wrote this thing, anyway?" one of them said, unaware that the culprit was standing next to him. The crew wasn't jazzed either, because the soundstage had to be swept within an inch of its life. Not a stray nail, not a single splinter, could be on the floor lest injuries result. The only one who was sanguine was Andreas, because I had deliberately written into the script that G'Kar had his boots on. Why? So costuming wouldn't have to manufacture Narn feet. (The business of G'Kar tossing fruit to Mariel to drop a hint that the two were involved was not in the script; I'm not sure who came up with it, but it was a wonderful subtlety.)

The reason John Flinn was up against the wall was that the shoot was running too long. The banquet scene was complicated, and it was the last day of filming. John had no leeway, and as the shoot crept toward midnight, there was still material that needed to be filmed if the show was going to be cut together properly. The problem was that if we went past midnight, we were into overtime costs. This would be A Bad Thing, to be avoided if at all possible. To go into overtime would not reflect well on John.

We were two minutes from midnight, and the Suits had assembled on the edges of the set, to make clear by their presence that midnight was the cut off. The fact was that John needed another hour to do things right, but we weren't going to get it. And we hadn't yet shot a crucial scene in which Londo collapses and Sheridan says into his comm link, "Medlab, this is Sheridan!" and summons help. John was being told that he would be allowed to shoot the master shot, but that was it. No close-ups, no nothing. He couldn't have the hour he needed. He was frustrated, and everyone knew it.

So we were filming the scene, literally down to the minute. Peter as Londo collapsed. Bruce leaned in. I was directly behind him, just out of camera range. Bruce hit his comm link and said, "Medlab! This is Sinclair!"

"Sinclair?!" John bellowed from off camera.

The place erupted in hysterics. I rested a hand on Bruce's back because I was laughing so hard I almost fell over. Bruce said in bewilderment, "Where did *that* come from?!" apparently unable to fathom why he had confused his character's name with that of his predecessor, Jeffrey Sinclair. John emerged from behind the camera and mock-strangled Bruce, and everyone was still howling.

Most significantly, the suits were laughing. Suits they may have been, but there were men in the suits, and even they could have a sense of humor. The take was blown, and there was nothing for it but to go into overtime. John would have the hour he needed to do things right, and if it cost the production some extra money, well, the Suits had a great anecdote and a terrific capper for the gag reel. Totally worth it.

Here's the thing: To this day, I believe Bruce flubbed the line deliberately.

I've never asked him about it because I thought it would be impolite. Come on, though: who forgets the name of his own character?

I think Bruce knew that John was feeling the heat and wanted to buy him the time he needed to do the episode right. If John screws up the episode by running over, maybe they aren't so eager to let him direct again. But if Bruce is the one who blows it, what are they going to do? Nothing. Nothing they can do. I believe that Bruce threw himself on the grenade of overtime, taking the hit so that John wouldn't have to. Can't prove it. I doubt he even remembers it. But that's my theory and I'm sticking to it.

While I was on the set, I noticed a few things that would become relevant later. The first was when they were filming sequences in the Zocalo. I would watch the background aliens walking around, and the assistant director would call out "heads off" or "heads on" depending upon whether they were filming or not. And it was odd to me to see Drazis pulling off their heads on cue to reveal humans underneath. I was chatting with Bill Mumy about it and said, "You know what I'd love to do? Write a sequence where there's a *Babylon 5* gift shop. And Ivanova is there shopping, looking at all the merchandise. And she turns to a Drazi and say, 'Can you believe all this stuff?' And the Drazi pulls off his head, revealing he's a human." Bill came up with the capper. He said, "Then you have Ivanova turn to a human and say, 'This place is nuts!' and the human pulls off *his* head and it's a Drazi."

I filed it away on my mental "to do" list.

Why did I zero in on Ivanova as the victim? Because I'd witnessed first-hand Claudia's wicked sense of humor. Claudia Christian has serious comedy chops. At one point I mentioned to her that they should cast her as Patsy in an American version of *Absolutely Fabulous* and she immediately started doing a dead-on Joanna Lumley impression. Also the entire *B5* crew always ate lunch together, and I'd watch in amusement while she would regale Bruce with her recent bawdy exploits and Bruce would be clapping his hands over his ears saying, "I don't want to hear this!" So I told myself that if I ever had the opportunity to do another episode, I'd try to give Ivanova some more comedy beats.

It happened far sooner than I could have expected.

While I was out there for the filming of "Soul Mates," Joe called me into his office and said that they had a hole in their shooting schedule. A script that had been in development simply wasn't working. "It's obvious that you 'get' the show, and I was wondering if you had any other ideas for episodes," he said.

Fortunately I did have something kicking around in my head. The news had been filled with stories of cops who had gotten into shooting incidents—typically a white cop shooting a black guy—and all manner of tension and anger ensued. Figuring it would be interesting to put it in SF terms, I said, "What if Garibaldi got into a shooting incident with a Minbari? And the incident put Sheridan in a very difficult position with the Minbari demanding justice?"

Joe considered it a moment and then said, "What if it were Sheridan instead? I could use a strong Sheridan episode, and then it would be Delenn who would be in the difficult position."

Garibaldi had been the one who occurred to me because basically he was a cop, but I could easily see how it could work with Sheridan. "Sure," I said, and Joe and I batted around general ideas of where the episode would go for a minute or two. Then I said, "Do you want me to write an outline?"

"We don't have time. Go straight to script."

It was astonishing to me how far I'd come in so relatively short a time. I'd gone from the guy who couldn't even get his outline approved to the guy who obviously "got" the show, was selling his second story in as many months, and was being told to skip the outline and start writing the script.

Upon returning home I proceeded to bang out the script that I entitled, "There All the Honor Lies." It derived from Alexander Pope's "An Essay on Man," in which he wrote: "Honour and shame from no condition rise; Act well our part, there all the honour lies."

Although the bulk of "Soul Mates" was mine, "Honor" was less so. Joe rewrote about half the script; he could easily have put his own name on it as co-writer, but he opted not to do so because it wasn't his style.

The gift shop storyline was mostly intact, although the ending was different than I'd conceived (more on that later). The removable head sequence went exactly as Bill and I had developed it weeks earlier. The sequence was brilliantly filmed, as the human pulled off his head to reveal a Drazi entirely in one take, with no cutaway. This was before the sort of morphing effects that would have made it easy to do in post-production. Instead it was done entirely live, in camera. Mike Vejar, the director, staged it so that Ivanova was facing the "human," who reached down to the base of his throat and started pulling away what appeared to be the bottom of a mask. The camera then angled around onto a mirror (which customers would presumably use to see how they look with a mask on) and the customer's reflected image pulled off the "mask" to reveal his Drazi face. It was simplicity itself to stage. The actor simply stepped out of the way once the camera moved away from him and the human-playing-the-Drazi-playing-the-human stepped in to be reflected in the mirror and complete the illusion, pulling off a mask modeled on the face of the other actor.

Some of the rewrites stemmed from necessity. There's a storyline in there involving Sheridan being taught by Kosh about a perfect moment of beauty. Every word of that was Joe's. I suspect that it was previously in the other script that "Honor" was replacing, and Joe felt it was necessary to have in my script because of arc considerations. That was what Joe had to keep his eye on: the overall story arc. The big picture was more important than my single episode, or any single episode really.

As a consequence, material in my script was tossed aside in order to make room for the Kosh scenes. The one who really got boned was the character of Guinevere Corey, Sheridan's lawyer, named after my second daughter and played by Julie Caitlin Brown, liberated from her Na'Toth make-up. Almost all of her scenes got written out, with the result being that she made a great entrance and then didn't really accomplish much of anything.

Some stuff got cut for time. I tried to give Stephen Furst more to do and had a storyline in which he's being consumed with guilt over the atrocities he's seen Londo commit. I wrote a scene in which Talia accidentally brushes against him and gets a glimpse into Vir's mind. What she saw was a surrealistic sequence in which Vir is falling, plunging into a bottomless vortex. In the aired version she bumps into him, but the fall was cut. It was, however, filmed, which involved hauling poor Stephen up in an uncomfortable harness, and dangling him in front of a green screen for about an hour, thrashing about and screaming and generally acting tortured (again, not much acting involved).

Other rewrites were a matter of characterization. In the aired version, Lennier tricks a Minbari, Ashan (the name of my eldest daughter, Shana, spelled sideways), into confessing that the dead Minbari was part of a vast scheme and Sheridan was set up. That wasn't the way I scripted it.

Earlier in the episode, Ashan speaks contemptuously to Delenn, referring to her as a "freak" because of the metamorphosis she has undergone. In my original draft, when Delenn comes to realize that Ashan was complicit in setting Sheridan up for a fall, she pulls out her gravity ring not seen since "The Gathering" and proceeds to use it to pummel Ashan for information. She makes it clear to him that if he doesn't start talking and fast, he's worm food. An agonized Ashan cries out, "But Minbari don't kill other Minbari!" To which Delenn icily replies, "That is true. But of what consequence is that ... *to a freak?*" And Ashan promptly spills his guts, metaphorically.

I loved that line, and the notion of Delenn hurling the "freak" slur back in the guy's face. I could hear Mira's voice saying it.

Joe hated it. He felt it was inelegant and brutal for a character to just beat the truth out of a suspect. He was the one who wrote the Lennier sequence. Just as he felt my original outline for "Soul Mates" was too *Star Trek*, I felt his resolution for "Honor" was too *Murder She Wrote*.

Was I angry over the change? Nope. A little disappointed, perhaps, and to this day I think my way was better. But *B5* was, and is, Joe's sandbox. It's not like *Star Trek* where you had a dozen or so writers going over every script and making all manner of changes, whether the script needed it or not. *B5* was the singular vision of Joe Straczynski, and any changes he made were in order to protect that vision.

Speaking of *Star Trek*, while I was working on "Honor," a documentary on Trek aired one night. There was much discussion of *Deep Space Nine*, and how the impetus behind the creation of the series was to find a way to continue "the Franchise." That pissed me off for some reason. The series was no longer a referendum of hope for the future or the grand vision of Gene Roddenberry. Instead the people running it considered it the Franchise, a vast money-making machine that nobody wanted to screw up. *DS9*'s purpose was to keep the Franchise going, period. Everything else was incidental.

That notion combined in my head with the earlier concept of a gift shop. I had Ivanova, upon learning of the intrusion of merchandising into the station, protest to Sheridan, "We're not some ... some deep space franchise! *This* station is *about* something!" I was positive Joe would cut the line rather than stoop to such a painfully cheap shot.

I should have known better. Joe loved the line. I think he would have filmed the whole episode just so he could get that line on the air.

What did Joe not love?

The bear.

The legendary *Babylon 5* bear, which was not in my original draft of the script. How it got in there, and blown into space at the end of the episode, is a story unto itself.

My then-wife was really into plush bears. Grateful that Joe had bought two scripts from me, and with the holidays approaching, she felt sending Joe a gift in appreciation was in order. After some thought, she decided that Joe would be sent a bear from the Vermont Teddy Bear Company. It would be clothed in a baseball jacket, carry the logo "Babearlon 5" on the back, and the initials "JS" on the front of the jacket.

The bear was ordered, produced and sent off.

I spoke to Joe about a week or so later. He sounded grave. "Peter ... I got your 'gift.'"

"Oh, good," I said. "Did you like it?"

"I'm not into cute," he said, sounding no less grave.

Apparently he was of the impression that this was common knowledge. I didn't know. "Uhm ... okay, well, if you don't want him, sent it back."

"No, no, I'm keeping it," he replied. Then he paused a beat and added ominously, "I'll get you for this."

"You're going to *get* me? For sending you a gift?"

"Yes."

And Joe wrote the bear into the script, the end of which was that John Sheridan took umbrage at the bear that had his initials inscribed on his shirt (Joe Straczynski.... John Sheridan.... Jeffrey Sinclair. Coincidence? Hell no). The result was that he had the helpless furball blown into space, ricocheting off the windshield of a Starfury and bouncing into the void.

Had I had a crystal ball and known the marriage would end in divorce, I would have shrugged it off. But when one's wife's gift has been dissed on national television, retaliation is in order.

So on the TV series *Space Cases*, which I co-created with Bill Mumy, an identical bear (sans cap and jacket at the insistence of Nick executives) was found floating in space by several of the kids on our ship, the *Christa*. The character of Rosie asked rhetorically, "What kind of dope would throw a perfectly good bear into outer space?" The answer, it was later learned, was that it was the work of an alien race called the Strazyn: would-be galaxy conquerors who were on a tight budget and therefore seeded their region of space with booby traps, including—in this case—a deadly virus contained within the bear.

I told Joe that now we were even. Joe informed me that, no, quite the contrary, I had now unleashed a force of nature. Actually, he was almost giddily up for it. He envisioned this back-and-forth as building into something genuinely entertaining, as fans would go to conventions and wonder what new prank Joe or Peter would pull in the name of the bear. He even wanted to get the bear onto other SF series. Have it show up on *DS9* or *Voyager*.

At the following San Diego Comicon, my antennae were most definitely up. I was doing a presentation about *Space Cases*. I had a video set up and had just started running an episode. I then proceeded to prowl the darkened room, searching for something. I wasn't sure what, but I knew I'd know it if I saw it.

Sure enough, in the back of the room, there was a young woman clad in a bear suit. I knew it was a woman because she was holding her bear head in her hands. Apparently, she had just arrived and was waiting there. There was another woman next to her. I walked up to her and said softly, "Can I help you with something?"

She said, "I'm supposed to deliver a singing telegram to Peter David."

I said, in as humorless a voice as I could affect, "I'm Peter David."

Even in the dimness of the room I could see the blood drain from her face. I'd caught her before she was ready to go on. "Oh, well, uh.... I'm supposed to sing and dance and embarrass you."

"I see," I said, sounding grave (it was easy; I just imitated Joe). "Well, I'll tell you, I just put on this video, and if you think I'm going to disrupt my presentation just so you can sing and dance and embarrass me, you can forget it. If you'd like, you can simply say you showed up to embarrass me but weren't able to."

The woman next to her was sort of an escort—someone from the company to verify that the telegram had been delivered. "No, she can't do that," said the woman. "We'll just have to wait until the video's over."

"Okay, fine."

"How long is it?" asked the costume-clad girl.

It was twenty-two minutes. Naturally I told her it was almost an hour. She leaned back against the wall and moaned softly.

The room temperature was not particularly cool, and she was starting to show the effects. I decided to help matters along. "Looks *reeeeeal* hot in that costume," I said, voice dripping with sympathy. "Man, you must be sweltering in that." She nodded. I continued, "I'm sure glad *I* don't have to stand around in a hot, sweltering costume for a *reeeeeal* long time." Perspiration was beginning to roll off her forehead. She looked like she was starting to melt. "Wish I could help you out, but it's gonna be a looooong time before that tape's over."

Her escort said, "Look, how about if we go into the hallway outside. She can do it there."

"Fine," I said quickly.

So we went into the hallway and the corridor was completely deserted, and no one saw it. So Joe's retribution was thwarted.

I was then planning retaliation, and I had a really neat plan in mind, too. But a few weeks later, a friend of mine, writer John Peel, called me with a disturbing story. He'd been asked by a convention to recommend potential guests, and he suggested they invite me. And what he was told was, "Well, gee, we like Peter as a writer and all, but our guest of honor is Joe Straczynski, and everyone knows that he and Peter hate each other's guts."

And I said, "Okay, that's it." After setting John straight, I immediately called Joe and told him what had happened. Joe promptly offered to get in touch with the convention and inform them that quite the opposite was true, that he and I were friends and that the whole bear thing was just for laughs—a mental exercise in ingenuity, as it were. I told him that that wasn't necessary, that I had it covered, and then I said, "As far as I'm concerned, it's over. I do not need the fan base thinking that you and I hate each other. So if you want to keep pulling bear pranks, you go right ahead, and I'll just keep taking it, but I'm not going to retaliate."

And Joe said, slightly disappointed, "Well, that wouldn't be any fun. Forget it, then."

And that was that.

Except it wasn't, quite. Because the bear had taken on a life of its own. One of the first questions Bruce Boxleitner received during a Q&A at a British convention was, "Do you think that the character of Captain Sheridan has been irretrievably damaged due to his abysmal treatment of the bear?"

As for Joe, at another convention he was doing a video presentation and, when the lights came up at the end, he turned to discover—to his chagrin—five stuffed bears had appeared on the on-stage table. Placed there by some stealthy fans, the bears just sat there, staring at him in a most accusatory fashion. Joe walked up onto the stage, grabbed one of the bears, and chucked it into the audience. Whereupon a little girl raised her hand and said, "If you're giving away the bears, can I have one?" Joe promptly scooped up the remaining four and dumped them on the delighted child. I later met her at the Orlando MegaCon and asked her if she had named the bears. She said no. And I told her she should name them Babearlon 1, 2, 3, and 5 because, y'know, 4 disappeared.

My one final regret about that episode is that I didn't get to keep any of the *B5* merchandise that was on display in the store. Not so much as a single shirt or baseball cap. Joe put the Londo Mollari action figure up on eBay a while ago and I bid furiously for it but didn't get it. I used to have two *Babylon 5* crew jackets, but my ex-wife got one (she promptly gave it away, which pissed me off no end) and an unexpected moth infestation destroyed the other. So I don't have any physical souvenirs from my time with *B5* (other than the bear, but I don't count that).

Still I have plenty of memories, and a place in *B5* history, even though Mira to this day gets cranky if anyone mentions the cramps line to her. The ironic thing is that fans of my *Star Trek* novels always said to me, "You should write *'Star Trek'* episodes." So here I wrote two episodes of *B5*, and what did the fans tell me? "You should write *B5* novels!" Which, as it so happens, I eventually did, including a three part "Centauri Prime" trilogy. Joe told fans that I was the natural choice to do so, saying, "Peter David practically *is* a Centauri."

All in all, one of the enjoyable and exciting creative experiences of my life. People ask me if I'm going to be working on any more *B5* material, and I always give them the same answer: If Joe wants me, I'm there. Otherwise, though, I'm perfectly content to be just another fan, waiting to see what is going to happen next in the *B5* universe.

Once Upon a Time, in a School in Outer Space

When I was a kid, I was hooked on *Lost in Space*. Although my parents had zero interest in *Star Trek*, they felt *LIS* was harmless childhood entertainment. Plus, lucky me, there wasn't anything on opposite it that my parents were interested in seeing, so I had a clear shot at the TV and could watch it with no problem.

Most people remember *LIS* for its campy excesses and its trio of Will, Doctor Smith and the Robot getting involved in absurd adventures with talking carrots and the like. But genuine scholars of those days will assert that the first season was damned good science fiction, and my favorite episode was episode 15, "Return from Outer Space." In that outing, Will Robinson stumbled upon a matter transmitter and wound up getting beamed back to Earth: specifically to the town of Hatfield Four Corners in Vermont. There the residents refuse to believe his story, thinking he's just a kid with an overactive imagination, because apparently no one had a damned picture of Will to compare him to. Will instead was stuck trying to avoid the annoying townspeople while he endeavored to return to his space-lost family.

And I, as a nine-year-old, desperately wished that I could have been in that stupid town. I knew that if he showed up at my door, I would believe his whole story and do whatever I could to help him get back to his loved ones. I desperately wanted to be Will Robinson's friend.

Then I grew up and became Will Robinson's friend.

I first met actor Bill Mumy, along with his close friend Miguel Ferrer (after whom I would later name Spider-Man 2099) at a comic book convention in Texas, I believe it was. We hit it off. It helped that Bill was a fan of my writing. He actually wrote a fan letter to a short-lived series I wrote called *Merc*, which naturally we ran in the letters column. Over the years our friendship grew stronger, and he even introduced me to some interesting friends of his.

Once Upon a Time, in a School in Outer Space

When *The Phantom Menace* came out, the original *Star Wars* was put into heavy rotation on TBS. One night I was channel surfing, came across it and thought, "God, I haven't seen this in ages." So Ariel and I settled in to watch it. As the battle of the Death Star ensued, the phone rang. I answered it.

"Peter, hey, it's Mark."

Hamill.

He was one of the friends that Bill had introduced me to. He had been appearing in a Broadway play, *The Nerd*. Bill flew in to see him, invited me along, and after that we'd gone up to Mark's gorgeous apartment and hung out. At one point he offered me a beer which I drank, and that is the single time in all my life that I've consumed a beer, because when Luke Skywalker offers you alcohol while Will Robinson is standing there, you drink the damned beer.

Anyway, I said into the phone, "Uh, hey, Mark, I'm watching you about to blow up the Death Star."

He said, "I can call back…"

"No, that's okay, I've seen this movie before. I know how it ends."

He had called because he was going to be producing a trade paperback of a comic series of his, *The Black Pearl* (no relation to the later Disney version) and wanted to know if I'd be interested in writing an introduction. I said sure, we chatted for a couple minutes, hung up, and then said, "What has my life come to that Luke Skywalker calls me while I'm watching him on television?"

It had gotten to that place because of Mumy.

Bill and I also enjoyed working together. We had teamed up on a handful of comic stories, and then one day, Bill's then-manager, Susie Dietz, had gotten Nickelodeon interested in working with him. They were interested in having Bill create a TV series about kids in space, because if that's what you want, you can't do better than asking Bill Mumy to come up with it. Bill, in turn, saw it as the perfect opportunity to embark on a major writing project with me.

That was how we came up with *Space Cases*. We worked out that our heroes would be a group of misfit students at the Starcademy, a deep space training school for students who were interested in becoming "Stardogs," the equivalent of Starfleet in this new universe.

Interestingly, Myra was very helpful in creating the original cast. She suggested that we have a series of opposites so the kids can be in opposition to each other and hence we would have drama arising from their interaction. That seemed a reasonable way to go with it.

Slowly the characters came into focus:

Rosie Ianni, the relentlessly cheerful resident of Mercury;

Bova, the perpetually dour inhabitant of Uranus;

Radu, the isolationist loner and Andromedan, member of a race that years earlier had been at war with the Stardogs;

Harlan Band, an Earther whose father had died in that war and consequently he despised Radu's presence;

Catalina, from the moon of Titan, an insecure engineering genius who heavily depended upon an invisible companion named Suzee who everyone else assumed was an imaginary friend;

T.J. Davenport, the very proper, very British principal;

Seth Goddard, the busted-in-rank Spacedog who hated being forced to teach a bunch of misfits.

Aiding them in their endeavors would be an android named Thelma, which stood for Techno Human EMulating MAchine. She would be aboard the ship, which we dubbed the *Christa* after the late astronaut, Christa McAuliffe, and basically serve as exposition on legs.

The bible and pilot script was assembled and we went to work with casting.

The show was going to be produced by a Canadian production company called Cinar, run by a woman named Micheline Charest. Since it was slated to be a Canadian production, half of everything involved had to be Canadian. Since Bill and I intended to write the majority of the episodes, every script written by us would have to be directed by a Canadian. Also half the cast would have to be Canadian as well.

We began the casting process, beginning in America and then moving on to Canada.

In Los Angeles, a guy who came in and read for Harlan was someone I instantly recognized: Walter Jones, the former Black Power Ranger. He and several of his castmates had been unceremoniously fired from the series because they'd had the nerve to ask for a very minor pay increase. Walter seemed very personable, and furthermore his extensive knowledge of karate and physicality would be a nice add to Harlan's character. He finished his audition and was immediately followed by a young Indian lad named Rahi Azizi. "Was that the Black Power Ranger?" he asked. When we confirmed his identity he said, "Cool!"

Rahi was there to read for Bova, and the kid was a godsend. Bova, whom we'd intended to be a human Eeyore, had thus far been the toughest role to cast. No kid seemed capable of providing the deadpan that we wanted. Rahi was the first and really the only kid to nail the role. At one point he said a line in a dour voice, then flashed a wide smile before retreating back to his vacant listlessness. It was hilarious.

From there we moved to Vancouver and found several interesting cast members. A young girl named Paige Heuser (who would change

Once Upon a Time, in a School in Outer Space 159

Walter Jones and me backstage at the filming of the "Space Cases" pilot. Note the totally different uniform, designed by George Perez.

her name to Paige Christina for no reason that I ever learned) read for the cheery Rosie, and to portray our Catalina we discovered an actress named Jewel Staite. Yes, that's correct, we reached through time and space and managed to rip off Joss Whedon ten years before he cast Jewel as a space going engineering genius in *Firefly*. I have to say, Jewel was amazing. In person she was a perfectly attractive enough girl, but nothing that would make you look twice at her. When she was on camera, however, there was a complete transformation. There's an old saying that the camera loves some people and it was clearly enamored of Jewel because when she was on camera she became absolutely gorgeous. It was astounding.

We also found an actor for Radu, a young British-Canadian actor named Kristian Ayre. Kristian grafted a kind of hesitant stammer onto his readings that played toward Radu's sense of being a cautious outsider.

We also found two actresses that we thought were perfect for Davenport and Thelma. We wound up casting one of them, Tamsin Kelsey, for Davenport and kept the other in mind as the most likely for Thelma.

Then we went to Montreal for further casting.

And in walked a young woman to audition for Thelma who was unlike any other that had come in. She had applied make up to her face to give her a robotic appearance and had even assembled a costume to convey a space-going look. Furthermore, whereas other actresses had portrayed Thelma as an efficient flight attendant, this one endeavored to put across that this was actually a machine that was attempting to look and sound human. Her name was Anik Matern, and we absolutely fell in love with her portrayal. She became Thelma.

In addition, we found our Commander Goddard. We met some interesting people during the casting of that. Erik Estrada came in but refused to read; he just wanted to talk to us about the part. Because when you were on the cover of *TV Guide* twenty years ago, I guess that means you're too fabulous to read for parts anymore. We also brought in Mark Goddard, "Don West" from *Lost in Space*, after whom the character was named. But he just didn't bring what Mumy called the "Don West magic" with him. We wound up casting a Canadian actor named Paul Boretski who'd done *Spacehunter: Adventures in the Forbidden Zone* and a variety of TV shows.

We needed some help in designing the costumes and I turned to George Perez, who did a terrific job designing Perezesque uniforms for them. Some weeks later we filmed our pilot, "Breath of a Salesman." Then we waited.

Now customarily when a network makes a pilot, they pay the actors a holding fee, so that for six months their services are tied to the show. They can't take any other gigs that would conflict. Nickelodeon, being a bunch of cheap SOBs, opted not to do that to save money. Subsequently Jewel made a pilot for Disney called *Flash Forward*, and when Nickelodeon finally gave the go-ahead to our series, she warned us that if Disney picked up *Flash Forward*, she'd have to leave our show because Disney *had* paid the holding fee.

We also hit another snag: Tamsin Kelsey had gotten pregnant. Because of that, we couldn't use her, because actors on a TV series have to be insured should something go wrong during filming, and no insurance company would cover her. We were basically screwed. So we sent out a frantic casting call in Montreal and got an actress named Cary Lawrence, who did a wonderful job affecting a British accent for the very proper Miss Davenport.

Some weeks later I moved up to Montreal. Since I was going to be working there, I was brought to a special customs agent who was in charge of processing me into the country. I had to pay $100, which was being held for me by a Cinar rep who was waiting outside. I told the agent that's where the money was.

"Sir," he said stiffly, "I am a special agent for the government, not a messenger. You have to pay me and then you can get reimbursed."

"Fine," I said in frustration, paid the money and entered Montreal.

We started filming.

It was the most brutal writing experience of my career.

I moved into an apartment that Cinar rented for me. This was a typical day for me:

Wake up at 6 a.m. Have breakfast. Be in the office by 7 a.m. Work until 7 p.m. Go home. Maybe heat up some leftover pizza for dinner. Work on comic book scripts, a novel, or my opinion column until 1 a.m. Fall asleep. Wake up five hours later and repeat.

I'd never been more creatively exhausted in my life.

Bill and I were determined to have a *Gilligan's Island*–styled theme song that set up our situation and cast. Nickelodeon wouldn't hear of it. They said we could hire a narrator to provide an introductory voice over that would then be accompanied by a dramatic orchestral theme. We tapped Harlan Ellison to record it, and he did so after rewriting our intro (naturally). Meanwhile Bill wrote a theme song that we dropped over the closing credits.

After the show started airing, Nickelodeon became so enamored of that theme that they scotched the opening that they had mandated and instructed us to move the theme song to the top of the show. Of course.

Mumy and I wrote nine of the first season's thirteen episodes. Sometimes he was up in Montreal with me. There was one script we were working on where I was writing the first half of it and he was writing the second, and at some point we both got kind of stuck. So we got up, switched places, and picked up where the other had left off.

Bill always preferred I drive whenever we went somewhere because Montreal had a layer of permafrost. We were told that every winter when the first snowfall hits, the guys who are supposed to plow go on strike in order to make sure they quickly get whatever demands they want. Consequently, since the temperature remains low throughout the winter, the first snowfall sticks. Bill, being a lifelong California guy, had no experience with snow and deferred to my driving experience. One evening we trekked through a fresh snowfall in the parking lot to the car. Bill remained resolutely silent until we got in the car, at which point he unleashed a string of profanity and stomped his feet furiously to get the snow off him. I waited until he calmed down and said, "We okay now?" He nodded and off we drove.

Bill and I were generally in accord on the show, except on one occasion when he wanted to do an episode where the *Christa* has gone dead in space and was squarely in the path of an oncoming comet. "The whole crew is going to be sweating as the giant flaming comet is closing in on them!" he said.

I said, "Comets don't flame."

"What do you mean?"

"I mean they don't flame. There's no air in space for them to burn. Comets are the exact opposite of giant balls of flame. They are giant balls of ice."

"No, they're not!"

"Yeah, Bill, they are."

"When we did the same story on *Lost in Space*, it was a giant flaming ball!" he protested.

"Bill, *Lost in Space* was not the bastion of accuracy you seem to think it was. And we are not going to put something as scientifically illiterate as a flaming comet into *Space Cases* so that some elementary school kid can flunk a science test because of what he saw on our show!"

We wound up having it be a ball of ice, but the ship was stuck in a warp bubble or some such that was causing it to overheat, so Bill got to have them all sweating as the comet approached.

Bill also acted in an episode alongside Mark Hamill as they portrayed two alien beings who, for no discernible reason, talked like they were members of the Beatles. That was fun.

As we approached the end of the first season, we had to prepare for the possibility that we might lose Jewel. We hit upon the ideal solution: we would establish that her imaginary friend, Suzee, was real. We'd have an episode where Catalina would seemingly die in a massive explosion and Suzee would wind up switching places with her. We wouldn't show her face at the end of the episode; that way if Disney didn't pick up the series, we'd simply put a different wig on Jewel and she'd play Suzee the next season.

We also decided to introduce a major enemy, the dreaded Warlord Shank of the evil race, the Spung. We'd introduced one of the lizard-like beings in an earlier episode, but we figured we'd bring in the big bad himself for our season ender. We wanted to have a major guest star with an identifiable voice because his face would be hidden behind the mask.

As Bill and I were talking, we had a movie on the TV in the background: *Kissinger and Nixon*. Suddenly I heard a familiar voice and my head snapped around. There was George Takei as Le Duc Tho. "George," I said immediately. "We get George to do it."

"Do you think you can talk him into coming to Montreal for a week?" said Bill.

I snorted derisively. "I talked him into coming to Romania for three months. This'll be a cakewalk." (More on that later.)

And so several weeks later the Cinar rep and I were waiting outside the gates at the airport for George to come through. George was going to have to pay the same $100 that I had. I was with the Cinar guy because I was the one who had talked George into it and felt I should be there to greet him.

We waited and waited and he didn't emerge. Then suddenly the same agent who had held me up a couple months earlier came running out and began to survey the crowd. I cleared my throat and said, "Excuse me ... we're waiting for—"

"Mr. Sulu?" he said immediately. We nodded. "Where's the money?"

Because the same guy who was too fabulous to let me go out and get the money when I came through didn't hesitate to do it himself on behalf of George. We gave him the money and he said with great excitement, "It's Mr. Sulu!" and vanished back through the door.

Welcome to life with George.

The cast was incredibly excited about the prospect of working with George. Everyone on our show was a Trekkie so this was a dream come true. John Bell, who had directed half a dozen episodes, was on board. That day we had our table read of the script.

Now understand that a table read is carefully timed because in a

(From left) Caroline, Brad Takei, me, George Takei and Kathleen.

half hour episode we have exactly twenty-two minutes to tell our story. When we finished the read through, we knew we had a problem.

It had run twenty-nine minutes.

The problem was George's delivery. As Warlord Shank, he spoke very menacingly and *verrrry sloowwwwwwly.* John could certainly have gotten him to speed up, but he loved the threat that George's delivery imparted. All eyes turned to me.

"I'll fix it," I said.

I then gutted the first act of the script. Shank originally didn't show up until the very end of it; now he first appeared maybe five minutes in. Meanwhile the cast was fully aware that the episode had run way over, and throughout the course of the day, everyone stopped by my office with the same question: "Did you cut my scene with George?" Because I'd made sure that everyone had had *their* moment opposite him. I assured every cast member that no, their scene was intact, everything with George was still there. Their earlier scenes were gone, but their George scenes survived. They didn't care. As long as they got to share screen time with a living legend, they were fine with it.

The shooting went fine. Meanwhile there were some moments of having fun with the cast. On one evening we went out as a group to play Lasertag at this great facility in Montreal. Walter was unquestionably the best at it, for two reasons: First, he had great aim, and second the entire place was heavily shadowed, and being African American, he blended into the darkness. So you'd be creeping along past what seemed an empty area, and suddenly you'd be zapped. You'd spin and all you'd see was Walter's smile disappearing into the shadow, like an armed Cheshire Cat.

By that time the show was on the air, and there was a heavily played commercial which included Bova grousing, "I hate being from Uranus. I'm the butt of every joke." We had gathered at one point in the lobby of the Lasertag place and suddenly a young guy, obviously American, spotted Rahi and he said, "Oh my God! You're from Uranus!" Standing nearby, I said, "Turn around." He did and Walter was right behind him, and the guy freaked out as he realized he was surrounded by the entire cast of *Space Cases.* So that was a fun moment.

Was it all fun during those months? Good lord, no.

Nickelodeon was a huge pain to deal with. Their calls for rewrites were incessant, insane. One executive sent notes with a cover letter saying, "I gave the script to my six-year-old. These are her comments. Please implement." There was another executive who was so scientifically oblivious that one time we had a script where at one point we had the kids land on a heavily vegetated moon, and the executive said, "Isn't there only one moon?" Incredulous, I lost it. "In the *galaxy*?! There's more than one moon in our *own solar system*! Catalina comes from the moon of Titan! Haven't you even read our own bible?!"

Between seasons, I was invited to a convention in England and wound up bringing Kristian with me. Not only that, but I somehow managed to pull some strings and arranged a visit with the cast of *Red Dwarf* and co-creator Doug Naylor. We got to visit the set and have lunch with all of them, and it was a terrific time.

We'd had a story editor during our first season: David Gerrold, widely renowned as the creator of "Tribbles." By the end of the season, David informed Nickelodeon that he really didn't think his services were still required; that they should just trust Bill and I to do the show and leave us alone. Naturally Nickelodeon went in the other direction. They brought in a new story editor, Valri Bromfield, a talented writer, comedian and actress who knew a lot about comedy and nothing about science fiction. She was also a lesbian. I mention this because she made a point of telling me this information thirty seconds after meeting me, which I didn't understand at all. It wasn't like I was hitting on her. But y'know, okay, whatever.

We also indeed lost Jewel to Disney. So we wound up finding another excellent actress, Rebecca Herbst, who went on to a very lengthy stay on *General Hospital* as "Elizabeth Webber."

Also, Nick wanted some changes. They decided they weren't wild about either Rahi or Paige, feeling they were both limited in their acting chops. We managed to stave off getting them fired by hiring Anik to tutor them in acting. They also had taken a dislike to Paul, and on this they wouldn't back off. They didn't like him as an actor and they didn't like spending money on him, so they wanted him out of most of season two. We managed to accommodate them, injuring him badly in an early episode and putting him on ice for half a dozen episodes. I wasn't thrilled about it, but it was either that or kill him off.

Furthermore, Nick wanted the series to be funnier. They wanted romance. And they wanted Bill and I writing far fewer episodes. We wound up doing only six in the second season.

My favorite episode that season was "Both Sides Now" in which all the characters wind up switching looks and personalities. It was a great episode especially for Rahi and Paige, because in real life Paige was always kind of dour while Rahi was genuinely upbeat, so for once they could play to their own personalities. The best was Anik, who played the now fully human Thelma. She was nervous about it because she wasn't accustomed to acting "without a mask." But she was so effective that I was actually asked by some fans who we had cast as the human Thelma, because they literally didn't understand it was the same actress. They might have genuinely forgotten there was a human being under the make-up.

My second favorite episode was our season ender, "A Friend in Need," because we cast my daughter, Shana, as a computer entity. She was on set the entire time, because even though all her on-camera material was shot later in front of green screen, she remained on the set to feed her lines to Rebecca (the main character to interact with her). The cast was impressed by the fact that Shana gave a full-blown performance with every line reading, even though none of that part would be used on the show. Had she decided to stick with acting, I've no doubt she could have forged quite a career.

Most of the rest of the episodes weren't as pleasant. There was one episode that was so bad, the characters so badly out of character in every way, that the actors staged a mini-strike. They went to Cinar and insisted I be brought in to rewrite it. Cinar was positive that I had put them up to it. I hadn't. I assumed it was spontaneous, but I was wrong; the director later admitted that he was the one who had convinced the actors to push back.

So they managed to get the rewrite, but the final result was me being thrown out of Canada. Cinar wanted me out and Nickelodeon instructed me to return home. I was no longer on set making changes, fighting for the show, and keeping everything on track.

At the end of the season, Valri Bromfield quit and told Nickelodeon the same thing David had: leave Peter and Bill alone to write the series.

Once again, Nickelodeon paid no attention to the suggestion and informed us some weeks later that they were cancelling the series. You see, all the "fixes" that Nickelodeon had demanded had backfired. The fans hated the change in tone and characterization and made it clear by no longer watching. Nickelodeon, unwilling to admit that their instructions had sucked, decided it was better to just dump the show.

It was a shame because Bill and I actually had a whole five-year plan worked out. I've never stated before what it was, but I might as well since we're never going to be able to do anything with it. Basically, the crew was going to become involved in a major war between the Stardogs and the Spung. They were going to be the ones who settled it and managed to bring eventual peace to the galaxy. They would eventually become the ruling council of the star system, and as adults they would wind up sending the *Christa* back through time to be found by their younger selves and thus set their future into motion. So our last episode would end in a callback to our earliest one.

That would have rocked.

Comics Stuff

I've written quite a few comic series in my career. There is literally no major character I have not put words into the mouth of, either in an ongoing title or in a guest shot. In this chapter, I'd like to go over my career and discuss the ups and downs on some of my various series.

The Incredible Hulk

I discussed in an earlier chapter how I wound up taking on the jolly green/growly gray giant.

I continued to write the series for twelve years. In those days I had access to sales figures, so I was able to monitor them monthly. If I saw that sales were starting to dip, I would come up with something big to skew the status quo in order to bring people back on board.

That formula worked and continued to work. Then one day my editor, Bobbie Chase, approached me to discuss upcoming story arcs, and she said tentatively, "I want to suggest something to you, and if I'm crossing a line here, feel free to tell me."

"Oookay," I said slowly.

"You've always said that Betty is your wife's favorite character, and because of that, nothing really bad would ever happen to her."

"Yeah?"

"Well ... your wife's divorcing you, so I wondered if that still applied."

I said, "Are you suggesting we kill Betty?"

"Well, that would be pretty major," said Bobbie. "If Betty died, the Hulk would freak. And—"

"Fine, she's toast," I said.

I wasn't being vindictive. Remember, Bobbie had suggested it, not me. Although I did have the exact date and time of Betty's death match up with the date and time that the divorce became finalized.

Unfortunately, it was right after that that it went off the rails.

Marvel upper editorial saw Betty's death as an opportunity. They wanted the Hulk to become a mindless rage monster and go on a destructive streak throughout the entirety of the Marvel universe. That idea went utterly flat with me. I had spent a dozen years writing deep psychologically driven stories. The notion of throwing all that out the window and having the Hulk become a destructive berserker was completely anathema to me. "No way!" I said to Marvel. "There's no way the fans will accept that! It's a completely terrible idea!"

"Well, that's what we want," I was told uncategorically.

"No," I said.

"Okay," was the response of the folks from Marvel upper editorial, "don't the let door hit you on the way out."

Bobbie Chase called me to tell me I was fired off the book. *She* was sobbing. *I wound up consoling her.*

She asked if I'd be interested in writing a final issue or whether I just wanted the death of Betty to be my last story. I did not. Now understand that I was planning to have issue #500 be my finale. So in issue #467, I basically summarized everything that I was going to do in the succeeding thirty or so issues. I figured that would give the fans a taste of what they would be missing.

Marvel then brought in other writers to provide exactly the stories that they wanted.

Sales tanked, as I knew they would. Part of it was loyalty to me, I suppose, but the bottom line is that fans care most about the characters, and they hated what was done to Bruce. They couldn't bail fast enough.

That finally turned around when British writer Paul Jenkins came in and started doing psychologically based stories again, including some nonsense that stuck: that Doc Samson had actually just crafted a new personality called the Professor. I'm sorry, no, my guy was the merged Hulk, and I felt some measure of vindication when my incarnation showed up in *Avengers: Endgame.* It should also be noted that every person who was connected with my being fired off "Hulk" is gone from Marvel—either fired or resigned—but I'm still there. So that counts for something, I guess.

Aqua-Stuff

I never understood why Aquaman got such a bad rep, dismissed as a lame superhero. "He can talk to fish, big deal. He's no Batman."

Yeah, okay, you know what? If you take Aquaman and drop him into the middle of Gotham City with nothing but the clothes on his back, he'll be fine. He's superstrong, can leap long distances, is fairly bulletproof. He would head back to the dock, clobber whoever stood in his way, leap into the ocean and swim off. If you drop Bruce Wayne off at the Marianas trench with nothing but the clothes on his back, you'll never hear from him again. Aquaman was, to me, the Tarzan of the DC universe. He can talk to animals and survive in terrain that would kill anyone else.

My first involvement with his world was when Bob Greenberger wanted a limited series about the history of Atlantis. At the time I was enamored of a BBC series *I, Claudius*, about the history of several Roman emperors. I wanted to do some major generational saga along the lines of that. I decided that the story would be told from the point of view of various historians, and that the nature of the events would be shaped by the prejudices and opinions of the writers. I called it "The Atlantis Chronicles." Bob selected Spanish artist Esteban Maroto to do the art. Esteban didn't speak English, so I wrote full scripts that his bilingual daughter would translate for him.

I also came up with an idea to create an artificial reality for the series. The first issue included a memo from Editor-in-Chief Dick Giordano, on DC letterhead, to Bob Greenberger. In the letter Dick said that a historian, Professor R.K. Simpson, had approached DC with a huge archaeological find: a series of books of actual Atlantean history. But he couldn't get anyone to publish them because the assumption was that they were fake. Dick contended that he didn't care; that he just thought it was a really good story. He then suggested about a dozen writers to handle the adaptation to comic book form, none of whom were me. There was a hand-written response from Bob in which he wrote, "None of them available. How about Peter David?" To which Dick hand wrote, "Okay, if he's the best we can get."

Now Dick's secretary really typed it up, but I was the one who wrote it. R.K. Simpson was named after my then-brother in law, Robert Simpson Kasman, a brilliant young man and a rabbi who was instrumental in providing advice for how I developed Atlantis and its religions. Dick and Bob actually handwrote the replies which were also exactly what I told them to write. To further sell the fiction that these were real books and Simpson was a genuine academic, each issue included an essay by the good professor (really by me) about Atlantean history. They all had footnotes, some of which were genuine but at least one of which was fabricated. Invariably the made-up one provided major support for a fundamental aspect of the article. But I figured that if people went to the library to research it, they'd find some of the footnotes and so assume they were all correct.

At the first convention I went to after issue #1 came out, a young lady came up to me and told me that she was quite upset that Giordano had suggested all these other writers, because clearly I was the best person "to bring Professor Simpson's discovery to comic books." She said it in all seriousness. I thought, "My God, I did it."

I didn't know the half of it. A couple months later, Atlanta retailer Cliff Biggers called me and asked me to settle a dispute in the store. Some fans were insisting that Simpson was real, and Cliff was certain he knew otherwise. "He's real," I said.

"Come on."

"No, he's real. That's all true."

"Fine," said Cliff. "I want to interview him for *Comic Shop News*," which was a comic-related publication that Cliff put out.

"Okay," I said, and arranged a day and time. I then immediately called Bobby and said, "Hey, wanna be Professor Simpson for an interview?"

"Sure," said Bobby.

At the appointed time, Cliff's phone rang and he fully expected to hear my voice speaking with an accent or something. Instead to his bewilderment he was being spoken to by someone whose voice was completely unknown to him. He asked Bobby some fairly educated questions, but Bobby was a rabbi. He'd studied this stuff and he answered them and built upon them. After the interview, Cliff called me and demanded, "Who the hell *was* that?!" "Professor R.K. Simpson," I said simply. To bring it full circle, we got Cliff's permission to run the subsequent interview in the last issue of *The Atlantis Chronicles*.

Producing the series itself wasn't without its bumps. For instance, I got a call from Bob about issue one. I had decided that I'd go with the theory of some Atlantean scholars and go with the notion that Atlantis was sunk by a huge asteroid. I had it getting progressively closer to Earth, and at one point, I wrote, "The asteroid has drawn closer. For the first time, we can see the face of it, its craggy surface and exterior."

Esteban's daughter had taken it literally. I had meant "face" as in front, but she took it to mean "visage." Consequently, the damned thing had a giant death's head skull face on its front. Bob sent me copies of the finished art and asked if I wanted to have art corrections fix it.

I decided I liked it. I mean, if you see an asteroid coming toward you but it's just a ball of rock, you can tell yourself you might survive. But if it has a death's head skull, the message is clear: you're done. Get your affairs in order, don't start reading any continued stories. Time to pack it in.

Interestingly enough, in the year 2018, asteroid 2015 TB 145 passed nearby Earth, and pictures of it clearly depicted a death's head skull on its surface. Fans with long memories called me prescient considering *Atlantis Chronicles* was published twenty-five years before the actual asteroid was even spotted.

After the book came out, DC decided they wanted a change in the writer of the ongoing Aquaman series and I was considered a natural fit for the job. I decided to do everything I could to beef up Aquaman's image and present him as a badass. Considering all the trauma he'd gone through in recent issues, I had him become a hermit in the Aqua-cave. I grew his hair and beard long so that even when he was standing still underwater, there would be constant movement. I also came up with a twisted visual idea: I was going to have piranha eat off one of his hands and replace it with a harpoon. I figured that would be the ideal weapon. A harpoon was a preferred weapon that humans used against sea creatures; what better way to turn that around. I loved the imagery. When short haired Aquaman entered a room, the response was, "Hi, Aquaman." When the long haired, bearded harpoon-handed Aquaman walked in, the response would be "Holy shit, what does *this* guy want?"

DC didn't buy it immediately. I had to go into a meeting with Paul Levitz and sell him on the idea, including a long-term storyline in which eventually he would die but wind up coming back to life with his hand intact. DC signed off on it and we were off to the races.

Fans freaked out, as I knew they would. What the hell had I done to Aquaman? For some reason many referred to the harpoon as a hook, which I didn't remotely understand. It wasn't a damned hook. It was a harpoon. How stupid can people be?

Nevertheless, sales were great. People might have been shocked by it, but they were fascinated by Arthur's new ass-kicking attitude. I even built upon things from *Atlantis Chronicles*, including an explanation of why the asteroid had a face.

Unfortunately, things began to get difficult. My editor was giving me consistently inconsistent instructions. At one point he wanted me to show Aquaman being a leader of men, but then he said he wanted stories where Aquaman was operating solo. He wanted stories of a political bent, but then said he didn't want stories set in Atlantis. The constant contradictions made it impossible for me to know which direction I was supposed to go. And then, when I finally began to embark on my death-of-Aquaman storyline, the editor refused to let me do it. "We killed Superman, so we can't kill Aquaman," he said. At which point I gave up and quit the book.

He brought in Erik Larsen who was on for a short while and then discovered the editor's constant contradictory instructions were hampering him as well as they had me and he likewise quit. So they brought in someone else and then eventually did the exact story I had wanted to do, except naturally I wasn't credited for it. The editor was eventually fired.

Many years later, when Zack Snyder first put up a picture of Jason Momoa as the king of the sea, modern day fans said, "That's not Aquaman!" But the older fans immediately said, "No, that's Peter David's Aquaman!" I am somewhat flattered that my version of Aquaman wound up earning over one billion dollars, and I fully expected he'll lose a hand in the sequel.

Supergirl

DC wanted to launch a new Supergirl series using the version created by John Byrne. And naturally they turned to John Byrne to write it.

John passed.

So honestly, I have very little patience if John bitches about what I wound up doing to his character considering that he was given the opportunity to write her and he turned it down flat.

John's incarnation had a hopelessly complicated origin. The original Supergirl was nice and simple: She was Superman's cousin. Easy to understand, boom, done. John's, by contrast, was, according to Wikipedia, "a man-made lifeform made of synthetic protoplasm created by a heroic Lex Luthor of a 'pocket continuum'" who was implanted with Lana Lang's memories, could shapeshift into Lana, and for a while even believed she was Lana.

What the hell was I supposed to do with that? Furthermore, she had assumed human shaped by choice. She could just as easily shift into anything else. How was I supposed to take seriously a character who didn't know who she was and was human arbitrarily?

I decided I needed to ground her, to lock her into a human shape by circumstance so that was all she could be. Plus, I wanted to give her a secret identity that actually mattered. Ultimately, I came up with the idea that she would merge her protoplasm with a dying human girl named Linda Danvers, the original secret identity of Kara Zor-El. I further posited that she would wind up in a town where weird stuff happened because the town sat on a tributary of the River Styx. I should point out that I was not watching *Buffy the Vampire Slayer* at the time and so was unaware of Sunnydale and the Hell Mouth, which didn't stop some fans of claiming I was ripping off Joss Whedon. Indeed, when I introduced a British bad boy to interact with my lead, they claimed that I was ripping off Spike even though my guy was actually created before Spike showed up. But, y'know, whatever.

However I wasn't content with my rejiggering. I was thinking bigger.

See, I wanted to explore things in *Supergirl* that no other "S" title had covered. I realized that the Super books tended to steer clear of magic, mysticism and matters of faith, and that was the direction in which I decided to go. I came up with an additional wrinkle: Supergirl was going to be an angel. An Earth-born angel, a previously unknown species that was created under very specific circumstances. I loved it. It would allow me to tell stories no one else was telling.

Fans didn't know what to make of it.

I was accused of having made the character's origin hopelessly complicated. I disagreed with that and still do. Before she was a protoplasmic being from a pocket dimension who thought she was Lana Lang. Now she was an angel. That's way simpler. You could summarize her with one word. Also I was able to tell stories with deeply philosophical underpinnings. I even introduced a kid named Wally, named after my brother, who purported to be God. You have to love the nerve of introducing God into a comic as a *supporting* character.

As the series progressed, I completed the story arc of her being an angel and made some changes to her, removing the divine persona and scaling back her powers to the levels of what Superman was when he was first created (he could leap an eighth of a mile! Nothing less than a bursting shell could pierce his skin!). We also adapted a costume that she was currently wearing in animation.

Fans did not seem enamored of the changes. Sales began to slide.

I came up with a storyline that I was sure would reinvigorate the book. I was going to have the original Kara Zor-El show up and come face to face with Linda Danvers. Initially this was considered verboten since Supergirl had died in "Crisis on Infinite Earths" and she absolutely could not be brought back. But I managed to convince Paul Levitz (yet again) to let me do it. The editor managed to line up Ed Benes to do the art, and I absolutely fell in love with his artwork. Leonard Kirk had done a fantastic job up until that point, and Ed was taking it to the next level. I was positive that sales would turn around.

And then the editor got the worst artist I've ever seen to do the covers of the first couple of issues. Why she didn't have Ed do it, I couldn't fathom. The art was cartoonish, stick-like, like Harvey comics done by someone tripping on heroin. It did not remotely represent the interior art, but it was the only visual that DC released.

Orders plummeted. DC of course assumed that my story concept had not done the trick, because that's SOP in comics. If a title is a success, praise the artist. If a title tanks, blame the writer.

By the time issue #75 came out, DC had already cancelled the title. It didn't matter that when it got to the stores and people actually looked at the interior pages, they were blown away. DC had pulled the trigger and there was no recalling it. The fact that the editor wised up and had Ed do the later covers didn't matter in the slightest.

It was a shame. My plan was to convince DC to let me keep Kara around, and have her, Linda, and Power Girl team up to be the "S" equivalent to *Birds of Prey*. The title for the proposed new book? *Blonde Justice*. Never happened.

Since then, Kara Zor-El did indeed return and become Supergirl permanently, because of course she did.

Fallen Angel

So Dan Didio took me out to lunch and asked me what I had had planned for *Supergirl*. I did have a back-up plan if we couldn't do *Blonde Justice* and outlined it for him.

"How about this," he said. "We're launching a new imprint designed to appeal to women. Why don't you create wholly new characters and we can launch it as part of that? And you'd own the characters."

That sounded good to me.

And thus was Lee born.

I was originally going to set the stories in San Francisco. Since we were going to be starting from the bottom up, I came up with a brand-new fictional city, Bete Noire. There would reside the Fallen Angel, whose origins were cloaked in secrecy because I wanted readers to think that she might actually indeed be Linda Danvers, whose full name was Linda Lee Danvers. Lee would be the court of last resort for the truly desperate. If she felt your situation was worth intervening with, then she would fight to the end to make things right. If, on the other hand, she believed you'd brought it on yourself, she would bring disaster crashing down upon you. So make sure your conscience was clear if you were seeking her aid.

The new label launched and naturally tanked within months, because when you start an entire line aimed at women, you are telling the vast bulk of comic buyers that they likely won't be interested. I knew we were dead from the very first reviews I read of issue #1. The consensus was the same across the board: "Great first issue, and I'm definitely going to read it when it's collected in trade paperback format."

See, trade paperbacks are slowly destroying the comic book publishing industry. Fans wait for trades and don't collect the monthly titles, except then sales on the monthlies drop so much that they are no longer profitable. So I knew that the fan attitude of "wait for trade" combined with the narrow fanbase at which DC was aiming meant the entire line of comics was doomed.

As it happens, mine outlasted pretty much all the others, which were cancelled after maybe six issues. *Fallen Angel* ran for twenty. After it was cancelled, I was contacted by Chris Ryall of IDW, who was determined not to let the series suffer such an ignominious fate. He was interested in seeing what happened next to the citizens of Bete Noire and IDW picked it up as on ongoing series.

The original series had been drawn by Dave Lopez, but artist J.K. Woodward took over for the IDW incarnation. J.K. fully painted the first five issues and they looked amazing. After that the monthly schedule precluded him from continuing in that format and he switched to straight up pen and ink.

Freed of any connection to the DC Universe, I gave my heroine an actual background and origin. She genuinely was a fallen angel, and her full name was "Liandra." I don't recall where I got the name from, although apparently it means "gift from God," which I suppose makes it a good angel name. *Fallen Angel* sold well enough for several years for IDW, although eventually that fell off as well and IDW decided to cancel the title.

In the meanwhile, David Uslan, son of "Batman" producer Michael Uslan, optioned it for a movie. That was three years ago and in that time we have no director, no screenwriter and no cast. So, y'know, other than that, it's going great.

Young Justice

Todd Dezago created a group called "Young Justice." It consisted of Robin, Impulse and Superboy (the Superman clone, not the kid version of Superman). They showed up in a one shot and when Todd passed on doing a monthly title, once again DC came to me. I committed to six issues because I wasn't sure what I was going to do with three characters who had their own titles. It meant I'd have to react to what other writers did and I couldn't really do anything especially dynamic to their lives.

I also quickly discovered that I was having trouble relating to the personalities and troubles of a group of teen boys. Yes, granted, I had actually been a teen boy, but I'd had virtually no friends or buds to hang around with. So as a species they were alien to me. I quickly fixed that by issue #4 when I introduced three females: Arrowette, Wonder Girl and Secret, the last of whom had been introduced during Dezago's first excursion. Teenage girls I knew: I had already raised two of them, so I knew what their minds were like.

The series was intended to be a bridge between the kids' level comics (such as *Scooby-Doo*, which DC produced) and the older skewing superhero comics such as *Teen Titans*. Basically what it meant was no profanity and no sex. That was fine with me. The last thing I would have needed was to write in a sex scene with underage teens anyway. Instead I had Secret crushing on Robin and Wonder Girl crushing on Superboy, but the guys were by and large too dense to be aware of it. Which made sense to me.

My favorite moment was when I sent the crew to New Genesis and had Secret meet Darkseid. For some reason I imagined that he spoke like Bela Lugosi, and so Secret misunderstood his name and thought it was Doug Side. She introduces her new friend to the team and cheerily informs them that "Doug" says he thinks she has potential. She sees that as a good thing and naturally the rest of the kids are trying not to freak out.

My artist for the entire series was Todd Nauck. Todd was wonderful; no matter what I instructed him to draw, he was able to do it flawlessly.

Indeed, some years later when I was writing *Friendly Neighborhood Spider-Man*, I was told we needed a fill in artist. I recommended Todd. I got pushback from editorial; they weren't thrilled with the prospect. But I insisted and so they wound up sending my script for the first issue of a two-part Mysterio story to him. Some days later I got a surprised call from the editor. "We've started getting in art pages from Todd really quickly and they're great!" he burbled. "Look, is there any way you could make this two parter into a three parter?" I said, "Sure," brought in the dead Mysterio through the typical means we use to revive dead characters and suddenly Todd was doing three issues. When the regular artist subsequently left, Todd became the ongoing artist. Later on Marvel did a comic book one-shot about President Obama and Todd was tapped to draw it, which in turn got him national attention. So I'm very pleased with the way Todd's career turned out.

Flash forward some years later and an actress named Stephanie Lemelin puts up on her website that she's been cast to play Arrowette in this new animated series entitled *Young Justice*.

I flipped out. The title was long gone, but it was still me who had written it. Why was I being cut out of the loop for an animated version? I called Paul Levitz and Paul put me together with a guy named Sam Register. That name may not mean anything to you, but if you watch the closing credits of pretty much any program on Cartoon Network, you'll see his name come up. Sam is the Grand Poobah there, and he put me together with the show runner, Greg Weisman.

Now I'd known Greg for years. His biggest claim to fame was writing the terrific series *Gargoyles* for Disney. And he knew me, but we'd never had the opportunity to work together. So I called him and he said, "Peter, the truth is that I have enough writers for the first season, but it's Young Justice and it's you, so if you want an episode, you've got it."

I flew out to LA on my own dime and found the episode he wanted me to write was called "Secrets." It featured not only Secret, but the villain Harm whom I had created for issue #4. I sat in with Greg, co-producer Brandon Vietti and the rest of the YJ writers and broke that episode and five others. I then flew back home and banged out the script in no time.

A couple weeks later Greg called me. The writer for a later episode, "Insecurity," had had some sort of a breakdown. They needed someone else to step in and bang it out, and apparently, I was the fastest writer Greg knew of. I agreed to take it on and pounded that one out for Greg as well.

The series was then renewed for a second season and Greg sorrowfully told me he couldn't hire me. He wanted to, but I had been blackballed by DC. Astounded, I emailed Mike Carlin and asked him why DC was preventing me from working for them. He said he'd check into it and get back to me.

He subsequently told me that DC had decided to preserve writing for their animated series as a perk for those folks who had signed exclusive contracts with DC. Since I had an exclusive with Marvel, that was obviously not happening. But in this instance, DC decided to grandfather me in so I could keep writing for *Young Justice*. Greg was ecstatic and brought me on for two episodes of season two, and one of season three. I imagine if there's a season four I'll be asked back. Now if only I could get the attention of someone on Marvel's side of the animation fence.

Green Lantern and Gilgamesh

Dick Giordano had been blown away by what I did in the Sin-Eater storyline and wanted something dark and gritty like that for the "Green Lantern" series that was going to be running weekly in *Action Comics*.

The editor, Denny O'Neil, didn't want me. He wanted Jim Owsley. He was overruled by Dick and so reluctantly offered me the title. I took it on and said eagerly, "What type of stories do you want me to write?"

And Denny, who should have passed on Dick's preferences, told me I was free to write whatever I wanted.

So I took the series in a humorous direction.

I decided that the notion of Hal Jordan being completely without fear was ludicrous. Everyone has to be afraid of something. Dying, for a start. Someone with no fear had to be monumentally stupid. So I theorized that the power ring was suppressing Hal's fundamental fears. He instructs the power ring to stop doing that, and when it does, he starts freaking out over stuff.

Dick hated it. It wasn't remotely what he wanted to see, and he asked Denny why I wasn't writing what he did want. Where were the grim and gritty tales he expected? Denny replied that I had proven utterly unwilling to do the types of stories that DC wanted, which of course was a complete lie. And Denny fired me off the book and replaced me with Jim Owsley, which is who he wanted in the first place.

I found out about this conversation some months later when I had the occasion to talk to Dick face to face.

I had pitched Denny on the idea of updating Gilgamesh. My brother-in-law, Bobby, had given me the idea. Gilgamesh, after all, was really the very first superhero, and Bobby saw me doing for him what I had done for King Arthur in *Knight Life*. I told the story to Denny and offered to write up a pitch. He said, "Hold off on writing it. I want to think about it a little."

He strung me along for several weeks, insisting I not write anything down. And I, because I trusted him, obeyed his instructions. Then one day he called me with bad news: by total coincidence, writer/artist Jim Starlin had *also* come up with the idea of updating Gilgamesh and he'd already done a bunch of work on it. So he was reluctantly going to go with Jim's version, "Gilgamesh II."

And I believed him.

Until I spoke to Jim, and I asked him where he had gotten the idea from.

"Denny," Jim said immediately. "He pitched the idea to me. I didn't have it until Denny suggested it to me."

I went ballistic. Denny had freaking stolen Gilgamesh out from under me. That was why Denny hadn't wanted me to write anything down. It was so there would be no evidence of his theft. It gave him deniability if there was nothing in writing from me earlier than the stuff that Jim turned in.

Furious, I went straight to Giordano and told him exactly what had happened. Dick was dumbfounded. It was at that point that he started asking me about Green Lantern and we realized that Denny had worked to get me torpedoed off that title as well.

Giordano wound up paying me a kill fee for Gilgamesh and Denny assured me that we were going to do my version of Gilgamesh after Starlin's, which of course never happened.

Understand, I don't think it's personal. I just believe Denny doesn't think much of my writing abilities and will do whatever he could not to work with me. Other than the fact that he screwed me out of two jobs and also torpedoed my relationship with John Byrne, I think he's great.

X-Factor

Andy Schmidt, an editor at Marvel, wanted to do a limited series with Jamie Madrox as a detective. He decided I'd be the ideal writer for it. Furthermore he saw it as a back door pilot for a new version of *X-Factor*.

I was onboard with the idea. My only concern was, What could I do with Jamie Madrox that would make him seem different?

It was Kathleen who suggested the underpinning of it. What if, she suggested, Jamie's duplicates start displaying different aspects of his personality? We all have different facets, after all. We behave differently with our parents than we do with our friends, differently with our spouses than with our children. Until now Jamie's duplicates had always been just like him. What if something happened so that they were different? What if one was gay? Hell, what if one was homicidal? It opened up all sorts of possibilities.

So I took Kathleen's idea with her blessing and ran with it.

The new version of Madrox became a fan sensation, and an *X-Factor* ongoing series was immediately green lit.

As I was selecting characters for the team, Brian Bendis was particularly interested in our including a character he had created for "House of M," Layla Miller. His reasoning was simple. If Layla became an ongoing character, then "House of M" would serve as her introduction. If she vanished from the Marvel Universe, then she would come across as what she truly was: a device Brian had come up with to make the plot for "House of M" to work. Obviously, the former was preferable, and so I agreed to bring her on board. I also brought in Rictor who had recently been depowered and was incredibly bummed out about it.

I had a ball writing the series, although I was a bit annoyed when I lost Layla after she was transported to the future as part of a crossover.

Another crossover seriously screwed up my series plans. I had Polaris get pregnant after an ill-advised midnight rendezvous with Jamie. Then I was told, after the story had seen print, that she couldn't have the child. Marvel was doing yet another crossover, "The Messiah CompleX," in which the first child born a mutant since "House of M" was going to be born, and Madrox's baby would overshadow it. So there couldn't be a Madrox baby.

I wracked my brains over what I should do. Then, while I was walking around the San Diego Comic-Con, the answer came to me: It wouldn't be a real baby at all. I would establish that Polaris had actually slept with a dupe, and the result had been a baby dupe, which Madrox would then—to everyone's shock—absorb. I ran around the convention, found Andy, and ran the idea past him. "My God, that's sick. Let's do it," said Andy.

Over the next months the book wound up going through several editors. In each case I had to bring the editor up to speed with the plan. The reaction was always the same: "My God, that's sick. Let's do it."

So we did it.

When the book came out, I put out a special request to the fans: please keep this under your hat. This was a major development and I wanted it to be a shock when fans got to that page.

I should mention that the biggest thing I ever did in *X-Factor* was out Rictor and Shatterstar. I brought back Shatterstar to give Rictor something new to do, and Marvel had been hinting about the two of them being a couple for well over a decade. I said to myself, "The hell with it. It's the 21st century. Let's just be out in the open about it." So I had the two of them kiss upon coming back together. To me, it was no big deal. It was panel five of a six panel page.

To fandom, it was a huge deal. Apparently, it was a slow news day and so it made the rounds, because it was the first time that two male mainstream heroes had liplocked in a comic.

It went through a normal news cycle, and then Shatterstar's creator, Rob Liefeld weighed in. No, no, Rob insisted, Shatterstar wasn't gay. No, he was like an ancient Greek warrior. Well, that kicked the coverage to a whole new level, because apparently Rob was unaware that ancient Greek warriors would typically bang the boys who carried their weapons the night before a battle. That catapulted coverage into the stratosphere.

But actually, I'm getting ahead of myself. Let's go back to Madrox absorbing the baby and my plea to fans to keep a lid on it.

There was a website called Scans_Daily that decided to take the opposite approach. They posted a page by page summary of the entire issue, including visuals from half the comic. Half.

Putting aside that I was pissed that they were so flagrantly ignoring my request, it also seemed like copyright infringement. As an employee of Marvel comics, I did exactly what I was supposed to do: I informed the publisher of apparent copyright violation. Legally, that was all I could do considering I was not the copyright holder.

Before Marvel's lawyers could do anything, however, Photobucket, the site that enabled them to put the pictures up, told them to take it down. They did so. Meanwhile I used my wife's LiveJournal account to comment on the site. Someone asked me point blank if I'd told Marvel about the copyright infringement. I said I had, but that Marvel as of that writing had not yet done anything about it.

Two days later, Scans_Daily was shut down completely. Apparently, their host had had enough.

What was the immediate takeaway? Not the fans going, "Wow, we really screwed up, violating copyright so flagrantly." No, it was "Peter David destroyed Scans_Daily." They stampeded my website, they wildly distorted my Wikipedia page, they declared open warfare throughout the Internet, determined to ruin my reputation and destroy me. Eventually they rebuilt their website and the first rule they came up with was that no one was allowed to mention any of my work, or me, again. Ostensibly it was self-protection. No. It was intended as punishment, pure and simple.

Because fans can be great.

And they can be incredibly entitled and remarkably petty.

Fans

I was walking around the dealer's room of a convention that was wrapping up, chatting with long-time friend Tom Galloway. Tom commented that I had worked my ass off during the convention and had made so many people happy.

"Yeah, but you won't hear from them," I said. "Instead there will be one guy who I pissed off somehow, and he's the one who's gonna go around and talk about what a dick I was."

As if on cue, a guy walked up to me and asked me to sign a comic.

I looked at it. I hadn't written it. It wasn't even published by Marvel or DC; it was some independent title.

"I didn't write this," I said.

"That's okay, just sign it."

"No, it's not okay," I said patiently. "If I sign it, it's like I'm taking credit for it. I'd rather not do that."

"Just sign it."

"Do you have anything else I could sign?" I asked. "A program book. A piece of paper."

"No, forget it." His face twisted in anger and contempt. "I'm sorry to have *bothered* you," and he stormed off.

Tom looked incredulous. I turned and said very calmly, "There he goes. He waited until the last minute, but that was him. That's the guy who's going to go on the Internet and say, 'I walked up to Peter David and he wasn't doing anything else but he refused to sign my comic.' And other people will immediately pipe up, 'Yeah, I heard he was really nasty.'"

Understand that I grew up as a fan way before I was a pro. I participated in conventions. One of my favorites was a small one called August Party that was designed as a con by fans, for fans. I wrote a number of sketches that were performed there, including one after *Empire Strikes Back* came out, in which I riffed the end of *The Wizard of Oz*. I had Luke Skywalker wake up back on Tatooine, burbling about this dream he'd had, and he says, "And you were there, Uncle Owen! And you, Han! And you, Dad," and he pointed at Vader and then Leia and said, "And you too, Sis!" Fans muttered "Sis?" because Leia's parentage wouldn't be revealed for another several years. Lucky guess.

As my writing career took off, I slowly was elevated in the August Party rankings and instead of being one of the attendees, I became someone that other fans were coming to meet.

The concept of acquiring fans was new to me. As far as I was concerned, I was just me. I was telling the same stupid jokes I always told, except now instead of people rolling their eyes or moaning, they were laughing at them. If I attended a party, I was suddenly holding court. People would cluster in groups to hear every word that might tumble out of my stupid mouth.

The Internet was a very different situation. Brother-in-law Robert informed me of this thing called rec.arts.comics, an internet posting board where people would comment about comics. And it appeared that my work on *Spectacular Spider-Man* was being very well received.

Grateful for the positive attention, I swung over to rec.arts.comics and greeted them.

I was immediately told to get the hell out of there.

Not by everyone, mind you. Some people seemed genuinely jazzed to "meet" me. But the majority of them proclaimed that I had no right to be there. That this was a preserve specifically for fans. That my presence would have a "chilling effect" and was not remotely welcome.

I know this must seem very odd considering the way the Internet functions now. Fans routinely interact with creators, actors, writers and directors. Far from presenting a chilling effect, the Internet is populated by trolls who delight in saying the most obnoxious things they can. Hell, as of this writing, the President of the United States utilizes the Internet to hold power over everyone he considers an enemy. Far from being a place of polite conversation, it's become a bastion of noxious behavior.

It wasn't like that back in the old days.

The truth is that, as years have gone by, the concept of taking responsibility for one's words and deeds has gone the way of the dinosaur. There is a vast sense of entitlement out there, that people feel is due them because of their education or skin color or the amount of money they have in the bank.

Let me give you an example. When science fiction author Roger Zelazny passed away, fans on rec.arts.scifi were in mourning. And one guy posted a comment in which he opined that it was good Zelazny was dead because he hadn't written anything decent in several years.

The guy was pummeled into oblivion. Fans online united and tore the guy apart and I never saw a posting from him again.

If I should die and someone says, "Good, he hasn't written anything entertaining since *The Incredible Hulk*," a chorus of people would chime in in agreement. Because that is how disconnected from simple human civility we have become as a nation. Let's face it: without the Internet, there's no way Trump becomes president and retains power.

Is this to say that the entirety of fandom is hopeless? No, not remotely.

Understand that I do not remember the vast majority of fans that I meet at conventions. There's a reason for that. Ninety-nine percent of them blend together into a vast haze of niceness. They love my work, they say nice things, they get autographs, and sometimes they buy stuff.

One percent of them do not fit into that category. They stand there and yammer and yammer about everything under the sun. Or they insult me. I attended a memorial service for Mark Gruenwald, and as I was studying one of the displays, a young woman walked up to me and asked if I was Peter David. When I confirmed I was, she said, "Your writing is terrible. Just awful." "Thanks for sharing that," I said.

When I was in England a guy showed up at a store signing. He insulted my work relentlessly, and then proceeded to challenge everyone standing on line as to what they could possibly see in my work. Finally, I got fed up and personally threw him out of the store. He went out with such a twisted smile that I was sure he'd be waiting for me outside with a gun.

Let us contrast that with a young guy who came up to me at one San Diego Con. He said, "Mr. David, that conversation we had last year turned my life around." He proceeded to tell me at length about how the things I had told him had enabled him to pull himself out of the hole he was buried in emotionally. I, of course, had no idea who he was, nor recollection of the conversation. But I was not about to let on because I was terrified I might send him into a spiral of depression. So instead I lied through my teeth, telling him I had thought about him often in the intervening year and hoped things had worked out for him.

Indeed, one has to be very careful not to give offense. A guy once came up to me with an issue of *Web of Spider-Man* I had written and told me it was his favorite comic ever. Me, I hated it. The story wasn't properly thought out; it was just a bad comic. And I was stupid enough to say so. I saw his face fall and realized that I had insulted the poor guy. I immediately said, "But I totally get what you like about it," and found things in it to praise. He brightened right up.

Some time later, I was at a store signing with artist Sam Kieth. A young fan brought a copy of one of Sam's book to him and said how much he liked it. Sam began to do the exact same thing I had done. Realizing it, I clamped a hand on his shoulder and said, "Sam, the young man has just complimented you. What do we say?" "Thanks!" Sam said brightly. I patted him on the back approvingly. So I'm not the only creator who can occasionally be insensitive when it comes to fans.

And there have been times when the fans came through for me in big ways. For instance, some years ago I ran into trouble with the IRS because a chunk of money I earned during *Space Cases* vanished during the divorce that was going on. It left me in the red; I still paid taxes every year but was unable to make up the shortfall from my one year of making a huge amount. When the IRS threatened to take my house away, I went public with my situation and money flowed in. Granted, it also gave haters a new reason to hate and twist the facts to suit them ("Peter David hasn't paid taxes in years!" was one of my favorites lies) but for the most part they came through.

And boy, did they pray for me vociferously when I had my medical problems seven years ago. Money came flowing in from people who wanted to help with medical costs, which was much appreciated, and fans worldwide prayed for me in their most aggressive fashion. I'm really not sure just how much miracles are really accomplished by prayers, but all I can say is that I'm fully recovered from something that the doctors told Kathleen there was a sizable chance I'd die from. So who knows?

Plus, I wind up having fans in the damnedest places.

Kathleen enjoys making puppets as I've said, and she loves making them of Doctor Who and various companions. David Tennant was going to be attending one Creation Con that I was going to be at, so Kath made a puppet of his incarnation of the Doctor and asked me to get it to him. I managed to arrange with the Creation folks to bring me straight over to him during an autograph session so I wouldn't have to stand on line for hours and miss being at my table.

At the appropriate time, they escorted me over to his table. There had to be literally a thousand people waiting for autographs. I was able to breeze past them because everyone knew I wasn't getting something signed. I walked up to him with the puppet and said my wife had made it for him. His handlers had closed in tightly around him, ready to shoo me away immediately since I wasn't going to be spending any money. David's eyes widened and he said, "How marvelous!" He started playing with the puppet and his handlers relaxed somewhat. I said cheerfully, "My wife's name is Kathleen David. My name is Peter David."

He looked at me, startled, as if seeing me for the first time. "Peter

Caroline, David Tennant and me. Kathleen is standing directly behind David operating the puppets.

David the comic book writer?" Surprised, I nodded. He broke into a wide grin and said delightedly, "I loved your run on the Hulk!"

Stunned, I turned to the crowd and shouted, "David Tennant's a fan of mine!" A thousand fans cheered.

Sometimes it's really great to be me.

I think a lot of my public persona has resulted from *Comic Buyer's Guide*. *CBG*, as it was called for short, was a weekly newspaper published by Krause press that covered the world of comic books. And I wrote a column for it.

A lot of stuff happened as a result of *CBG*.

"But I Digress"

When I launched "But I Digress" in 1990, I wasn't sure what in the world I would talk about. There was no limit on the range of opinions to be discussed; I was limited only by my imagination. Yet with a few rare exceptions, such as the birth of a child, I always found something to write about.

In retrospect, I have to say that my employers were incredibly good sports about it. I did not hesitate to attack Marvel or DC in "But I Digress" when I felt they were doing something worthy of being criticized. I consistently tried to remain fair minded in all things. What I did in every column was give thought to things that other people were not giving consideration to, and the result was always entertaining.

I've already described one of the most memorable uses to which I put my column: Destroying the Enemies of Ellison. Indeed, Harlan passed away a year ago as of this writing and there's no word of the posthumous slam book being revived, so I'm hoping we can safely say that's gone.

But a second entertaining use of the column was when I began writing about Image Comics. Image was formed by a coterie of Marvel artists who basically wanted to produce their own intellectual property and make money from it.

Uhm ... okay. No problem with that.

What I had an issue with was the way they said it. Erik Larsen, for instance, claimed that for years the Image boys had been "holding back" their best creations. I commented on that, asserting that I had never held back in all my years as a writer; that I had given my all, every time. I never just dogged it for a paycheck. Image also asserted that they were friends going into business together. I expressed great skepticism at that, stating that friends and business was a dangerous mix and I hoped they all that their lawyers up to speed. They roundly castigated me for that. This was of course before, a couple years later, they would evict Rob Liefeld from their ranks. They also claimed that there was no one spokesman on their behalf. I stated that was insane; they need one person to speak for all of them. They roundly derided me for that as well … before they decided that Jim Lee, one of the most reasonable of them, would be their spokesman.

So basically, they did everything I predicted they would do, and yet found novel ways to criticize and attack me. How dare I hold Image to the exact same standard of analysis that I hold Marvel and DC? Who the hell did I think I was? If I was going to be writing articles about them, why didn't I call them and interview them? Well, I wasn't writing articles, I was writing opinion pieces that were based on statements they themselves said. Wasn't my job to call them individually and demand to know what the hell they had been talking about.

The one who took it most personally was Todd, the artist whose career at Marvel I had helped launch when I'd signed off on him drawing the Hulk. Todd loudly asserted that I was dealing with Image unfairly and challenged me to a debate at a 1993 Philadelphia comic book convention. If I'd had a shred of brains, I would have told him to forget it. Instead I let my ego get the better of me and agreed to it, although I stipulated that we had to debate an actual topic: Namely whether the media as a whole had treated Image fairly.

To give an indication of how seriously I took this challenge, here's what I did: First, I read four books on debating, argumentation, and speech. Then I organized a strategy session at my house wherein half a dozen folks whom I collectively referred to as "The Brain Trust" assembled, to work out directions to take and anticipate possible lines of attack from Todd. I poured over interviews Todd had done, finding contradictions and gaps in logic. I then retyped pertinent sections, pasted them onto index cards and referenced them by topic. Ultimately, I wound up only using half of them.

The high point of the debate came when Todd was trying to make assertions about truth-telling versus lies. There he was, standing there in boxer shorts with boxing gloves, talking about veracity, and I was standing there in a sports jacket and necktie trying to take in the absurdity of the encounter. Harlan had provided me with a clinical definition of the term "paralogia" which I had on an index card on the stand. In my rebuttal, I observed that Todd the truth-teller had labeled both myself and John Byrne as being "psychotic," which was demonstrably false. Then I said that if you're going to slam someone using psychological terms, this is how you do it.

I then read the definition of paralogia, which is false and illogical thinking. I provided examples of it which all suited Todd's history of delivery, which set the audience howling. Then I got to this part:

"Another characteristic of paralogia is its false, dream-like logic. In his study of schizophrenic thinking, Mueller, 1911, cited a patient who was convinced he was Switzerland. Such a false logic could not be entertained by the normal mind. But this patient's thinking followed the line, 'Switzerland loves freedom. I love freedom. Therefore, I am Switzerland.'" I then pointed dramatically toward Todd and said, "Ladies and gentlemen: Switzerland."

Well, that was pretty much that. The debate went on for another half hour, but it was effectively over from that moment.

Some years later, both Todd and I were going to be attending the San Diego Comic-Convention. They were going to be holding a Todd McFarlane Q&A and they wanted me to be the emcee, to field the questions. I guess they believed that if there was anyone who the audience was convinced would be even-handed with Todd, it would be me.

Todd's reputation was somewhat shaky at the time because he had spent $2.7 million in 1998 to buy the 70th homerun baseball hit by Mark McGwire. Let us put aside that some years later McGwire fell into disrepute because of his admitted use of steroids. In 1998 it was a pretty big deal. A number of fans were offended by the notion of spending such a huge amount of money on a piece of sports memorabilia.

It was one of the first things that Todd was asked about during the Q&A. Todd began to give a choppy answer, but I interrupted and said, "I actually have no problem with Todd having spent that much money on the baseball." The crowd lapsed into stunned silence and I continued, "Yes, he spent $3 million on a baseball. And he's gotten, conservatively guessing, $50 million of publicity from it. He's being talked about on ABC, NBC, CBS, CNN, NPR, and God knows ESPN. His name is everywhere. This has done wonders for his name, his brand, his notoriety. There's an old saying that you have to spend money to make money, and the odds are huge that he's going to make a ton of money for his initial investment. I take no issue with him buying the baseball. However," I added, referencing an interview he had given, "I don't think you spend $3 million on a baseball without telling your wife first. You don't spring that on her." Which was indeed what Todd had stated in an interview that he had done. That his wife had learned about it when it had broken on the news.

His wife, Wanda, was seated in the audience when I said that, and immediately her head bobbed up and down most definitively. I suspected that there had been some rather lengthy and heated discussions in the McFarlane household about that very topic. Now I have no idea what Wanda's impression of me was before she met me. Doubtless it was filtered through Todd's prism. But I'm pretty sure she liked me a lot after

Bill Sienkiewicz (left), Todd McFarlane and me at the after party for the "Remembering Stan Lee" celebration at the Ambassador Theater.

that Q&A, and I ran into her and Todd fairly recently during the party that was held after the Stan Lee Memorial held at the Ambassador Theater. We got on great.

So the days of Image hostilities are long gone. Their launch remains one of the shakier in the history of publishing but say what you will about them: They're still around. Many other publishers have come and gone in the intervening years, so I suppose they're doing something right.

One of my favorite things I ever did in my column was when Rob Liefeld distributed at a convention art pages of his upcoming "Captain America" series, without dialogue. So I ballooned it, having a field day. For instance, Steve Rogers is shown at a payphone, complaining about being unable to dial "Operator." Why? Because Rob had simply drawn the buttons for one through nine but had neglected to include the asterisk, hashtag and operator buttons. He also makes observations about his shifting physiology or complains because he's holding a knife in his hand in one panel and a fork in the same hand in the very next panel. Fans loved it; Rob, less so. I'm sure the editors who wound up art correcting most of the details I made fun of certainly appreciated my help.

Meanwhile not everything that happened as a result of *CBG* was because of my column.

For instance, back when I was writing *Captain Marvel*, I had developed what I thought would be a very exciting storyline. My reasoning was that if, with great power came great responsibility, then with too much power came too much responsibility. I was going to have Cap's Cosmic Awareness overwhelm him and he was going to be driven completely insane.

Why? Because when I work with artists, I try to cater to their strengths. I came to the realization that my artist, ChrisCross, had one strength: drawing people who looked nuts. Everyone he drew looked crazy: Rick, Marvel, everybody. So I figured that I would really have Marvel go around the bend to play to that.

But that was when Joe Quesada decided to announce that he was going to be increasing *Captain Marvel*'s cover price because sales had dropped off. I felt that was crazy; if you take a book that isn't selling and raise the price and make a point of announcing that's what you're doing, you are informing the buyers that they might as well just stop buying it. It's slated for cancellation.

Since Joe had publicly announced the price increase, I took my response public. I wrote an open letter to Joe that was published in *CBG*, complaining that he had just put a death sentence on *Captain Marvel*. I contended that if he needed to raise prices, he should bump up the price on *X-Men*, which could certainly endure a small mark-up and not lose any sales. That he should use the sales of top selling books to support those that were critically acclaimed but struggling sales-wise.

At first Joe was less than thrilled. He was pretty much ready to fire me from Marvel for opposing him publicly. But then he realized that

I was simply using the same tactics that he and Marvel VP Bill Jemas were routinely employing, attacking people publicly in order to drum up publicity.

Joe called me and proposed a contest called "U-Decide." Marvel would relaunch *Captain Marvel*, maintaining the current price. It would also launch two other titles, *Ultimate Adventures* by Ron Zimmerman and *Marville* by Jemas himself. The two lowest selling books would be cancelled after six issues at most, while the winner would stay around. He also proposed that the losers volunteer to go into dunk tanks. Still feeling burned after the McFarlane debate, I passed on that aspect, but agreed to the rest of it. It was certainly better than being fired.

Well, *Captain Marvel* was the best-selling, of course, although two dozen issues later sales again wilted to the point to where Marvel just cancelled it. *Marville*, however, may be the best remembered, since Wikipedia describes it thusly: "The book is regularly considered one of the worst comics of all time due to its confusing and rapidly-changing plots as well as its blatantly promotional nature."

At least *CBG* always treated me well. Indeed, most comic magazines did, *Comics Journal* being the obvious exception. Once *Comics Journal* ran an entire fake letter purporting to be from me that criticized them. Rather than do basic journalism and check with me to make sure that I had written it, which I most certainly had not, they printed it and Gary Groth ran a scathing reply to it. Some months later they eventually ran a tepid and half-hearted withdrawal without actually apologizing for the entirely unprovoked attack. Groth naturally blamed the whole staff rather than taking any responsibility for his assault.

Wizard inadvertently gave me some problems. At one convention, a kid came up to me with a copy of *X-Factor* and asked me to sign it. It was an issue or two after I had left the book. "I didn't write this one," I said. "*Wizard* says you did," the kid replied.

"But I'm saying I didn't."

"*Wizard* says you did."

I flipped the book open to the credits page and pointed to the name other than mine. "See? Not me."

"*Wizard* says you wrote it," he assured me.

"*Wizard* is wrong," I said.

His eyes widened. I thought his brain was going to explode. I had suggested the unthinkable. Suggesting that *Wizard* could be in error was enough to shatter the poor kid's entire worldview.

I miss *CBG* to this day. First it went from weekly to monthly, and then collapsed entirely. One day I received a general email telling me that they had published the last issue. They gave us no notice; not even the opportunity to write a closing column. I have to say, it was a major accomplishment for me, writing that column for twenty five years without let up. Indeed, perhaps this autobiography is nothing more than a final, lengthy "But I Digress."

Various Things

In preparing this manuscript, I put up on my Facebook page a general call for things that fans were interested in reading about. In this chapter I am going to do my best to accommodate as many of those requests as I can.

Mystery Trekkie Theater

I've made several mentions of this undertaking, but it's worth talking about in a bit more detail.

Bob, Mike and I had a field day as, every year at Shore Leave, we would snark on some episode of *Star Trek*. I came up with the undertaking because I wanted to come up with something that would make Shore Leave want to invite me every year since on occasion, they would skip bringing me out. I brought in Bob Greenberger and Mike Friedman as my creative cohorts and we covered a vast range of episodes from *TOS*, *DS9*, *Voyager* and *Enterprise*. We would also have a deranged opening sketch. One of my favorites was "Riverborg" in which Bob, Mike and I, none of whom can dance, much less stepdance, came out as Borg soldiers and attempted to imitate Riverdance. My sister Beth came in as the Borg queen in a sweeping dress and did her own part of the number while the three of us went into the audience and pulled people out to get up and dance with us.

One of my favorites was not a *Star Trek* episode, actually. In our opening sketch, Mike claimed he didn't want to play along. That he was tired of making fun of Trek. Whereupon our mad scientist, T. Alan Chafin, emerged and said, "You're tired of Trek? What do you think of ... *Alexander*?" At that time, the Brad Pitt film *Alexander* was in the theaters. There was stunned muttering from the audience. Were we really going to riff on the two-hour movie still in the theaters?

The film began and what they saw was a black and white opening, with an announcer informing the viewer that we were in Persia and proceeded to do some sort of opening narration. We cracked jokes but the audience sat there in dead silence. They had no idea what the hell they were watching.

Then a soldier on screen shouted "Alexander!" and Alexander the great rode onto screen.

It was William Shatner. Shatner from 1963. They were watching a busted TV pilot with a pre–Trek Shatner.

He rode his horse at high speed, and we started singing the theme song to the TV show *F Troop*, but nobody heard us because the audience was howling in hysterics. Most, if not all, of them were unaware this thing even existed.

The opening credits ran and I said, "Y'know, we've got to hand it to the Mad Scientist. He's outdone himself. This could not possibly get any worse."

The co-starring credit came up: Adam West. As the audience erupted, we sighed unanimously, "It's worse."

After twenty years, we finally decided to put an end to *MTT3K*. I came up with the perfect conclusion. Joel Hodgson, with whom I had formed a friendship at conventions, had brought back *MST3K*. I came

Caroline, Kath and me at a performance of *Mystery Science Theater 3000*, with the cast.

up with the idea of having Joel record a video in which he asked us to shut down *MTT3K* because it presented competition to the original. Joel recorded it perfectly. One of the first things I had him do was say, "Please, hold your applause," and my guess had been right. The audience applauded when his image appeared on the screen, and when he told them to stop, they gasped and I heard several mutter, "He's live!" Which he wasn't, but he held his responses for the perfect amount of time so it seemed as if we were actually having a conversation. The audience bought it one hundred percent.

I still miss *MTT3K*. It even affects the way I watch Trek to this day. I was watching *The Wrath of Khan* and when Joachim dies in Khan's arms, I suddenly said, "By Grabthar's hammer ... by the suns of Warvan..." and then Khan says, "I shall avenge you!" Part of me now wants to do *MTT3K* with that film just for that line.

Klingons

I was at a Friendly's nearby Shore Leave one year, and there were a group of Klingons there who were acting very much in character as they sat around a table eating. As I was getting ready to leave, I strode over to them and said, "Today is a good day to die!" "Yes!" they chorused. "Tomorrow is also a good day to die!" They again declared, "Yes," although they seemed slightly uncertain.

Then I said, "Now let's look at the five day forecast." At which point I talked about how the rest of the week was going to remain warm, causing blood to flow faster and thus make dying good. But then the predicted cold snap was going to roll in, which would cause blood to flow much more slowly and make dying more prolonged and painful. "So in summary, three good days to die followed by two not-so-good days to die. Back to you, Roger." At which point the Klingons burst into applause.

Not bad for something I came up with off the top of my head. I later wound up using it in a sketch called "Bye Bye Buffy" and had a complete Klingon weather report, which had a Klingon weatherman and an actual projected chart.

What can I say? Klingons amuse me.

Plays

I've done quite a bit of community theater in my time.
I performed in several productions of *1776*. In one show I played

the Scots-accented Colonel Thomas McKean. His name was mispronounced as McKeen in the feature film instead of McCain, like the late John McCain. I've no idea if the two are related but that's how you say it. In addition to normal performances, we did several for elementary schools and did Q&As afterward. I maintained my Scots accent. I also carried a prop flintlock and the kids naturally asked me if it was real. I told them it was because it made the conversation more interesting.

Even better was when I played Richard Henry Lee of Virginia. That's the best role in musical theater. You're one of several dozen representatives in the opening number, "Sit Down John." You come out in scene two and sing the best song in the show, "The Lees of Virginia." Then you miss half of the interminable scene three which is the longest scene with no song break in the history of musical theater. You come in, declare that Virginia resolves that America has a right to independence. You wait out the remaining ten minutes of the scene, inform your colleagues that you're going to return to Virginia to serve as governor, and then you get to hang out until curtain call. I wrote an entire Trek novel in the dressing room during one run. Indeed, I populated a whole bridge crew with characters named after my fellow actors.

I also portrayed "Marrying Sam" in several productions of *Li'l Abner*, and "Sancho Panza" in two productions of *Man of La Mancha*. I still remember bringing little Ariel to one of our rehearsals. We were performing a full run through of the show, and even though we weren't in costume and in a large classroom rather than on stage, she was sobbing during the final scene with Quixote's death. That's when I knew we had a winner on our hands.

Perhaps my favorite was when I played a detective sergeant in a production of Agatha Christie's play, *The Unexpected Guest*. The director handed out the scripts but didn't include the last several pages which contained the revelation of the murderer. He challenged all of us to read it and endeavor to solve the murder; at the first rehearsal we would then come together, pitch our resolutions, and then read the actual revelation. This was before the internet, so there was no way we could cheat and look it up. Of all the cast members, my conclusion was the only one that everyone else derided. They thought it was ridiculous and couldn't possibly be correct. Then we read the ending. I was right. I can't recall the last time I was so happy with my predictive powers.

(Generally speaking, it's pretty hard to fool me. I still remember watching *The Sixth Sense*. We were a few minutes into the film, we see Bruce Willis sitting on a park bench, and I muttered to Myra who was seeing it with me, "I bet he's dead." I won't say that's what caused the divorce, but going to see movies with me couldn't have been a lot of fun for her.)

I remember one actor from community theater, Joe Mankowski. I invited him and his wife to my wedding to Kathleen. I'll always remember George walking over to him and saying, "Hello, I'm George Takei, and you are…?" Joe, a huge Trek fan, was stunned into silence.

I was also in several shows with a guy named Joe Morris. He played Adams in *1776* and Quixote in *Man of La Mancha*. He was a dentist by trade and always swore that he would never play the role of the dentist in *Little Shop of Horrors*. I was in the audience when he did, in fact, play that role because his girlfriend was playing "Audrey" and she talked him into it. I wonder if the clothes he wore were his own dentist outfit.

I still remember running into George Perez at a Dragon Con and mentioned that I was playing Marrying Sam at that particular moment. George immediately said, "I played Abner in community theater!" We promptly launched into a rendition of "The Country's in the Very Best of Hands," Abner's and Sam's duet. This was before cell phones, which is a shame; we would have lit up YouTube with that.

Broadway Bound

I am one of those rare beasts: a straight white man who loves Broadway musicals. For years we regularly attended the Broadway Bears auction from Equity Fights AIDS and acquired a host of custom bears ... including one of Morticia Addams, which we actually showed to actress Bebe Neuwirth at a Broadway street gathering.

Caroline and Bebe Neuwirth, along with Bebe's Broadway Bear of her as Morticia Addams.

My most memorable encounter happened at a New York Comic Con one year when these two gentlemen came up to my table to get me to autograph their comics. One of them was wearing a t-shirt that looked like a stylized Jafar and I asked about it. The larger of the men said, "This is the stage manager for the Broadway show *Aladdin* and I'm the genie."

I blinked and said, "Wait, what?"

He repeated himself, and introduced himself by name: James Monroe Iglehart. I said, "My God, I saw you on the Tonys!"

He said "You watched the Tonys?!" with some surprise, as if it aired on Hulu or something.

We chatted for a few minutes and then I said, "I haven't seen your show yet because every time I check, tickets aren't available." Which was true. James cocked his head and said, "You need tickets?"

Tony-award winning actor James Monroe Iglehart, who came up to me at a New York Comic Con and told me what a big fan he was of mine. The following Sunday Caroline, Kath and I were his guests at a Broadway matinee of *Aladdin*, where he was the Genie.

A week later we were seated in his house seats watching the show. And when he finished "Friend Like Me," as the audience applauded and howled its approval, he shouted, "Thank you! You're all wonderful! Peter David, I love you!" My jaw dropped. I spun and said to Kathleen and Caroline, "Did you just hear that?!" Kath hadn't, but Caroline had.

Since then James has remained a good friend. And now he's in *Hamilton* so we've seen *that* three times. It's good to have well-placed comrades.

My Tattoo

At San Diego Comic-Con, I was doing a signing at the Comic Book Legal Defense Fund table. And there was a sign that read: "Now signing Peter David." Wendy and Richard Pini, the creators of *Elfquest*, happened by and Richard said, "Who's signing Peter David?" Wendy immediately took my left arm and autographed it.

I said, "Can you do a sketch?"

So she did a big bold sketch of Cutter on my forearm.

"You should have that tattooed on," someone said.

Now at that point, the CBLDF was still about a thousand dollars behind on where we'd wanted for fund raising. So I said, "If someone donates a thousand dollars to the CBLDF, I'll have it tattooed permanently."

Unbeknownst to me, there was a reporter from Comic Book Resources there. He immediately put "Peter David issues a challenge!" up on CBR and suddenly the whole damned internet was up to speed on it.

Meanwhile Wendy and Richard were trying to find someone to cough up the thousand. Who would be willing to spend a grand for me to be in pain for half an hour? Naturally they thought of Joe Quesada, but he'd already left. So they went to Paul Levitz, but Paul said he'd have to run it through legal and it would take a couple of weeks to get back to them.

At which point Wendy and Richard returned to the CBLDF and said they'd decided they were going to donate the thousand dollars themselves. "Why give someone else the publicity bump?" they reasoned.

Wendy then began to think better of the image that she had drawn on my forearm and suggested that she make a second, better and more detailed drawing further up my arm, so that it wouldn't always be exposed. I agreed and on second thought decided that I'd rather have a tattoo of Leetah, a female elf, on my arm. She drew it in careful detail on my upper left arm. I then asked a passing fan whose body was adorned with tattoos if she could recommend a good tattoo parlor nearby and she recommended one that was literally across the street.

The Pinis accompanied me over there and even paid to have the tattoo done. Honestly, I was petrified of the prospect because I have (a) a low pain threshold and (b) a fear of needles. But I sucked it up and endured it, and I must admit it was actually less painful than I thought it was going to be. The tattoo artist kept commenting about what a "sweet drawing" it was and wanted to add shadings and shadows, but Wendy wanted to keep it simple. Since she drew it, we all respected her wishes and it came out beautifully. Wendy and Richard then took me out for dinner and Maggie Thompson joined us.

Kathleen saw it and said she was going to have Wendy draw a matching Cutter on her arm. Some years later Kathleen and I were attending San Diego together, having dinner with Maggie Thompson and Mark Evanier. (It's worth noting that Mark was responsible for me getting SDCC's Inkpot award. I had mentioned to him wistfully that I wondered why I'd never gotten one, he asked SDCC, and they replied, "We gave him one years ago." "Check again," he said. They did and said, "Whoops.") And who was eating at the same restaurant? Wendy and Richard. I said, "Hey, Kath! Great opportunity here!" Wendy dutifully drew Cutter on Kath's arm and the next day she had it tattooed, so now we match.

Of course, when I die, I have to return my arm to Wendy, but that's another day's problem.

Kath's and my matching tattoos.

Band on the Run

I wrote several movies for Charles Band, the owner of Full Moon Entertainment. I was actually paid for them, which makes me somewhat unique in Hollywood since I'm told that Charlie is as good as Donald Trump when it comes to paying people who have worked for him.

The first two movies I wrote were the fourth and fifth installments of the *Trancers* movies. These starred actor/comedian Tim Thomerson as Jack Deth, a tough as nails guy who fought creatures called Trancers because they absorbed the life force of their victims, or something like that. I got them to hire a then-struggling director named David Nutter who since then went on to a good deal of fame directing everything from *The Sarah Conner Chronicles* to *Game of Thrones*. I was told that both films were going to be made in Romania and so tailored the movies to take advantage of what we have around us.

Our budget was insanely low. Allow me to illustrate: remember the first five minutes of *Raiders of the Lost Ark*? Imagine the following: no money for stunt men. No money for caves. No money for a giant boulder. No money for extras. The opening of *Raiders* would have been Indiana Jones creeping through a forest. He finds the idol on a pedestal in the middle of a clearing. He does the switch, smiles, suddenly the camera shakes and he runs away, dropping the idol as he goes. The end.

That's what writing *Trancers* was like. Charlie told me to let my imagination run wild and then provided no money to take advantage of it. *Trancers IV* was bad and *Trancers V* was even worse. I wrote a sensational script and nearly half of it—all the action sequences—were never filmed. The movie ran sixty-five minutes, and that included a ten-minute recap of the previous film. So not the best time I ever had.

Although there were some bright moments.

One of the actors who joined us late was a young guy named Lochlyn Munro. Modern fans may know him as Betty's homicidal father on *Riverdale*. When I first met him at the hotel, for reasons that I cannot fathom to this day, I affected a Romanian accent and introduced myself as Mister Vlad, a production assistant who worked for the company. I kept this going for two days, dragooning all the Romanian crew into going along with it. I would hold entire conversations with them using the few Romanian words I knew. The biggest deal was when we broke for lunch and I automatically started to sit with the Americans. Thomerson immediately said, "Vlad, we didn't invite you here; you should sit with the other Romanians." I instantly realized Tim was right and obediently went and sat with the Romanian crew. This was a *huge* deal to them, because their world was very much divided by class and having one of the high-class Americans sitting with the lower-class crew was simply unheard of.

The fact that I did not consider myself above them in any way immensely endeared me to them. On the second night, one of them came over to me and said, "Mister Vlad, come, come." I followed him and found that some of the crew had caught and cooked a fish they'd pulled from a nearby pond. They wanted me to share their meal with them. Now I'd seen dogs pissing in the pond, plus I really don't like fish, but there was no way I could turn down their offer. It would have been hugely insulting to them. So I gamely ate some of the fish and then spent the next twenty-four hours waiting for some sign of food poisoning, which fortunately never happened. Eventually we sprang the revelation that I was the American writer just having fun on Lochlyn, which David filmed, so that's around somewhere.

Oblivion and *Oblivion 2: Backlash* were far more entertaining.

Oblivion was basically cowboys and aliens years before the movie "*Cowboys and Aliens*," and also years before the Tom Cruise film of the same name. The director for that was Sam Irvin, who was a great guy. Full Moon actually spent a little money on these two films and it showed. Casting it was also fun. We had one role "Doc Valentine," who was the town doctor and drunk. John Astin was originally cast and then pulled out, and I was talking with Sam about who we could get. I suggested George Takei and Sam immediately embraced the idea. I called George and pitched the role to him.

"I don't know," he said hesitantly. He was daunted by the prospect of a two month shoot in Romania.

I said, "George, when was the last time you got to play someone who was not specifically written to be Asian."

"1963," he said immediately.

"Thirty years ago. Doc Valentine isn't Asian. He's just a guy. Wouldn't that be a nice change of pace?"

"Send me the script," he said, which I did. Within two days he signed on.

In order to have some fun, George kept sliding in "Star Trek" references. He makes his entrance drunk, holding a bottle of Jim Beam whiskey, and his first line was to stare at the bottle and mutter, "Jim, Beam me up." I wasn't thrilled. "They're gonna blame me for those," I said. Some months later we attended a fan screening of the completed film. I was seated next to George, and when he said his first line, the audience moaned and I heard someone say, "Oh, Peter!" I turned to him and said, "Told you!"

This time out Full Moon was going to fly me out to Romania for two weeks to be on set, and they were giving me two tickets. I decided to bring my father and I asked Sam if he could have a cameo in the film. After all, my father had come to America to be in movies; I could finally make his dream come true. "He has to have a beard," said Sam. "I want pretty much all the guys in town to have beards. Would he grow one?"

I said, "In the entirety of my life, I have never seen him with anything more than five o'clock shadow. But to be in a movie, yes, he'll grow a beard."

I met my father at the New York airport six weeks later. He looked like Tevye.

What Sam and I worked out was that my dad would be a customer in the general store. I mentioned Carel Struycken some chapters back; he played "Mr. Gaunt," the psychic funeral director who would always show up when someone was about to die so he could catch the body. Consequently, whenever he showed up anywhere in town, most people would turn and run. My father would be a customer who would do exactly that.

As we prepared to shoot his scene, my dad said, "What's my line?"

"What?"

"What do I say?" he asked.

He didn't have a line. He was just supposed to see Mr. Gaunt, turn and run. I told him to hold on a moment and went over to Sam. "My dad wants to know what his line is," I said.

"You're the writer. Give him a line," said Sam.

I went back to my dad and said, "You say, 'I think I'll come back later.'"

"Got it," he said.

We finished shooting the master take, and then Sam said, "Okay, let's go in for Gunter's close-up."

These were words my father had literally been waiting decades to hear. "My close-up? I get a close-up?" he said.

My dad learned quickly. On the master take he had said his line quickly and got out of the store. On the close-up, he stuttered and stammered in terror, which served to prolong his screen time. He milked it for all it was worth. I'm pleased to say that they did indeed use his close-up in the final film (it was the second movie).

The capper was that some weeks later I brought my rolls of film, pictures I'd taken, to a local film development place. When I came to pick them up, the counter guy said, "Were these taken on the set of a movie?" "Yes, they were," I said. "Yeah, I thought so, because I recognized one of the guys!" He pointed to a group photo of a number of the cast members, including George and Carel, and he said, "This guy." He pointed to my father.

"No, *him* you haven't seen," I assured him. But the guy insisted that he had.

My father later wrote an entire essay about his appearance in the film which was published in one of the "Chicken Soup for the Soul" collections. My dad, the movie star. At last.

Looking Back

I look back on my life and I have trouble believing it.

When I was a kid, I wanted to be Will Robinson's friend. Now I am.

When I was twelve, I wrote and drew my own comic books. I realized that I hated drawing and decided to focus on writing. Now I write comic books for a living.

When I was a teenager, I read the works of Harlan Ellison, and I had a signed poster of George Takei up on the door to my bedroom, and I enjoyed *Star Trek*. Harlan was the best man at my wedding and George attended mine and I was at his, and I've written several dozen *Star Trek* novels.

My first wedding, we were all talking about this new movie called *Star Wars*, long before it was "Episode IV." Years later, the star would call me while I was watching him on TV.

There was a study done that shows that something like eighty-five percent of the people in this country hate their jobs. That they do it just to pay the bills but have no real emotional attachment to it. I am among the lucky fifteen percent who loves his job. Who is living a life that is quite literally a series of dreams come true.

I'm not really sure how I did it.

I know that when I was a teenager, I resolved I would never do drugs. Considering I grew up in the '60s, that was a hell of an accomplishment. It's just that I realized the only reason that mankind is the dominant species in the world is because of our brains. Other animals are faster, stronger. Monkeys have opposable thumbs. It is our brain that gives us our advantage, and therefore anything that interferes with our ability to think is, by definition, a bad thing and should be avoided. Plus, I knew that I would eventually have kids and I didn't want them to do drugs. And I didn't want them to be able to say, "Well, when you were our age, you experimented with drugs!" I wanted to be able honestly to say that I hadn't. Once Bill Mumy told me that I was the only person he knew who had not seen *2001: A Space Odyssey* while stoned. I dunno;

maybe I should have. I saw it twice. Once when I was a teenager and knew nothing about science fiction, and I was bored by it. And once when I was in my twenties, was an experienced fan, had read the Arthur C. Clarke story, and was still bored by it.

Whatever.

Yes, I've had setbacks in my life. When my first marriage was ending, I seriously contemplated suicide. The only thing that prevented me was that I did not want to leave my children behind.

I still remember driving down to Pennsylvania to visit my parents. They were incredibly upset because Beth's first marriage was falling apart and I couldn't bring myself to tell them that mine was spiraling down the toilet. Not only that, but Shana wasn't even speaking to me, and Gwen was following her lead.

While I was down there, my father found something that he gave me. It was a wristwatch that my grandmother Shanedel, after whom Shana was named, had given me for my bar mitzvah. It was inscribed to me on the back. As I drove home, my mind whirling, trying to figure out what to do, I did something that was rare for me: I prayed. I didn't pray to God; I figured he was busy. Instead I prayed to my grandmother. "Help me," I said. "Help me find a way to fix things with my children."

When I got home, I walked into the kitchen. Myra and Shana and Gwen were there. Conversation was polite but strained as it typically was back then, and as we chatted, I swear to you, I suddenly heard a voice in my head. Nothing like it has ever happened before or since, but a voice whispered to me: "Give her the watch."

I pulled the watch out of my pocket and said, "Shana, it occurs to me that you don't have anything of your grandmother's, for whom you were named. She gave this to me when I was bar mitzvahed. It's inscribed from her on the back, and I'd like you to have it." I handed her the watch.

Shana stared at it and then, to my utter astonishment, she burst into tears and embraced me as if I had just returned from the dead.

It turned out that Myra had been filling her head with nonsense about how I didn't consider her my real family and didn't really love them, blah blah blah. By giving her the watch, I had proven how utterly untrue that was.

The point of the story is not to badmouth Myra, but instead to underscore how I've managed to get through most of my life: By doing what felt right at the time. Whether it was the realization that I didn't have what it took to be a reporter, or the marriage that produced three wonderful kids, or the remarriage that not only gave me a fourth great child, but also helped save my life—because let's face it, if I'd been home by myself when the stroke hit, I would never have understood what was happening and likely just died in my bed at the ripe old age of fifty-six—I've endeavored to act in accordance with my instincts.

They have yet to steer me wrong.

I have no idea what's going to be happening to me after this. It's getting harder to sell books, I know that. Nowadays you no longer sell to editors; instead book sellers, people who do the job that I used to do for Marvel, weigh in and make decisions based not on the quality of the work, but purely and exclusively on sales. And unless you're a Stephen King/J.K. Rowling top seller, well … here's what happens. You put out a book and they publish, oh, let's say fifty thousand copies. Half of those get returned for credit.

So the next time you publish a book, the book buyers for stores check your name, they say, "Oh, he sold twenty-five thousand copies last time" and they will order twenty-five thousand copies of the next book. Let's say you have two-thirds sell through of that title, which is a lot. So what happens? Your next book, they order sixteen thousand copies, and so on until publishers literally can't put out your book and get sufficient initial orders to make it profitable. It leaves a long-standing author with only two choices: publish under an assumed name that has no sales record, or self-publish. That's what I've been doing lately with Crazy 8 Press, the self-publishing imprint that Mike Friedman drafted me, Bob Greenberger and others to participate in.

Mostly I just got tired of the dumbass reasons publishers manufacture for not buying my books. For instance, I wrote a satirical vampire novel called *Pulling Up Stakes*. Some rejected it for being too humorous. Others said it wasn't humorous enough. My favorite was the idiot who declared that if it was a vampire novel, the author had to be female. I'm sure that would be quite a shock to Bram Stoker, or even Joss Whedon.

I have to say, I've often scoffed at the idea of writing an autobiography. The implication to me is that you're basically admitting that your life is over. You've done everything that would be of interest to people, so you're going to write it down and then die. I wasn't ready to believe that I've done everything that's going to be important.

But after my parents passed away, I thought back on all sorts of things I wanted to ask them about. Fragmented memories of things that had been said or done many years ago. Things that were hazy to me, but I knew they would be able to recall.

Except they're gone and I can't ask them.

Kathleen describes me as a raconteur. She said that's what her parents like about me, that I have all these stories that I'm able to recount so vividly. Anecdotes of people I've met, things that I've done.

When I'm gone, those stories will cease to be. I won't be able to sit in a chair in a living room and recall the time when I did such and such or this amazing thing happened or did I ever tell you about when...?

And I'm reminded of Roy Batty's wonderful monologue right before he passes: "All those moments will be lost in time, like tears in the rain."

I don't want my memories to vanish. I don't want my stories to die. I don't want my kids to say years from now, "Dad used to tell this story about ... what was it now? I forget." I don't want my grandchildren to grow up and have no idea who their grandfather was.

Right now, Orson, Gwen's son, loves Spider-Man. He's three years old and he adores the Spider-Man pillow pal we bought for him. He's looking forward to going to his first comic book convention in July where he's assured he'll be able to meet Spider-Man, which I'm sure will happen because *someone* will be cosplaying him. At age three he's too young to understand what his grandfather does for a living. Kids that age can't wrap themselves around the idea that Spider-Man is fictional, that someone comes up with his adventures. But eventually he'll be able to understand it, and if I'm not around to explain what I do and what I've seen and experienced, perhaps this book will help him to understand.

I still remember when I attended a memorial service for Julie Schwartz. Neil Gaiman and I, who were both on the board of directors for the Comic Book Legal Defense Fund at the time, were walking down the street engaged in conversation. Kathleen was walking behind us, and here's what she saw: Some guy in a suit was walking past us and suddenly his head snapped around. Either he recognized Neil or myself or the two of us together. He was so distracted that he walked directly into a lamppost.

Then there was the time at San Diego where I was coming down in an elevator at my hotel and I ran into Misha Collins, "Castiel" from *Supernatural*. We were heading to the convention center and were chatting politely, and then Misha's cell phone called. He glanced at it and said, "It's Ben Edlund."

"Tell him Peter David says hi," I said.

He answered the phone, they chatted, and then he passed on the message. I could hear Ben's voice on the other end. "Peter! He's a terrific writer! Just fabulous! A wonderful guy!"

Misha now looked at me with much greater respect. One of *Supernatural*'s top writers had just raved about me; that kicked me up several notches in his estimation. After he got off the phone, I said, "Have you actually seen the convention center yet?" "No." "Want me to show you around?" "Sure!"

So we walked around the dealer's room, and very slowly, we started to pick up followers. It reached a point where I was worried we were going to be mobbed, so I said, "I think we better duck somewhere for cover." So I brought him backstage to the Marvel Comics booth. The reaction of the Marvel guys was priceless. "Oh, hi, Peter, who's your frie ... holy crap! Misha Collins!" He wound up leaving with armfuls of Marvel swag, which was amusing considering he was heading over to the DC booth, so they must've loved that.

In the course of the conversation I asked Misha if he'd be interested in a puppet of Castiel. "Absolutely," he said. I said I'd have Kathleen make him one.

Flash forward to Dragon Con. Kath and I get in the elevator to go up to our hotel room and who's in the elevator? Misha. Again. We greeted him and I said, "Kath made the puppet! It's up in our room! Want to get it?" "Okay," he said. We went up to the hotel room and she was teaching him how to use it, and there was a knock at the door. "That's my sister," I realized. I knew that she and Rande were attending the con and had given her our room number.

Kath and I both looked at Misha and he immediately understood. He got up, crossed to the door, and opened it. To this day, Beth swears that she maintained her cool, but I'm sorry, no. Her jaw dropped and her eyes looked ready to leap out of her head.

My life is filled with moments like that. Where I've met and formed friendships or working relationships with hosts of people, and also provided hope and inspiration for others. After I outed Rictor and Shatterstar, multiple fans came up to me in later years and told me that they had been considering suicide over their sexuality and my stories had given them strength or resolution to continue. You have no idea what it's like to have total strangers come up to you and tell you they owe you their lives.

* * *

Where will my life go next? What's my next project? Well, I've finished a book called *Spoken Word*. It's unlike anything I've ever written, which is probably one of the reasons why I'm having trouble selling it. Here's the first chapter:

First

People make a huge deal about the first word that a baby says. Mothers always remember it; fathers usually do. There's a kind of unofficial competition between parents, lobbying to see whether "mama" or "papa" are the first syllables the baby's able to utter in sequence and have it mean what it sounds like it means. If it's a random word, like "light" or "yes," then a lot of meaning can get attached to it.

Mickey's first spoken word was "fart."

He was however the hell many months old he was, and he was bopping around on the floor, doing the whole baby thing. It was after Thanksgiving dinner, and his Uncle Tommy, he did his usual thing of sitting in an easy chair, his legs splayed to either side (which he also used to do stark naked in steam rooms, to the appreciation of absolutely no one). He undid his belt and the top of his pants, and sighed lustily, scratching his ample belly, and then he uncorked a ripe one that supposedly went on for, like, a year, to hear Mickey's mother, Tommy's sister, tell of it. She yelled at him, "Tommy, for the love of God!" and Tommy apologized without really meaning it, and Mickey's father walked in and said, "Good Christ, who died in here?" and Mickey's mother started yelling at him, and his dad was saying, "What the hell did I do? I didn't fart!" and his mother was saying, "You're treating it like a big joke," and Uncle Tommy said, "For crying out loud, Brenda, it's just a damned fart," and temperatures were blowing through the ceiling all because of gas passing, with this terrific dinner that his mother had produced being completely forgotten in the wake of Tommy's faux pas.

And Mickey was sitting there, playing with blocks, and he looked up at all the ruckus and growing anger. Mickey tilted his cherubic little face up to the chandelier and cooed, "Fart."

Everything froze. Every eye was on him. "Did ... did he say—?" began his father.

He didn't have to complete the sentence. "Fart," Mickey said again.

Tommy started to laugh.

"Shut up!" said Mickey's mother.

Her brother tried to do so. He really did. He clamped both hands over the lower half of his face, at which point Mickey's aunt Susan, his wife, walked in from having gone to the bathroom. She stared at her husband, who looked like he was trying to smother himself, and she said, "Tommy, what in God's name..." Then her noise wrinkled and she said, "Ewww ... did you—?"

"Fart," Mickey piped up. His comedy timing was already solidly in place.

His father immediately said, "I'm getting the video camera..."

"Oh, the hell you are!" His mother was livid.

"It's Mickey's first wor...!"

"No way." His mother shook her head with such determination that it almost toppled off her neck. His dad was a head and a half taller than his mother, but she stomped up to him and practically had to stand on her toes to wave her finger in his face. "There is no way that my son's first word is going to be—"

"*Faaaaaaaaart!*" Mickey said, and his voice kind of went up and down in the middle. Mickey was singing it like an aria.

His aunt Susan completely lost it. She had a huge belly laugh and she unleashed it then, and that set off Uncle Tommy who had come close to controlling himself but lost it. He was laughing so hard that he slid off the recliner so that his ass was on the carpet and his torso supported by the chair.

This got Mickey's father going, and he started laughing. His mother looked around like a trapped tigress, overwhelmed by events that were spiraling completely out of control. Whereupon Mickey crawled over to Uncle Tommy, who was on the floor, remember, and Mickey started thumping on his chest saying, "Fart, fart, fart, fart," rapid fire, like bullets from a machine gun.

Now naturally Mickey didn't remember any of it firsthand; most of it is what became family legend, repeated at subsequent gatherings.

But Mickey still felt a sense of empowerment, as if an understanding was being engraved in his baby brain that he could control crowds of people by reducing them to hysterics.

Three adults that Thanksgiving were helpless with laughter, putty in his baby hands, and only his mother was keeping it together, scolding, scowling, telling everyone to knock it off which only got them going all the more, because this kind of thing feeds on itself.

And finally, she glared at her son, the source of all this chaos, and Mickey paused in the thumping on his uncle's chest, looked up at her with wide-eyed innocence, and said, "Fart?"

At which point Mickey farted. Nothing remotely as magnificently sustained as what his uncle had unleashed upon an unsuspecting world. Just a quick, sharp "poot" that issued from his diapered backside.

And that was it for his mom.

Apparently, she'd been suppressing it, but his final little button on the scene pushed her over. She let out a loud bark of laughter, like a hopped-up seal, and like her brother had, covered her mouth with both hands as if trying to shove it back down her throat. Then her chest started shaking violently, and if she hadn't let it out her mouth, it probably would have just torn out of her chest, like in *Alien*, smashing through her ribcage and running around the living room. So she did, and she was laughing so hard there were tears running down her face. Her legs gave way and she sank to the floor, hysterical with laughter. And whenever the laughing came close to subsiding, he'd declare "fart" and it would start all over again.

This went on for anywhere from five minutes to half an hour, depending upon who you ask and at what point in the family history the question is being posed.

The point of all the above—which we admittedly made right up front, but is worth mentioning again since it was, like, a thousand words ago, is that first words can be important. If you want further proof that they can be relevant in the long term, you should know that Mickey went on to become a comedian. Not an especially good one, or even a full time one, but "comedian" is right there on his resume, along with about nine other different jobs, including "father." The job title resulted from the birth of his own son, Jordan. This was a compromise name. His wife and Mickey worked out the potential names of their child long before the birth. For some reason they settled on a girl's name pretty quickly: Catherine. A name for a potential boy, however, prompted far longer debate. His wife wanted to name him Daniel, after her father, and Mickey wanted to name him Jor-El, after Superman's father. This remained unresolved up until their son's birth. He wound up become "Jordan," which seemed a fair compromise. In short order his nickname became Jordy, because he seemed more like a Jordy than a Jordan. Plus Mickey felt like he'd got more of his way, because in his head it made his name Jor-D, which is like Jor-El. So, like they say, close enough for jazz.

Jordy's first word was likewise very important.

He didn't speak it until he was eight years old. And after he did, it set a whole series of events into motion that wound up with Mickey in jail.

This is how it started, and this is where it went.

Not bad. I can still write.

When I was twenty I went to a Stephen King autographing and told him I was an aspiring writer. He signed my book with "Best of luck on your writing career." I mentioned earlier how Stephen King autographed my copy of *Danse Macabre* with "Best of luck on your writing career." Nowadays fans will come up to me and tell me they are aspiring writers and bring me books to sign. I always tell them about how Stephen signed my book and I will then write the exact same thing to them. Then I will say that it's their job to get to the other side of the table and when some aspiring writer identifies him or herself, tell this story and sign the same thing to them. Keep the chain going.

I impart that to you now. I have led a life interesting enough that you felt prompted to buy an entire book so that you can read about it. The stories I tell about myself will never die. Now it's your turn. Do things interesting enough in your life so that people will want to cough up money to read your life's story.

And when you do, be sure to dedicate it to me. That way when people are paging through your book, they'll look at the dedication, wonder who the hell Peter David is, and want to find out.

Because in the final analysis, that's the best any of us can do. Make people wonder who the hell we were and want to find out.

If we work hard enough, maybe we can even figure it out for ourselves.

Index

Aarenberg, Lee 103
Abbott & Costello 112–113
Adventurers Club 78, 85–90
After Earth 22–25
Ali and Sara 100
Alpha Flight 38–39
American Gods 122
Amos, Tori 133
Aquaman 11, 60–61, 168–169, 171–1727
The Archetype 41
Arrowette 175
Asimov, Isaac 45, 111
Astrid (*How to Train Your Dragon*) 79–80
Atlanta, GA 3, 38, 73, 82–83, 90–92, 95, 170
Atlanta Fantasy Fair 82–83
Atlantis Chronicles 169–171
August Party 182–183
Avengers: Endgame 168
Ayre, Kristian 159, 165
Azizi, Rahi 158, 164–165

Babylon 5 83, 91, 122, 139–155
Band, Charles 201
Band, Harlan 158
Barrett, Majel 131–133
Batman 11, 60, 168, 175
Baumann, Fred 31, 37, 53
Bell, John 163–164
Bendis, Brian 179
Benes, Ed 173
Berlin, Germany 8
Bete Noire 174–175
Biggers, Cliff 170
Biggs, Rick 146
Bingham, Jerry 43
Bleeding Cool News 39, 99
Blish, James 110
Bloch, Robert 118
Bogart, Dave 98
Boogie Knights 103
Boretski, Paul 160, 165
Both Sides Now 165
Bova 158, 164
Boxleitner, Bruce 144, 148–149, 154

Breath of a Salesman 160
Bromfield, Valri 165–166
Bronsky's Dates with Death 115
Brooks Rehabilitation Center 99
Brown, Julie Caitlin 150
Buchanan, Ginjer 52
Buss, Mary Aileen 116
But I Digress 117–118, 187–193
Byrne, John 35, 38–39, 55, 172, 179, 188

Captain America 44, 60, 191
Captain Marvel 191–192
The Captain's Daughter 3
Carlin, Mike 60–61, 177
Carr, Jane 145
Castiel 208–209
Catalina 158, 159, 162, 165
Cavalieri, Joey 59
Celebration Hospital 96
Cermak, Kim 125
Cermak, James 125
Chafin, T. Alan 194
Chapin, Harry 70
Charest, Micheline 158
Chase, Bobbie 167–168
Chicago Comic Con 31
ChrisCross 1 91
Christa 152, 158, 161
Christian, Claudia 143, 149
Cinar 158, 160–161, 163, 166
Cinderella 78–79
Claremont, Chris 32–33, 37, 55
Collins, Misha 208–209
Colonel Sunchbench 85, 87–90, 97
Comic Shop News 170
Comic Book Legal Defense Fund (CBLDF) 100, 200, 208
Comic Book Resources 200
Comic Buyers Guide 116–117, 186–192
Comics Scene 29, 53, 128
Corey, Guinevere 150
Coronado Springs Hotel 95, 98
Crazy 8 Press 207
Creation Con 132, 185
Crisis on Infinite Earths 173

215

Index

Dark Tower 101
Darkseid 12, 61, 176
Davenport, T.J. 158–160
David, A.J. 75
David, Ariel 20, 34, 72–75, 79, 87, 90, 93–97, 99, 116, 121, 140, 157, 197
David, Caroline 23–24, 34, 64, 66, 75–81, 91, 94–95, 97–98, 119, 163, 186, 195, 198–199
David, Dalia Rojansky 8, 9–15
David, Gunter 8–9, 11–15, 105, 108, 112, 116, 203–204
David, Hela 8–9, 66, 206
David, Kathleen 1, 3, 7, 21, 23, 64, 76–99, 101, 103, 116, 118–119, 123, 163, 179, 185–186, 198, 201, 207–209
David, Leliana 74
David, Martin 8–9
David (Massett), Shana 28, 35, 52, 66–69, 72, 76, 85, 87–88, 90, 95, 97, 114, 133–135, 151, 166, David, (Mayhew) Guinevere (Gwen) 52, 69–72, 87, 89–90, 150, 206
David, Myra 52, 64–70, 72, 73–75, 82–84, 121, 157, 197, 206
David, Walter Charles 11, 13, 14, 173
Day, Felicia 103
DC Comics 1, 11–12, 26, 28–29, 35, 50–53, 60, 63, 128, 130, 142, 168, 171–178, 182, 188, 209
DC vs. Marvel 60, 63
Death of Jean DeWolff 45
DeFalco, Tom 39, 46, 48
deLancie, John 133
Delenn 142, 144, 147, 149, 151
Delta Airlines 101–102
Dezago, Todd 175–176
Didio, Dan 174
Dietz, Susan 157
direct market distributors 29
Discon II 115
Disney company 32, 68, 72, 78, 85, 87, 90, 95–97, 157, 160, 162, 165, 177
Disney Magic 92–93
Disney World 18, 68, 78, 85–86, 95
Ditko, Steve 58
Doctor Who 72, 185
Doohan, James 135–136
Doran, Colleen 62
Doyle, Jerry 146
Dragon Con 73–74, 80, 83, 198, 209
Dunst, Kirsten 134–135

Edlund, Ben 208
Ellison, Harlan 4, 40, 91–92, 114–127, 140–141, 143, 161, 187–188, 205
Ellison, Susan 4, 114, 121, 124–127
The Essential Ellison 116
Evanier, Mark 201

Falk, Lee 53
Fallen Angel (Lee/Liandra) 174–175

Farpoint Convention 103
Fearless 68
Ferrer, Miguel 58, 156
Finkel, Fyvush 65
Firefly 158
Fletcher Hodges 86, 88, 90
Flinn, John 143–148
Florida Hospital 97
Foreigner 46–47
Fort Wilderness 85, 87
Fox, Gardner 28
Frakes, Jonathan 44
Franklin, Doctor 146
Friars Club 1, 4–5
Friedman, Mike 22–24, 82, 194, 207
Friedrich, Mike 30
Friends of Ellison (FOE) 117–118
Full Moon Entertainment 201, 203
Furlan, Mira 143–144, 151, 155
Furst, Stephen 150

Gaiman, Neil 118–119, 122–123, 126–127, 208
Galloway, Tom 182
Galton, Jim 35
Garfunkel, Art 125
Geppi, Steve 124
Germantown Courier 15, 27
Gerrold, David 165–166
Gilgamesh 177–179
Giordano, Dick 169–170, 177–179
G'Kar 139, 147
Goddard, Seth 158, 160
Gold, Mike 53
Goldman, William 124–125
Goldstein, Wendy (Wedge) 113
Goodwin, Rande 86–90, 209
Gottfried, Gilbert 4
Green Lantern (Hal Jordan) 177–179
Greenberger, Bob 22–24, 29–30, 53, 66, 82, 92, 103, 128, 169–170, 194, 207
Gruenwald, Mark 60–61, 184

Hama, Larry 43–44
Hamill, Marilou 84
Hamill, Mark 36–37, 84, 157, 162
Harvey Comics 10
Harras, Bob 49
Hauman, Brandy 92
Hauman, Glenn 92, 103
Herbst, Rebecca 165–166
Heroes Initiative 99
Heuser, Paige Christina 158–159, 165
Havok 54–55
Hitler, Adolf 8
Hobgoblin 46–47
Hobson, Mike 35
Hodgson, Joel 82, 195–196
Holstens 10
Howling Mad 52

Hulk (Incredible) 27, 49–52, 60, 167–168, 184, 186, 188
Hurowitz, Paul 28–29

Ianni, Rosie 152, 157, 159
I-Con 124, 132
IDW Comics 175
Iglehart, James Monroe 199
Image Comics 187–188
Impulse 55, 175
Imzadi 133–134
Inkpot Award 201
Irvin, Sam 203–204
Ivanova, Susan 142, 144, 146, 148–151

Jack O'Lantern 47
Jacksonville, FL 69, 95, 99, 101, 115
Jarvis, Sharon 28, 42, 50
Jemas, Bill 192
Jenkins, Paul 168
Johnston, Rich 99
Jones, Rick 50, 61, 191
Jones, Walter Emmanuel 158–159, 164
Jurasik, Peter 145, 147

Kalish, Carol 29–32, 36–37, 41, 49, 53–54, 75–76
Kasman, Robert Simpson 169–170, 178, 183
Katsulas, Andreas 91–92, 144–145, 147
Keith 105–106, 108, 110
Kelsey, Tamsin 159–160
Kieth, Sam 185
King, Stephen 100–102, 207, 212
Kingpin 48
Kirby, Jack 11–12
Kirk, Leonard 173
Kitty, Steve 111–113
Klingons 82, 112, 196
Knight Life 42–43, 52, 178
Koenig, Walter 4
Kosh 150

Lane, Lois 41, 73
Lang, Lana 172–173
Larsen, Erik 171, 187
LaVelle, Alice Eve 113
Lawless, Lucy 73–74
Lawrence, Cary 160
Lee, Gordon 100
Lee, Jim 188
Lee, Stan 11, 32–33, 54, 58–59, 62, 190
Lemelin, Stephanie 176
Lennier 147, 151
Leonardi, Rick 59
Leopold and Loeb 44
Leva, Scott 44–45
Levitz, Paul 29, 171, 173, 177, 200
Liefeld, Rob 180, 187, 191
Li'l Abner 197–198
Lobo/Li'l Lobo/Slobo 61
Lopez, David 175

Lord of the Rings 3, 80
Lost in Space 156
Lucas, George 36
Luce, Clare Booth 140
Ludlum, Robert 108
Luthor, Lex 172

Madcon 118
Madrox, Jamie 54, 179–180
Magazine of Fantasy and Science Fiction 41, 115
Maguire, Tobey 58, 134
Man of La Mancha 197–198
Mankowski, Joe 198
Mantlo, Bill 51
Maroto, Esteban 169–170
Marvel Comics 11, 27, 30, 31, 33, 35–39, 42–43, 48–50, 53–54, 56–60, 63–64, 84, 95, 98, 128 168, 176–177, 179–182, 187–188, 191–192, 207, 209
Marville 192
Marz, Ron 60–62
Massett, Tim 69
Matern, Anik 160, 165
Max, Peter 124
Mayhew, Heath 34, 72
Mayhew, Orson 72, 208
McAuliffe, Christa 152, 158, 161, 166
McFarlane, Todd 46, 51, 188–190
McFarlane, Wanda 189–190
McIntyre, Vonda 2
Mednitsky, Adria 108
Men in Black films 22–24
Merc 156
Meyer, Nicholas 2
Michelinie, David 46
Milgrom, Al 45, 49–50
Miller, Layla 179–180
MIT 122
Mollari, Londo 139–140, 145, 147–148, 150, 155
Momoa, Jason 172
Montreal, Canada 71–73, 159–162, 164
Moore, Ron 22, 25
Morris, Joe 198
Mosesson, Gloria 27–28
Mumy, Bill 91, 141–142, 146, 148, 150, 152, 156–158, 161–162, 165–166, 205
Munro, Lochlyn 202–203
Murphy, Graham 78, 88–90, 97
Mystery Science Theater 3000 82, 195
Mystery Trekkie Theater 3000 22, 82, 194–196

Nauck, Todd 176
Naylor, Doug 165
Nettleton, Lois 146
Neuwirth, Bebe 198
New York City 1, 9, 12, 16, 19, 28, 36, 42, 53, 60, 65, 71, 75, 82, 84, 99, 102, 111, 124–125, 134, 204

Index

New York Comic Con 62, 199
New York Times 3, 67, 138
New York University 16
New York Mets 33–34, 54
Nichols, Nichelle 4
Nicieza, Fabian 12
Nickelodeon 152, 157, 160–161, 164–166
Northstar 57
Nutter, David 202–203

Obama, Barack 176
Oblivion 146, 203
Oblivion 2: Backlash 2 03
Ockstadt, Karl 90, 97
O'Hare, Michael 83
O'Neill, Denny 32, 38–39, 178–179
Ordover, John 137
Orlando, Joe 53
O'Shea, Helen 78, 83, 92, 96
O'Shea, Donald 83
O'Shea, Patrick 83
O'Shea, Rozana 116
O'Shea, Sean 83
O'Shea, Sheila 83, 86, 116
Oswalt, Patton 126–127
Overbrook Entertainment 23
Owsley, Jim 43, 46–49, 178

Paramount 3, 128, 132–133, 137
Paul, Sara 113
Peel, John 154
Perez, George 80, 159–160, 198
Peter, Paul and Mary 68
Peters, Evan 57
Phantom 53, 118, 128
Pini, Richard 28, 200–201
Pini, Wendy 28, 200–201
Pinkett, Caleeb 17–23, 25–26
Pinkett, Jada 17–18
Playboy Paperbacks 28–30, 42
Pocket Books/Simon & Schuster 2–3, 128, 131–133, 135–137
Poe, Edgar Allan 68
Polaris 54, 57, 180
Portman, Natalie 69
Priest, Christopher see Owsley, Jim
Pulling Up Stakes 207

Q-in-Law 131–133
Q-Squared 129
Quesada, Joe 191–192, 200
Quicksilver 54–57

Radu 158–159
Raiders of the Lost Ark 202
Raimi, Ted (Joxur the Mighty) 74
Rec.arts.comics 183
Red Dwarf 165
Reeves, George 10, 73
Register, Sam 177
Rictor 179–180, 209

The Rift 136
Robin, the Boy Wonder 175–176
Robinson, Will 156–157, 205
Rock and a Hard Place 130
Roddenberry, Gene 111, 129–131, 133, 137, 151
Rojansky, Aaron 9
Rojansky, Claire 9
Romania 146, 162, 202–203
Ryall, Chris 175
Ryan, Kevin 2–3

Saffel, Steve 75, 134
Samson, Doctor Leonard 56, 168
San Diego Comic-Con 57, 97, 116, 139, 141, 153, 180, 184, 189, 200–201, 208
Sapphire Star 42–43
Scans_Daily 180–181
Schechter, Sandy 31, 37, 53
Schmidt, Andy 179–180
Schwartz, Julius/Julie Award 73, 118, 208
Science Fiction Writers Association (SFWA) 125
Secret 176–177
Secrets 177
Seuling, Phil 12, 29
1776 195–196, 198
Shank, Dreaded Warlord 162, 164
Shatner, William 5, 108–109, 195
Shatterstar 180, 209
Shepherd, Bill 85–88
Sheridan, John 139, 144, 147, 149–152
Shooter, Jim 33, 35, 48
Shore Leave Convention 22, 82, 194, 196
Shukin, Ed 31
Shyamalan, M. Night 22, 24–25
Sienkiewicz, Bill 12, 190
Sim, Dave 38
Simonson, Louise 35–37
Simonson, Walt 32
Simpson, Professor R.K. 169–170
Sinclair, Jeffrey 144, 148
Sir Apropos of Nothing 120, 122
Sirtis, Marina 132
Skywalker, Luke 45, 84, 157, 182
Smith, Jaden 22–25
Smith, Trey 20–21
Smith, Will 16–26
Smith, Willow 24
Snyder, Zack 172
Soul Mates 142, 146, 149, 151
Space Cases 52, 73, 124, 152–153, 157, 159, 162, 164, 185
Space-Time Continuum 113
Spector, Warren 91
Spider-Man (Peter Parker) 27, 44–46, 49, 51, 54, 58, 60, 86, 134, 176, 183–184, 208
Spider-Man 2099 (Miguel O'Hara) 58–60, 156
Spike 173
Spoken Word 209–212

Staite, Jewel 159–160, 162, 165
Star Trek 1–3, 5–6, 12, 22, 29, 65, 82–83, 103, 105, 108–114, 128, 1320–132, 135–138, 140, 151, 155, 156, 194, 197–198, 203, 205
Star Trek: The New Frontier 137–138
Star Trek VI: The Undiscovered Country 2, 6
Star Wars (general) 37, 45, 84, 157, 205
Star Wars, Episode VI: Return of the Jedi 36–37
Starlin, Jim 178–179
Stern, David 128–130
Stern, Howard 3, 6
Stern, Roger 46–47
Straczynski, Joe 12, 83, 122, 139–143, 146, 149–155
Strike Zone 130
Stroke, Having A. 24, 90, 94, 96–101, 103–104, 207
Strong Guy (Guido) 54–55
Struycken, Carel 146, 204
Sulu, Hikaru 1–3, 138, 163
Superboy 175–176
Supergirl (Kara Zor-El/Linda Danvers) 11, 172–174
Superman 10–12, 27, 35, 41, 55, 60–61, 73, 136, 171–173, 175, 212
Supernatural 46, 208
Suzee 158, 162
Szarabajka, Keith 146

Takei, Brad Altman 1, 3–4, 7, 163
Takei, George 1–7, 91, 162–164, 198, 203–205
Teenage Mutant Ninja Turtles 10
Temple University 15–16
Tennant, David 185–186
Thanos 61
Thelma 158–160, 165
There All the Honor Lies 149
Thomerson, Tim 202
Thompson, Andrea 146
Thompson, Maggie 116–117, 201

Trancers (IV and V) 202
Trimble, Bjo 105

U-Decide 192
Ultimate Adventures 192
Uslan, David 175
Uslan, Michael 17, 175
USSR 137

Valk, Blair 146
Vejar, Mike 150
Venom (Eddie Brock) 46
Vietti, Brandon 177
Vir 150

Wacker, Steve 59
Web of Spider-Man 184
Weisman, Greg 177
Weisman, Sandy 113
Weinstein, Howard 29
West, Adam 195
Whedon, Joss 146, 159, 172, 207
Wikipedia 172, 181, 192
Williams, Robin 120
Windsor-Smith, Barry 51
Winters, Talia 142, 146, 150
Wizard Magazine 192
Wolfsbane (Rahne Sinclair) 37, 55, 57
Wolverine 27, 46–47, 51, 57, 61
Wonder Girl 176
Woodward, J.K. 175

X-Factor 37, 54–55, 64, 98, 179–180, 192
Xena, Warrior Princess 73–74

Yeoman Rand's Room Number 3C-46 111–112
Young Justice 175–177

Zack, Andy 17–18
Zelazny, Roger 115, 183
Zimmerman, Ron 192

www.ingramcontent.com/pod-product-compliance
Ingram Content Group UK Ltd.
Pitfield, Milton Keynes, MK11 3LW, UK
UKHW041955140426
5217IPUK00015B/805